treehouse™

iOS 6
Foundations

treehouse™

iOS 6
Foundations

Jesse Feiler

WILEY

A John Wiley and Sons, Ltd, Publication

This edition first published 2013

©2013 John Wiley & Sons, Inc.

Registered office

John Wiley & Sons Ltd, The Atrium, Southern Gate, Chichester, West Sussex, PO19 8SQ, United Kingdom

For details of our global editorial offices, for customer services and for information about how to apply for permission to reuse the copyright material in this book please see our website at `www.wiley.com`.

A catalogue record for this book is available from the British Library.

ISBN 978-1-118-35657-9 (paperback); ISBN 978-1-118-57008-1 (ebook); ISBN 978-1-118-57010-4 (eMobi); ISBN 978-1-118-57009-8 (ePDF)

Set in Chaparral Pro Light 10/12.5 by Indianapolis Composition Services

Printed in the U.S. by Command Web Missouri

About the Author

JESSE FEILER is a developer, consultant, and author specializing in Apple technologies. He is the creator of Minutes Machine for iPad, the meeting management app available in Apple's App Store. He is also Software Architect for PlattInfo, the network of walk-up touch-screen kiosks in downtown Plattsburgh, New York. As a consultant, he has worked with small businesses and nonprofits on projects such as production control, publishing, and project management, usually involving FileMaker.

His books include:

- *iWork For Dummies*
- *Dashcode For Dummies*
- *FileMaker Pro in Depth*
- Sams *Teach Yourself Core Data in 24 Hours*
- Sams *Teach Yourself Objective-C in 24 Hours*
- *The Bento Book*

He is heard regularly on WAMC Public Radio for the Northeast's *The Roundtable*. He is a member of the City of Plattsburgh Planning Board and the Saranac River Trail Advisory Committee. A native of Washington DC, he has lived in New York City and currently lives in Plattsburgh, NY.

He can be reached at northcountryconsulting.com.

The photos in Chapter 17 show one of the City of Plattsburgh's PlattInfo kiosks. PlattInfo is a network of walk-up touch-screen kiosks powered by FileMaker. Jesse Feiler is Software Architect for PlattInfo. PlattInfo artwork by Kelly Chilton (hey@kellychilton.com or www.kellychilton.com). You can find out more about PlattInfo at PlattInfo.com.

Publisher's Acknowledgments

Some of the people who helped bring this book to market include the following:

Editorial and Production

VP Consumer and Technology Publishing Director: Michelle Leete

Associate Director–Book Content Management: Martin Tribe

Associate Publisher: Chris Webb

Associate Commissioning Editor: Ellie Scott

Development Editor: Kezia Endsley

Copy Editor: Kezia Endsley

Technical Editor: Aaron Crabtree

Editorial Manager: Jodi Jensen

Senior Project Editor: Sara Shlaer

Editorial Assistant: Annie Sullivan

Marketing

Associate Marketing Director: Louise Breinholt

Marketing Manager: Lorna Mein

Senior Marketing Executive: Kate Parrett

Marketing Assistant: Tash Lee

Composition Services

Senior Project Coordinator: Kristie Rees

Compositor: Indianapolis Composition Services

Proofreader: Linda Seifert

Indexer: Potomac Indexing, LLC

Author's Acknowledgments

Many people have helped to make this book possible. At Treehouse and Wiley, Chris Webb and Kezia Endsley, brought the book from the initial idea to fruition. My agent, Carole Jelen, as always has been creatively supportive as the book has proceeded.

The tech editor, Aaron Crabtree, was great to work with, and I appreciate his help enormously. (You can find Aaron on Twitter at @aaron_crabtree and on the web at www.tap dezign.com.) Notwithstanding the help of so many people, any errors are mine. If you do find an error, please contact me through northcountryconsulting.com so that we can correct it in the next printing. And if you register on northcountryconsulting.com, we'll let you know of any updates.

Contents

Part 3: Building the Party Planner App

Part 4: Using Table and Collection Views

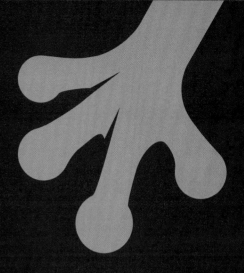

Introduction

GETTING STARTED WITH iOS 6 is easier than ever. Long-time iOS programmers who started programming with iPhone OS all those years ago (in 2007) might
scarcely recognize the tools at their disposal. Some people thought that programming
iPhone—and later, iPad—was just too hard. And maybe it was, but the engineers at
Apple were working feverishly to transfer major aspects of app development from
external developers to in-house Apple engineers. The process accelerated with iOS 5
and, with iOS 6, newcomers to iOS development have a wealth of riches in the frameworks and tools at your command.

Who Should Read This Book?

This book is for people who want to learn about developing iOS apps. It provides a
hands-on tutorial for you to develop your first app. Some people will use the book to
launch themselves on a career as an app developer. For others, the book will serve to
introduce the basics of iOS. This means that managers, clients, marketers, and others
who need to work with iOS can get up to speed

The assumption in this book is that you know a programming language and the basics
of computer programming and software development. You don't need an in-depth
knowledge of a programming language, and, in some cases, that may actually be a dis-
advantage. It doesn't particularly matter which programming language you're familiar
with, although if it is a modern object-oriented programming language such as C++,

C#, Java Python, and Ruby, that's great. If you are familiar with the object-oriented features of Perl and PHP, that knowledge will help you along the way.

What about "the basics of computer programming and software development"? Many people (including many people in the technology world) don't understand how software is developed today. Unfortunately, you can still find many books and courses that begin by teaching you how to develop a basic program to do something like balance a checkbook. Leaving aside for the moment the fact that most people don't balance a checkbook manually any more (online banking has changed all that), if your goal is to build the next killer app in the music world or to manage a recycling center or whatever, that checkbook-balancing app may not be relevant. However, if you want to write innovative apps for the 21st Century and the great iOS operating system, this book is for you.

What You Will Learn

The first thing that you'll learn is right here in this paragraph. iOS is the operating system of iPhone, iPad, and iPod touch. It is written in Objective-C. The iOS software is developed with the Xcode integrated development environment (IDE). iOS (as well as OS X) is a product of Apple, as is Xcode. Although Objective-C is not an Apple product (there are several implementations), most people refer to Apple's documentation for the last word on Objective-C and its features. (There is no single published standard other than the Apple documentation.)

As a result of these three points, it is sometimes hard to discern where the operating system and its frameworks end and the language begins, not to mention which features are implemented in Xcode and which features are part of the framework or even the language. They all work together in a seamless fashion. Don't try to tear them apart and learn the language separately from the frameworks or Xcode. Just remember that they are all part of an extraordinary whole. As you work through the book, you'll see how things fit together.

In Part I, "Introducing iOS 6," you'll see how the key components of your development environment fit together. You'll learn about the structure of iOS 6, and you'll see how to use Xcode. You'll walk through the process of thinking about an app and see how to begin defining it.

In Part II, "Storyboards: The Building Blocks of iOS Apps," you get to work designing your app's interface. Some people think of the interface as an add-on, thinking that the code you write is the real thing. Don't fall into that trap; the interface *is* your app. It's what people see and use. The interface comes first, and the code is used to support it. This is particularly important with iOS because, as noted previously, the functionality can be implemented in the iOS framework itself, in the Objective-C language, in Xcode, or in some combination of them. But the storyboard—a step-by-step walk through the interface—brings them all together.

And, yes, if you're wondering if these storyboards are anything like storyboards for movies or games, you're right. Today's storyboards can be traced to the Walt Disney studios in the 1930s. Look up storyboards in Wikipedia and you'll see that long before iOS, they were used to plan *Gone with the Wind* (1939). You'll also find earlier references such as Constantin Stanislavski's use of storyboarding in theatrical productions in the 1890s.

In Part III, "Building the Party Planner App," you'll use the Core Data Model editor in Xcode to build your data store using graphical tools. From there, you'll move on to customize the Xcode template that will become your app. In this section, you also learn how to save and restore data and how to use the debugger.

In Part IV, "Using Tables and Collection Views," you'll see how to use a critical component of iOS. Structuring data and allowing users to edit it is a common task for developers and users. With the built-in table functionality, much of your work is already done for you.

Finally, in Part V, "Interacting with Users," you circle back to the world of storyboards. There are a number of specific user interface elements that need to be covered so that you can complete your app. Here is where you find them.

How to Use This Book

There are no "reading police;" you can read this (or any) book when, where, and how you want to. (Actually, there is one generally accepted taboo with regard to reading a book — do not look at the last page of a murder mystery until you've read everything that comes before.)

That said, it's important to note that the practical example in this book—the Party Planner app— is built, chapter-by-chapter, as you read through the book. However, if you spot something that you want to explore out of sequence, it's easy to do so. The example code in each chapter is posted at `wiley.com/go/treehouse/ios6foundations` as well as on my website at `northcountryconsulting.com`. If you want to jump into Chapter 12, for example, you can download the code from Chapter 11 and modify it as you read on. (Note that the code posted on the web for each chapter represents the code as it is at the *end* of the chapter.)

This book describes iOS 6. Many of the concepts have been introduced in previous versions, but there also are new features that make their debut in iOS 6. This badge identifies those new features.

Using This Book with Treehouse

Just to be clear, you don't have to be a Treehouse member to use this book. However, the online videos at `teamtreehouse.com` do supplement the content quite nicely. When there is a video that covers the same content that is being covered in the book, you will see the Video icon in the margin and a link to the relevant video. Viewing all the videos and completing badges is a good way of testing what you have learned in the book (and of showing off your new skills to others).

If you ever get stuck on a concept in the book, Treehouse has a great community of members who would be more than happy to help you. You can find them in the official Treehouse members group on Facebook.

Ready to go? Let's get started.

part 1
Introducing iOS 6

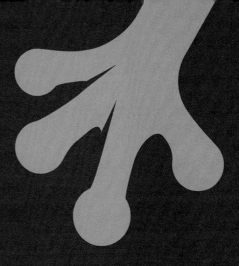

chapter one
Getting Started with iOS 6

WELCOME! IT'S GREAT to welcome new developers to the world of iOS 6, and I'm happy to help you get started. For most developers with experience on other platforms, iOS is unlike the development environments they are used to. For starters, it lets you build apps for some of the most exciting products today (and, indeed, for many, many days). When you build an app for iPhone, iPod touch, or iPad you become part of the exciting ecosystem centered on Apple's extraordinary technologies and designs. You can find many books, articles, and media stories about Apple, its products, and their designs. There is analysis and prognostication; there are books and training materials for users. And there are books and training materials for that special cadre of people who extend Apple's handiwork: the developers.

This chapter gets you started as quickly as possible. You'll see how to register as a developer. After that, you'll be able to download tools and documentation from developer.apple.com. In this chapter you learn the basics of the Objective-C programming language and the highlights of the history of iOS 6—how we got here. Then you'll find a high-level overview of the Xcode integrated development environment (IDE). Before you know it, you'll be following the steps at the end of the chapter to build your first iOS 6 app.

Doing Your Homework

How did you decide to start developing for iOS? Some people use iOS devices and just want to find out more about what makes them tick. Other people have an idea for a great app and would like to build it themselves. Still others are IT professionals who want to expand their skills to this new platform. And others are IT professionals who have been asked to find out how to port an existing or planned project to iOS devices.

Getting Yourself Ready

No matter which category you find yourself in, you probably need to do a bit of homework before you start. You should have some background in programming. It can be long ago or recent, and it can be in advanced languages derived from C or in scripting languages such as PHP. (As noted in the Introduction, some experience with object-oriented programming can definitely help.)

You should be familiar with iOS from a user's perspective. If you plan to develop for only one of the devices (iPhone or iPad, perhaps), you can just explore that device and its features. However, to fully understand the iOS ecosystem, it's good to have both devices and to share data between them using iCloud.

Apple has fairly aggressively pushed out new versions of its devices on roughly an annual basis. It has followed a pattern of dramatically lowering the prices on the previous version of each device as a new one becomes available. You may be able to find a model that is several years old (you may even know someone who can give you one) that you can use for testing. As long as you can install iOS 6 on it, you'll have a test device and not have to worry about mixing up your actual data with test data.

Adopting a Developer's Point of View

When people use computers, they usually focus on a task that they need to accomplish. As a developer, you need to learn a secondary focus: watch *how* people do things rather than *what* they do. Develop this skill and use it to observe how people behave with iOS devices. You have a perfect test subject: yourself.

When something goes wrong or doesn't work the way you expect it to, don't just push on to try it another way. Take a moment to think back not so much about *what* you did wrong but *why* you did it. Did you mistake one icon for another? (Perhaps the icon's meaning wasn't clear.) Did you assume that an action would be carried out differently than it actually was? It doesn't matter if you made a mistake or if the app has a bug in it; in either case, something broke the chain of logic in the user interface and the app. Get used to spotting and analyzing these little glitches. Each one is a learning experience if you just pay attention to it before moving on with the task at hand.

Exploring the App Store

As of this writing, Apple's App Store has surpassed three quarters of a million apps. There are all kinds of apps for all kinds of purposes. Explore the App Store to see what people are writing. If you have an idea for an app, look to see how other people are approaching the topic.

Even if you have an idea for your own app, continue browsing in the App Store in other genres. Many apps are free, so download and install any that seem interesting in any way. If you are planning to build an app for people to use for keeping track of livestock breeding, you may spot an interface element in a game or other app that would be useful in your own app. You can't see every app in the App Store, but keep yourself up to date.

Reading Reviews

Read reviews on the App Store as well as reviews in the media, including blogs. Remember at this point that you're looking for points that reviewers pick up on, both good and bad. Listen to friends as they point out what they like and dislike about the apps they use.

Understanding the App World—
Past, Present, and Future

For most people, the app world began in the summer of 2008. On July 10, the App Store opened (it's part of iTunes which received an update). The next day, July 11, the iPhone 3G went on sale. It ran iOS 2.0.1. The phrase "there's an app for that" was a key part of the marketing of the new iPhone 3G. Before long, people around the world understood the basics of apps that could be downloaded from iTunes directly onto an iPhone.

The app world is just a few years old. Every day, new people join it as they get their first iOS device or, as in your case, they decide to start developing apps. As you explore this world, keep a few critical milestones in mind to help you to make sense of information that you find in your studies:

- As noted, the first release of iOS to developers was iOS 2 in July of 2008.

- iOS 3 in June of 2009 added new features such as copy-and-paste. (Yes, in case you didn't know or have forgotten, you didn't have them at the start.)

- iOS 4 was released in June of 2010. iOS 4.2.1 in November supported the iPad.

- iOS 5, released in October of 2011 was the first unified release for iPhone, iPad, and iPod touch.

- iOS 6 (the subject of this book) was released in September 2012.

Along with new versions of the iOS operating system, the engineers at Apple were updating OS X as well as Xcode, the tool for developers of both operating systems as well as third-party apps. (Xcode is discussed later in this chapter and in Chapter 2, "Getting Up to Speed with Xcode.")

Xcode changes less frequently than the operating systems, but there have been very significant changes accompanying the unification of iOS for all the iOS devices, as well as major changes to the structure of Xcode itself.

Looking at the Master-Detail Application Template

All of this background information matters because, as you browse the web and discussion groups, it's important that you know what version you're looking at. Here's an example of how the evolution has taken shape. Xcode contains a number of templates that you can use as the basis for your apps. One of the commonly used templates today is the Master-Detail Application template for iOS (discussed more later in this chapter). It often serves as the basis of apps, and it will serve as the foundation of the app that you will build throughout this book. When you build the app, you can run it on the iPad simulator. Figure 1-1 shows it running in the simulator in landscape mode.

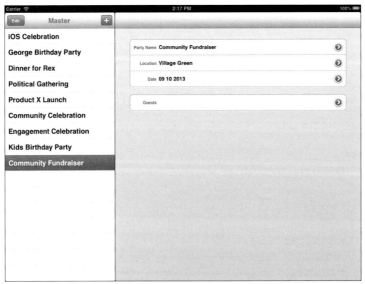

FIGURE 1-1 Master-Detail Application template running on the iPad simulator in landscape mode.

What you see in Figure 1-1 is an iPad feature called a *split view*. It combines two views in one. (Settings uses this architecture so you may recognize the bare bones of the design.) On the left, a *master* view lets you look at an overview; on the right, a *detail* view shows details for the selected item in the master view. When you tap the + at the top of the master view, a new item is added to the list. By default, the template simply inserts placeholder data (a timestamp).

When you rotate the simulator (you'll learn how to do that in Chapter 2), you'll see that the master view disappears (because there isn't room for it). Figure 1-2 shows the simulator in portrait mode.

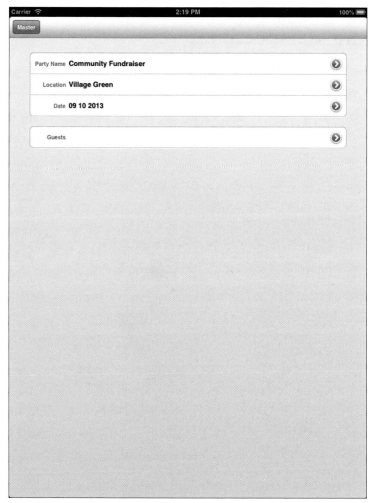

FIGURE 1-2 Master-Detail running on the iPad simulator in portrait mode.

However, there's a Master button in the top bar that will let you open a popover with the data. Tap the button, and the master view slides in from the left as you see in Figure 1-3. You can push the master pane back to see whatever it hides.

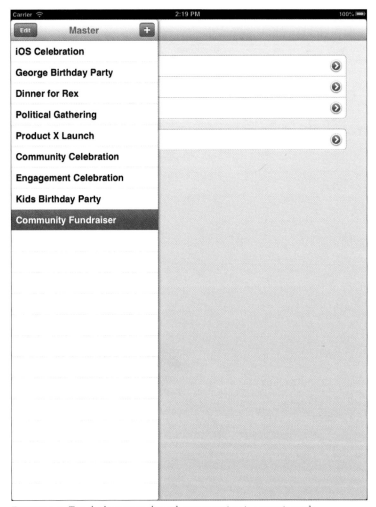

FIGURE 1-3 Tap the button to show the master view in portrait mode.

One of the architectural changes to both Xcode and iOS is the result of the introduction of *storyboards* and the concept of *universal apps*. You can use that combination to write a single app that behaves and looks right on both iPhone and iPad. Furthermore, with the Auto Layout features introduced in 2012, apps can also adjust to changing screen sizes, as happened with iPhone 5 and with iPad mini. Auto Layout lets you handle both changes in screen size and changes in aspect ratio (the latter being reflected in the difference between iPhone 5 and previous models).

Because the template has universal code in it, you can run the same code on the iPhone simulator. However, because the screen size in iPhone is smaller than in iPad, you can see only one view at a time. Figure 1-4 shows the master view.

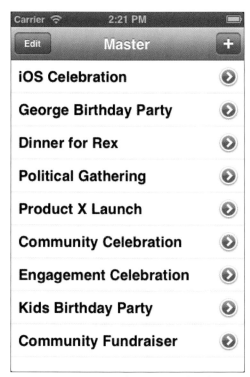

FIGURE 1-4 Master-Detail running on the iPhone simulator in portrait mode, in master view.

From the master view, tap on the item you want to switch to the detail view, as shown in Figure 1-5. You can click the Master button to toggle back.

Also, as part of the template, the views adjust to device orientation as you see in Figure 1-6.

All of this is part of the template: you don't have to write anything.

The reason for showing you this sneak preview of the tools you have available is to point out that much of what you're seeing is very new. In some cases, the best advice from two years ago is outdated today.

FIGURE 1-5 You can toggle between the master and detail screens on iPhone.

FIGURE 1-6 The views rotate properly.

Registering as a Developer

Have you registered as a developer at `developer.apple.com`, the website of Developer Technical Services (DTS)? It's a simple process, and it formalizes your status in the community of developers. Actually, there are several statuses for you to choose among. Most people register as an individual; at the time of this writing, it costs $99 for a year. That entitles you to online access to Apple's documentation, the critical development tools that are centered on Xcode, developer previews of new technologies including the operating systems, and, occasionally, invitations (free or priced) to certain Apple events. Most important to many developers, you gain access to the App Store so Apple can distribute your apps whether they are free or priced. (And you get 30 percent off the price of the app as well as 30 percent of the price of in-app purchases.)

In addition, you get two technical support incidents that you can use to ask Apple engineers for advice. You can send them your code and ask them why something is happening (or why something isn't happening). You can purchase more incidents for $50 each. There are separate programs for iOS, OS X, and Safari (Safari is free).

When you look at `developer.apple.com`, you'll see that you have other choices than an individual program. You can register as a business (if you are legally constituted as a business). You can register through an educational institution that pays the fee for all of its students, and you may find other options on `developer.apple.com`. Take the time now at least to register on `developer.apple.com`. You can come back later to choose which program(s) you want to join. The basic free registration gives you access to the basic resources (but not the App Store). Free registration consists of providing or creating an Apple ID. At that time or later, you can associate that developer account with a specific program.

When you become an iOS developer, you're not alone. There are online communities and discussion boards where you can meet other developers. In many places, there are local organizations of developers. You can find a local group by looking on sites such as `meetup.com` or by asking in an Apple Store or a third-party store that sells Apple products. If you can't find a local group but are planning to travel to a larger city nearby, take the time to inquire in that city's Apple Store; you may get a suggestion of a group near you or the email address of someone else who is interested.

While on the topic of traveling, as a registered developer you may get an invitation to Apple's Worldwide Developers Conference (WWDC). It is usually held toward the beginning of June in San Francisco. As of this writing, it's limited to 5,000 attendees, and in 2012 it sold out in less than two hours. To date, the limit on attendees has depended both on the size of the venue and on the fact that scores of Apple engineers attend both to present sessions during the week and to be available for consultations with developers. There are drop-in labs for just about every aspect of the operating systems, where you can ask your questions and ask for advice. It's an in-person version of DTS.

If San Francisco seems far away (or tickets are not available), have no worries—videos of the sessions are posted usually within two weeks of the conference. The entire conference is covered by non-disclosure agreements, so the only legal way to access these videos is by being a registered developer. (An exception is the keynote opening session; reporters are invited to it and are invited to write about it. You can usually sit comfortably at home and get the highlights of the keynote on your TV news.)

WWDC affects every Apple developer because it serves as the annual conference to bring developers up to date. Having so many developers together either on-site or through video means that Apple has a chance to preview new features and to explain existing ones. A public release of one of the operating systems (often OS X) within a month or so after the conference is common. In 2012, OS X 10.8 Mountain Lion was released a few weeks after WWDC, and iOS 6 was released three months later. Apple's hardware announcements have recently come in the fall and spring.

That's the crux of what you need to know as a new Apple developer. And here's a tip for you: When you meet other developers at any kind of event such as a Meetup, an Apple Store, or an Apple event, you will always be asked the same question. Don't be surprised. Now that you're part of the community, you'll be asked if you're working on an app. The answer is "Yes." You're reading this book and starting on the road to your first app.

Introducing Basic Programming Concepts

Many people begin learning the basics of programming by writing a short program—often one that displays simple text, such as "Hello, World." Depending on the language, you can do this in a single line of code or a few (see the article "Hello world program" on Wikipedia to find out much more). This is the basic code:

```
main()
  {
        printf("hello, world");
  }
```

It's been more than a quarter century since the first days of Hello World, but many people still learn with this first step in programming. Unfortunately, programming today isn't the linear step-by-step process that Hello World suggests. Technology has moved beyond the linear process of early programming languages into a world of objects and non-linear control.

In its developer documentation, Apple has a 20-page document that shows you how to write a Hello World program. In part, the difference between 20 pages and three lines of code reflects the development environments. In order to write a Hello World program, a few lines of code is sufficient; on the other hand, to use the panoply of developer tools in Xcode and iOS to do that is overkill. However, what developers have learned over the last decades is that the line-after-line model of writing code doesn't scale well. If you want to write an app in the style of Hello World, you'll be at it for quite a while.

In order to build the powerful, complex, and attractive apps that people want today, you need more complex tools than a keyboard and an empty file. In this section, you visit some of the concepts behind the tools. The details are covered in the remaining chapters of this book.

Object-Oriented Programming in Objective-C

If you have experience in programming languages (and you should know at least one to get the most out of this book), you may be put off when you first see the language of iOS, Objective-C. What jumps out at people the first time is the brackets. Here's a line of Objective-C code:

```
self.detailViewController =
  (DetailViewController *)
    [[self.splitViewController.viewControllers lastObject]
      topViewController];
```

Don't panic. Before long you'll understand the brackets and be able to parse that line of code.

Objects in Objective-C

Object-oriented programming is the predominant programming style today. In it, *objects* are created that combine data and logic. A code object often corresponds to a real-world or on-screen object. In Figure 1-1, you see a split view. At the left, you see a master view, at the right, you see a detail view, so you have a total of three views. These are objects on the screen as well as objects in the code.

Objects can refer to other objects, and they do not have to be visible. The three views shown in Figure 1-1 are each contained within another object—a *view controller* object that's not visible itself. People usually talk about the view controllers rather than the views they contain. Thus, it is appropriate to say that the split view controller in Figure 1-1 contains both a master view controller and detail view controller. Each of those three view controllers contains a view, and those views are what the user sees.

In Objective-C, an object is defined as a *class*. You write code for the class. The code defines the logic of the class, which is embodied in *methods*. (These are somewhat analogous to functions in C++ and similar languages, but they differ in a critical point, which is explored in the following section, "Messaging in Objective-C.") A class may also have *properties*. These define data elements (more specifically, they provide accessors to the class's data elements).

When the code is executed, a class can be *instantiated*. This means that there is a memory location set aside for the code and properties of the class. It is real. An instance of a class can store data in its properties, and it can execute the code in its methods. It is common to have multiple instances of a class at runtime, but in some cases there is only one (and in many cases, you write code for classes that are instantiated only under specific circumstances).

As in any object-oriented language, objects can be based on other objects. In Objective-C, a built-in class such as a view controller embodies the basic functionality required for all view controllers. In your own app, you may *subclass* the built-in `UIViewController` class that is part of Cocoa Touch with your own class. In fact, the Master-Detail Application template does it for you: you have a `MasterViewController` and a `DetailViewController` class. They are subclasses of `UIViewController`, and they inherit the methods and properties of `UIViewController`. You can see these files at the left of the Xcode window shown in Figure 1-7. (You learn more about Xcode in Chapter 2.)

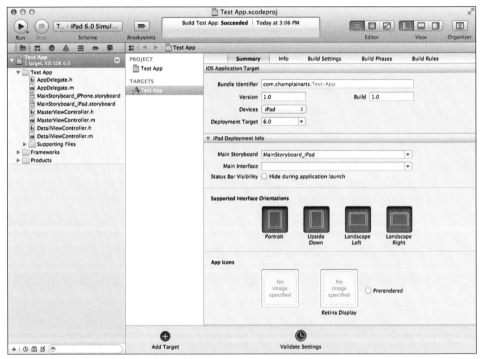

FIGURE 1-7 The project's files are shown at the left of the Xcode window.

You may notice that there are pairs of files for the classes. A file with the .h extension contains the headers—the declarations of the class's methods and properties. A file with the .m extension contains the definitions of the properties and methods—the code that implements them.

This is a very high-level overview of Objective-C. As you read on, you'll find out more about these basic principles.

Messaging in Objective-C

The most important point to understand is that Objective-C is a dynamic, messaging language. In traditional programming languages such as C, each line of code is executed, one after another. Control statements let you alter that line-by-line execution. You can go directly to another line of code (a technique now frowned on) or you can execute code conditionally or in loops.

You an also write functions or subroutines. They are executed line-by-line, just as your main program is. However, they can be called from your main program. Thus, in your main program, you execute the code line by line, but, if you call a function or subroutine, control passes to that code and then returns to the next line in your main program.

The `printf` function in the Hello World program shown earlier is a built-in function of C. Control is transferred to `printf` and, when it's completed, it returns to the main program.

In other object-oriented languages such as C++, you can instantiate an object just as you can in Objective-C. Once you have an instance of an object, you can call a function within it just as you call the `printf` function. When your code is compiled, these links are set up.

Objective-C uses a *messaging* model rather than a calling model. At runtime, you create an instance of an object just as you would in another language. However, rather than calling a function, you send a message to the object. That message causes a method in the object to execute. It is very similar to calling a function, but there is a critical distinction. When you call a function in another language, the function you are calling must be defined, and your main code must identify the function to be called. In Objective-C, you send a message to an object, and, it is quite possible that what that object is will not be defined until runtime. Thus, some of the error checking that occurs in the compiler for other languages is done at runtime. This allows for a great degree of flexibility.

For now, just remember that you are sending messages rather than calling functions. As you start to develop code, the distinctions will start to make more sense.

Frameworks

When you're writing an app, you rarely start from a blank piece of paper or an empty file. Xcode has built-in templates that are functional, so your job is to enhance and customize them. As a developer, you have access to a great deal of sample code on `developer.apple.com`. There is also more code on the web (but remember to be careful to use only current code).

Within iOS, you will find a number of *frameworks*. These are collections of classes that can work together to provide functionality. You can also develop your own frameworks, but in this book, the emphasis is on the provided frameworks. As you start to get a sense for the major frameworks, you'll see what is already built into iOS.

iOS is the operating system for iPhone, iPad, and iPod touch. You implement your apps using the Cocoa Touch application programming interface (API). Cocoa Touch—the API—is the language used by developers. iOS is used by developers, marketers, and users.

Graphical Coding

There's another difference between developing with Xcode and iOS and writing Hello World—some of your coding doesn't involve typing code. When you get around to developing your interface, you draw it with Interface Builder, which is part of Xcode. When you want to link objects in the interface such as buttons to the code that runs them, you simply drag from the button to the code in your file.

You also use graphical coding to set up data relationships; you use graphical elements such as checkboxes to manage your project's settings. There is a lot of code to type, but there is also a lot of non-typed coding to do.

Model-View-Controller

The last major concept to think about is *model-view-controller* (MVC) architecture. It was developed in the 1970s at Xerox PARC, and was first used in the Smalltalk language. When Objective-C was designed in the 1980s it adopted MVC, and it remains a linchpin of the architecture.

MVC organizes the objects in an object-oriented system. This organization creates triplets of objects that implement a model, a view, and a controller. Simply put, a *model is data*. A *view is a representation of the data* along with the controls to work with it. The model knows nothing about the view, and the view knows nothing about the model. This makes for highly portable and maintainable code. It also reflects the fact that with both models and views, you, the designer, can exercise a great deal of logical control. In addition, as you will see with Xcode, graphical user interfaces to design your model and your view are available for you.

The complexity lies with the controller object. The controller knows about both the model and the view. Most of what seems like "real" coding is done in the controller.

You have already seen views in Figure 1-1. Although there is no visual representation of a view controller itself, you have learned that each view has a view controller. As for the model, when you build a project from an Xcode template, you often have a choice of using Core Data for the model or of using another technique.

In the next section, you will see how to set up your data model. It's not terribly complicated: just a checkbox. So it's on to building your first project. It will be the Master-Detail Application shown in Figures 1-1 to 1-7.

Installing and Using Xcode

Until Xcode 4, installing Xcode was a bit complicated. Now, Xcode is installed just as any other app from the Mac App Store. Go to the Mac App Store, and search for Xcode. Then "buy" it, and it will be downloaded and installed automatically. You're ready to go.

Xcode is free, but the operation of installing software through either app store (Mac or iOS) is called a purchase even if there is no charge. It is also important to point out that from time to time, developers have access to pre-release versions of Xcode. They are available for download from `developer.apple.com`.

The following steps walk you through an overview of the Xcode process that will enable you to build the Master-Detail Application and run it as you have seen in this chapter.

1. Buy and install Xcode.

2. Launch Xcode. You will see the screen shown in Figure 1-8.

FIGURE 1-8 The Xcode Welcome screen.

3. From the menu, select Create a new Xcode project.

4. As shown in Figure 1-9, you can select from the built-in templates for iOS and OS X. Select the Master-Detail Application in iOS, and click Next at the lower right.

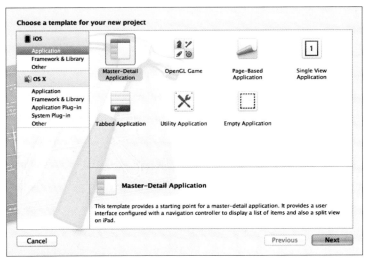

FIGURE 1-9 Select the Master-Detail Application template.

5. On the next screen, fill in the information requested, as shown in Figure 1-10.

   a. The name of the product and your organization name are up to you.

   b. By convention, the company identifier is a reverse domain name, which is guaranteed to be unique.

   c. You can omit the class prefix.

   d. For devices, choose universal to create both iPad and iPhone versions.

   e. Mark the checkboxes at the bottom to use storyboards and use automatic reference counting. If you want Xcode to flesh out your model with Core Data, check that checkbox. (It is not used in the example files you can download for this book.)

6. Click Next to continue.

7. On the next screen, choose the location for the project's files. Click Next. Xcode creates the files for you and opens the project, as you saw in Figure 1-7.

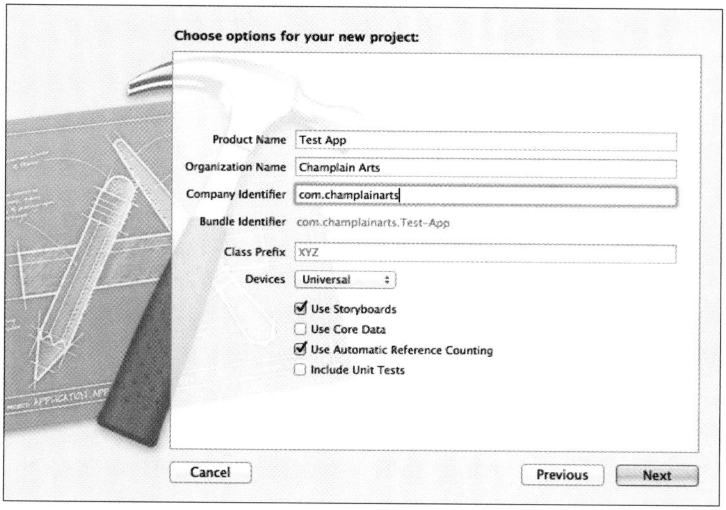

FIGURE 1-10 Fill in the project's options as indicated.

8. Click the Run button at the top left of the window shown in Figure 1-7 to build and run the project. Use the pop-up menu to the right of the Run button to choose whether to run the project on the iPad simulator or the iPhone simulator.

9. Run your project. You'll see the precursors of the images you see in Figures 1-1 to 1-6.

Summary

This chapter showed you how to prepare to be an iOS developer. You should practice looking at apps with a new eye—look at *how* they do things in addition to *what* they do. You have some familiarity with the basic principles and concepts of iOS; you'll learn more about the specifics later in the book. You also should have installed Xcode as described in this chapter. You should follow the steps to build your first project from the built-in Master-Detail Application template. It's important to do this now so that if, by some chance, there is an error in your Xcode installation, you catch it before moving on.

In Chapter 2, you explore Xcode itself. It has powerful tools to help you build your app. (It is actually the same tool that the engineers at Apple use to build iOS itself.)

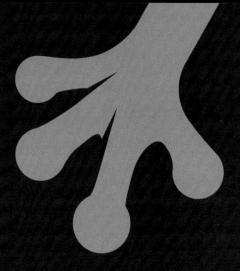

chapter two

Getting Up to Speed with Xcode

YOU'LL BE SPENDING a lot of time with Xcode, the integrated development environment (IDE) for iOS and OS X. Xcode is one of the three interlocking pieces of iOS development (the other two are the Cocoa Touch framework and the Objective-C language). This chapter guides you through using Xcode. In Chapter 1, "Getting Started with iOS 6," you saw the basics of how to create a new project with Xcode (refer to "Installing and Using Xcode" in Chapter 1). You even created a fairly complex project from a template and ran it with a click of the Run button.

Now it's time to look deeper into Xcode. In this chapter, you'll look at the Xcode interface and the tools that are available to you. By the end of this chapter, words and phrases such as "project," "workspace window," "navigator," "inspector," "library," and "utilities" will be familiar to you, and you'll see how to use these Xcode tools.

One chapter—or even one book—can provide just an introduction to Xcode. Bear in mind that Xcode is used internally by the engineers at Apple for the software that they build. This means that it's designed not only to help you build your own apps, but it's also designed to let the engineers build OS X and iOS, too, along with other Apple software such as the iWork suite, iBooks Author, and the built-in iOS apps such as Messages, Calendar, and Reminders. You don't have to worry about getting stuck building a project that outpaces Xcode.

Many tools for analyzing code and performance are built into Xcode or are provided as additional tools. What you'll learn in this chapter and in the rest of this book is how to build a basic iOS app. When you want to move on to more complex apps, Xcode and the `developer.apple.com` website will be there for you.

Using the Workspace Window

Xcode has a single window with a multitude of sections, each of which lets you manage different types of operations. It's called a *workspace window*. You can show or hide various parts of the workspace window as you see fit. You can open several workspace windows at a time if you are working on several projects. Xcode supports full-screen views, and, in fact it is one of the apps that most benefits from the use of the full screen.

This section introduces the basic controls for showing and hiding the parts of the workspace window. Following sections delve into the specific areas that you use to edit code, work with project files, and perform operations on your code and objects.

Most people who use Xcode show and hide the various sections of the workspace window as they go along. Perhaps the easiest way to introduce you to the window is not to show the full window with a lot of arrows and labels, but, rather, to start by showing you the smallest possible workspace window and then show you how you can add components to it.

Figure 2-1 shows you a workspace window. The *Editor area* takes up most of the window. At the very top is the *jump bar*.

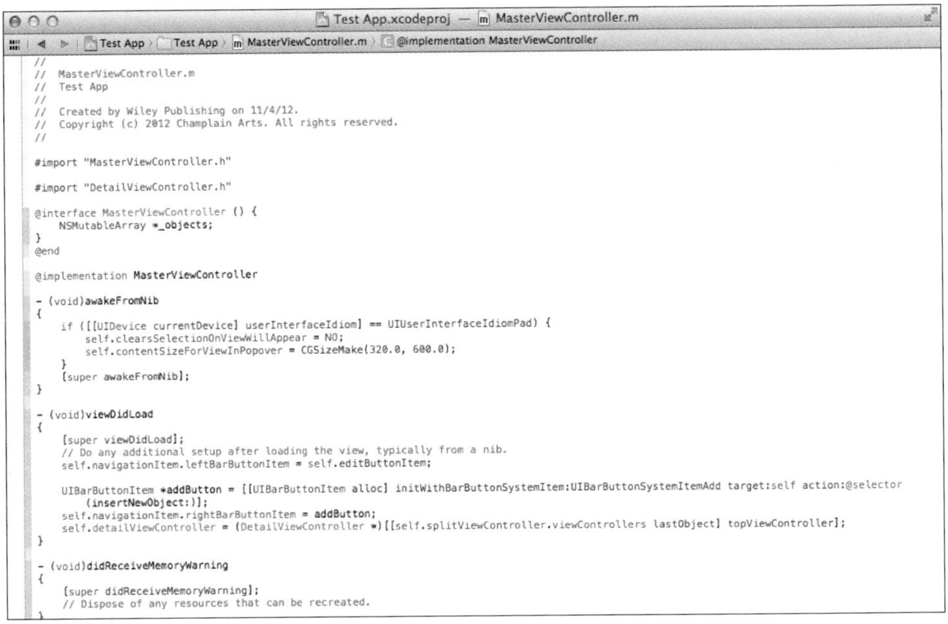

FIGURE 2-1 Editor in a workspace window.

Note the full-screen control in the top right of the window. It lets you switch back and forth between a window view and a full-screen view.

Most people find that to get the most out of Xcode, using the on-screen controls is often more efficient than using the corresponding menu commands. In this chapter, Xcode and its workspace window are presented based on what you see. Menu commands, where they exist, are noted. The first part of this chapter walks you through the interface. In the second part, you'll see how to perform common tasks such as editing your code. You may want to switch back and forth; indeed, you may want to bookmark this chapter and refer to it periodically as you encounter new tasks in the course of this book.

Exploring the Jump Bar

The jump bar appears above the Editor area at all times. It consists of three basic sections. From the left, they are the related items pop-up menu, the back/forward navigation buttons, and the navigation levels.

Related Items Pop-up Menu

Figure 2-2 shows the related items pop-up menu in action. Based on the file that is shown in the Editor area, you can choose from various types of related files and open them directly from the pop-up menu.

FIGURE 2-2 The related items pop-up menu.

This is an incredibly powerful tool that can save you an enormous amount of time as you are working in Xcode. However, there is much more you can do to improve your productivity. In Xcode's General preferences, shown in Figure 2-3, you can choose the behavior of modifier keys when you open a file—including from the related items pop-up menu. You open all the Xcode preferences using Xcode➡Preferences or ⌘-, (comma).

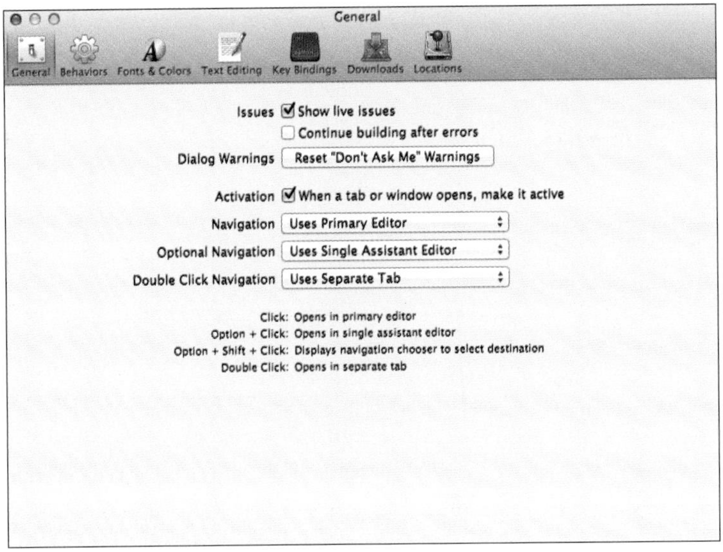

FIGURE 2-3 Set General preferences.

It is worthwhile exploring the preferences as you work with Xcode because you will gradually see how they work together. In Figure 2-3, for example, you can see that the option is set for optional navigation (holding down the Option key) so that the file that you're opening will open in a single assistant editor. An assistant editor shows two files side by side (or above and below) one another. Thus, you can look at an interface file next to its implementation, as shown in Figure 2-4.

You can also choose a separate assistant editor, as shown in Figure 2-5. This will add another assistant editor to the window. (Note, too, that editors need not be text only—in Figure 2-5 you see Interface Builder, which lets you use a graphical user interface to edit your app's interface.)

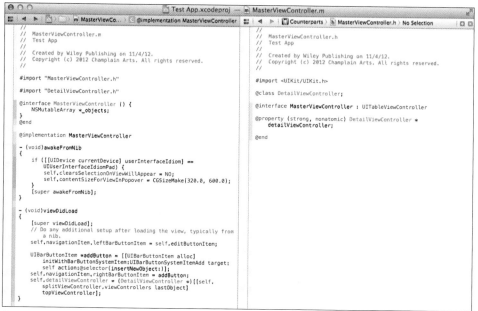

FIGURE 2-4 Use a single assistant editor.

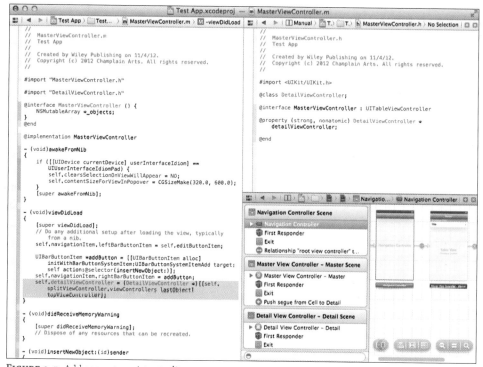

FIGURE 2-5 Add separate assistant editors.

To revert to the standard editor shown in Figure 2-1, choose View→Standard Editor→Use Standard Editor. Alternatively, use the small X at the top right of each assistant pane to close that pane. When you close the last pane, the standard editor will be shown.

Back/Forward Navigation Buttons

The related items pop-up menu lets you navigate easily through your code based on the relationships among your files. Sometimes, you want to simply go back to the previous file. The back/forward buttons to the right of the related items pop-up menu function the way that similar buttons work in web browsers.

Using the Jump Bar to Navigate

The main part of the jump bar lets you navigate through the levels of your code. Each of the levels in the jump bar lets you choose from the relevant files. From the left of the jump bar levels, the first item lets you choose top-level items such as your project. Next, you can choose from the groups in your project (groups are discussed in the Navigator area later in this chapter). From within a selected group you can choose the specific document you want to view. And, if applicable, a final button will let you choose among the syntactical elements in that document (methods, for example).

Exploring the Toolbar

Xcode has a toolbar at the top of the window. You can show or hide it in a window view; it is always shown in full-screen view. If you switch into full-screen view with the control at the top right of the window, the toolbar will appear, as shown in Figure 2-6. The menu bar at the very top of the screen appears only when the mouse is over that area. Otherwise, it is hidden. In a window view, you can show and hide the toolbar with the commands in the View menu.

The toolbar has seven areas.

- Building and running projects
- Choosing a scheme
- Enabling and disabling breakpoints
- Status
- Editor buttons
- View buttons
- Organizer

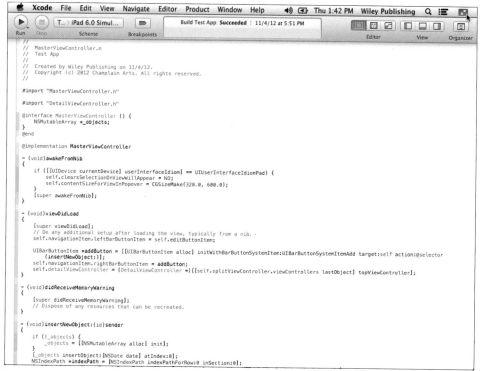

FIGURE 2-6 The toolbar is always present in full-screen views.

Building and Running Projects

The most commonly used controls for most people are at the left of the toolbar. The Run button builds and runs the current project. The Stop button stops it.

There are commands in the Product menu that that also let you build and run the project. Product➜Build (⌘-B) and Product➜Run (⌘-R) are the most commonly used. Another frequently used command is Product➜Clean (⌘-K), which cleans out all compiled code and recompiles everything. Sometimes, if you've been doing a lot of reorganizing in your code, cleaning it will get rid of some miscellaneous errors that have arisen.

Choosing a Scheme

The scheme lets you select where your app will run. As part of the standard Xcode installation, you have a simulator for both iPhone and iPad. You can choose to run it on either one. You also can attach an iPhone or iPad to your Mac with a cable; in that case, you can choose to run your app on the iOS device. These options are shown in Figure 2-7.

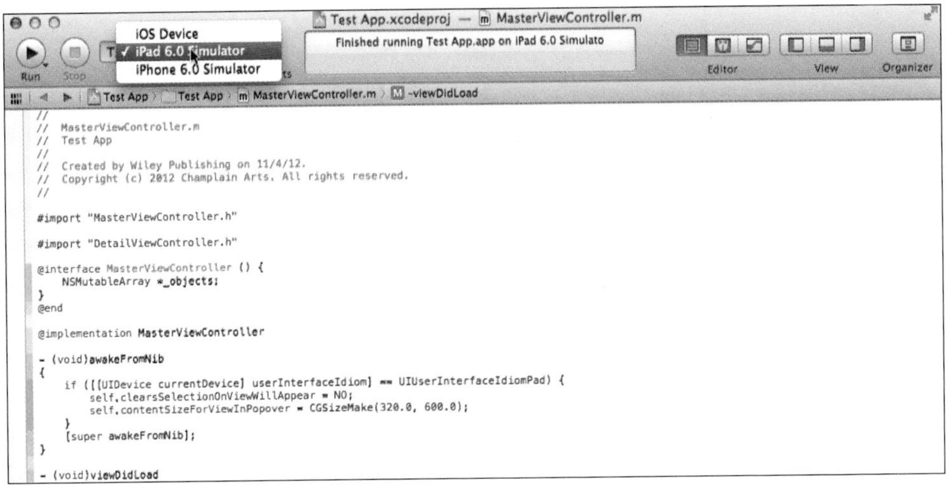

FIGURE 2-7 Select the scheme to use.

Running on a device requires that it be provisioned through `developer.apple.com`. There is more information there for registered developers.

Enabling and Disabling Breakpoints

Breakpoints are covered in Chapter 11, "Testing the App with the Debugger." The Breakpoints button in the toolbar simply turns them all on or off. It's often faster than modifying settings in the debugger.

Activity Viewer

In the center of the toolbar, the Activity Viewer lets you see what's happening inside Xcode. When you are building an app, a progress bar tracks its progress. If you encounter warnings or errors, the number of them is shown in the Activity Viewer. You can click on the number to view the issues.

Editor Buttons

To the right of the Activity Viewer are the three Editor buttons. You use them to switch among the standard editor, the assistant editor, and the version editor. The standard editor, shown in Figure 2-1, is where you normally edit and view your source code. As you saw in Figure 2-4 in the section, "Related Items Pop-up Menu" earlier in this chapter, you can open related items side by side (or above and below) so that you have multiple files open at a time.

I chose to set up the preferences as shown in Figure 2-3. Thereafter, I can simply open the necessary file. However, if you want, you can use an Editor button to switch between the standard and assistant editor and then, in a second step, you can choose the file(s) to show.

The version editor is used to compare changes in a single file shown in before and after versions.

View Buttons

There are three View buttons farther along the toolbar to the right. As shown in Figure 2-8, the first of these shows and hides the Navigator area at the left of the workspace window.

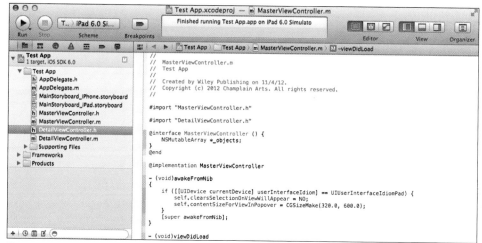

FIGURE 2-8 Show the Navigator area.

The View button on the right side of this group of buttons shows and hides the right-side Utility area of the workspace window, as you see in Figure 2-9.

The button in the center lets you show and hide the Debug area below the Editor area. You can use these buttons in combination. Figure 2-10 shows a full-screen view of the workspace window with the left-side Navigator area and the right-side Utility area both shown, along with the Debug area below the Editor area. (The Editor area can never be hidden.)

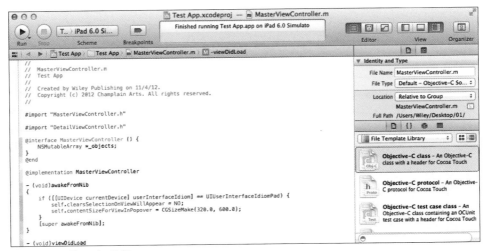

FIGURE 2-9 Show the Utility area.

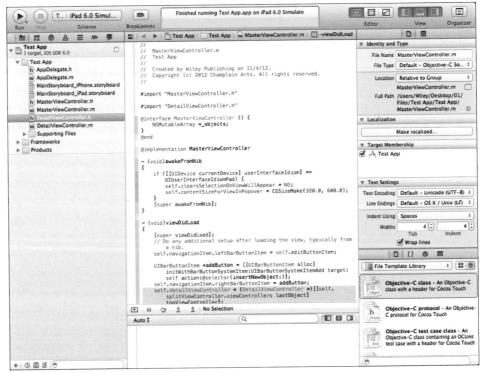

FIGURE 2-10 You can show any of the areas as you want.

Organizer

The Organizer, shown in Figure 2-11, always opens in its own window. It lets you organize devices and documentation. You'll find out more about it later in this chapter in the section on Quick Help.

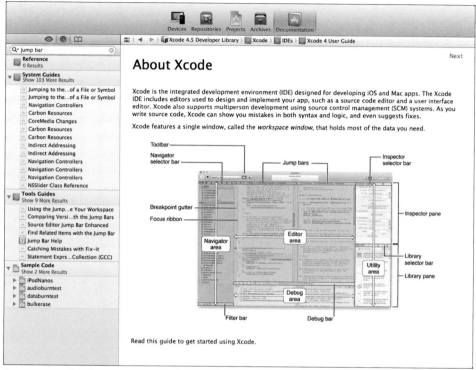

FIGURE 2-11 Use the Organizer.

Selector Bars

Finally, note in Figure 2-10 that at the top of the Editor area, you have the jump bar. At the top of the other areas, you have small selector bars with options and icons in them that let you control those areas. These bars will be discussed in the appropriate sections later in this chapter.

Exploring the Tab Bar

The tab bar, which can be shown or hidden from the View menu, appears just below the tool-bar and above the jump bar in the Editor area (as well as above the selector bars in the Navigator and Utility areas if they are shown). You can see the tab bar in Figure 2-12.

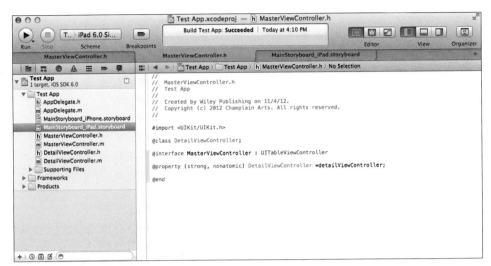

FIGURE 2-12 Show the tab bar.

You can use General preferences, as shown in Figure 2-13, to open files automatically in tabs.

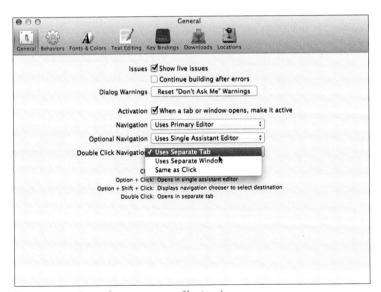

FIGURE 2-13 Set preferences to open files in tabs.

Using Projects

When you create a new Xcode project from a template, you may see the project summary, as shown in Figure 2-14.

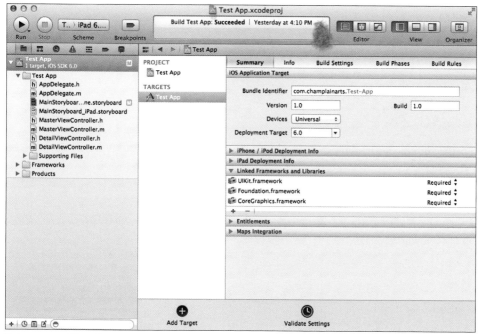

FIGURE 2-14 View the project summary.

For most of the templates you'll be using, you will have a single project and a single target—both have the name you provide when you create the project, as described in "Installing and Using Xcode" in Chapter 1. The default settings are usually correct, so you can just continue to write your code.

You should be aware, however, that Xcode can handle much more complex projects. You can have a project with multiple targets—for example, different devices or different versions of iOS. You also can have a workspace that contains several projects. The most common configuration is a workspace that contains one project for OS X and another for iOS. Such a workspace may often have a third project that contains shared code.

For now, a single project and target is a good way to get started.

Exploring the Editor Area

The heart of Xcode is the Editor area where you edit your code. You have probably used editors before in other programming environments. Xcode may be a little different. For starters, the Editor area displays a different editor for each type of file you edit.

Figure 2-15 shows one of the editors: Interface Builder. It lets you build your interface graphically. You'll find out more about it in Part II, "Storyboards: The Building Blocks of iOS Apps."

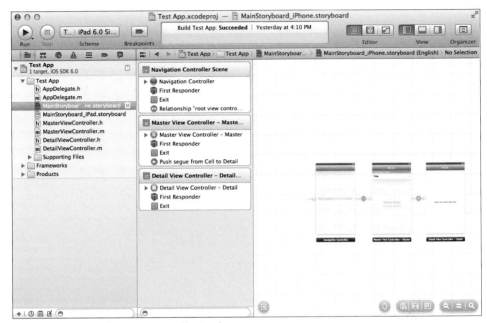

FIGURE 2-15 Set preferences to open files in tabs.

Figure 2-16 shows the Core Data Model editor—another graphical user interface to your programming. Core Data can be the topic of an entire book, but you'll find an overview in Chapter 10, "Saving and Restoring Data."

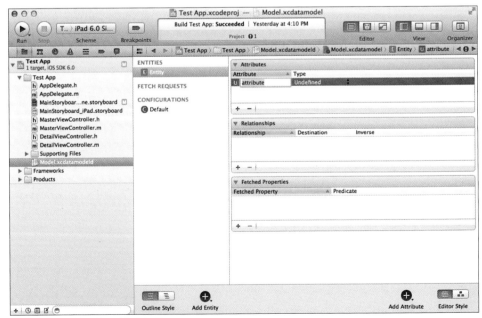

FIGURE 2-16 Core Data Model editor.

Using Editing Preferences

Many people use the standard editor with the default settings. This means you can just start to enter code (or, more likely, modify code in a template). If you do want to customize the Text Editing preferences, you find them in Xcode➜Preferences. There are two tabs for text edit: Editing and Indentation. Figure 2-17 shows the Text Editing preferences.

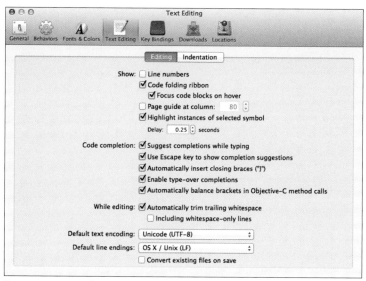

FIGURE 2-17 Set editing preferences.

Many of these are fairly standard code-editing settings that you may have found in other development environments, and they are self-explanatory.

Using Code Completion

What is likely to be new to you is the code completion section. Xcode monitors your keystrokes and can alert you to potential errors. It also can suggest completions for what you're typing. You'll find out more about this in the section called "Using Fix-It," later in this section.

Handling Indentation

As you can see in Figure 2-18, Xcode is able to smartly indent your code. This is because it is constantly monitoring what you're typing to determine what the syntax is. It is important to note also that you can choose to have the Tab key use tab characters or multiple spaces to manage indentation.

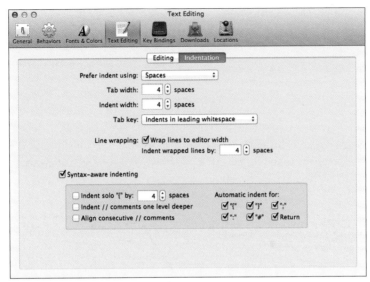

FIGURE 2-18 Set preferences for indentation.

Using Fix-It

As you can see in Figure 2-19, Xcode's Fix-It feature can flag potential errors and suggests fixes.

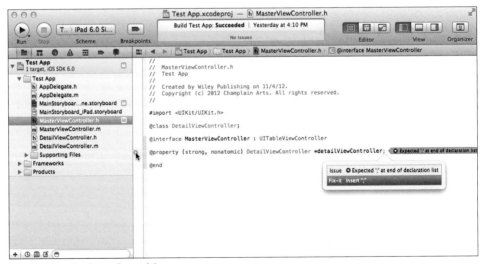

FIGURE 2-19 Fix-It can flag and fix errors.

If you want to accept the Fix-It suggestion, just press the Return key. As you get used to working with Fix-It, you'll notice that as you type, Fix-It may discover errors that will be solved as you continue typing. Don't automatically accept Fix-It suggestions, because sometimes they are just a result of your typing speed. However, you'll soon see that when that bulls-eye symbol pops up in the gutter at the left of the editor, you can quickly prevent or fix an error. In general, the closer the correction is to the moment at which you cause an error, the easier it is to fix.

Using Code Completion

Code completion (shown in Figure 2-20) suggests one or more completions for the code you are typing. The more characters you type, the fewer the number of suggestions that are available to you because you are narrowing the scope of what code completion needs to do.

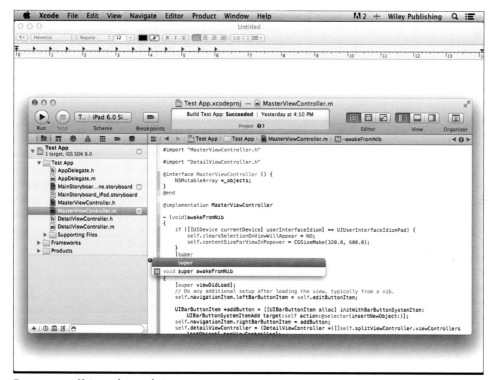

FIGURE 2-20 Using code completion.

Code completion often takes the format shown in Figure 2-20. This is the declaration of a method (the M indicates method). The actual code completion if you press Return or click that line will be super awakeFromNib because the void is part of the method declaration. Having the full declaration can help you decide which of several possible completions you want to use.

The "Using Quick Help" section, later in this chapter, is relevant to editing code. You may want to jump ahead to that section now.

Exploring the Navigators

You can show or hide the Navigator area with the View button in the toolbar or by using the View→Navigators submenus. The buttons in the selection bar at the top of the navigator correspond to the submenu commands and their keyboard equivalents:

- Show Project Navigator ⌘-1
- Show Symbol Navigator ⌘-2
- Show Search Navigator ⌘-3
- Show Issue Navigator ⌘-4
- Show Debug Navigator ⌘-5
- Show Breakpoint Navigator ⌘-6
- Show Log Navigator ⌘-7

Using the Project Navigator

The project navigator is where you manage your project's file. Located at the left of the workspace window, it can be shown or hidden with the left-most View button at the right of the toolbar as long as with the keyboard equivalents shown previously for individual navigators. The keyboard equivalent to hide the Navigator area is ⌘-0.

At the top of the navigator, you will find the project itself. A disclosure triangle lets you open or close the project. If you select the project, you see the summary shown at the right of Figure 2-21.

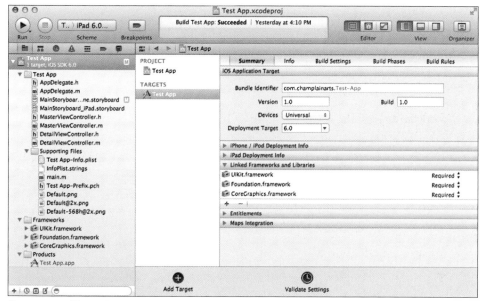

FIGURE 2-21 The project navigator.

Using Groups

You can organize your files into *groups* in the project. In the project navigator, those groups are indicated by folder icons that you can open or close. However, if you look on disk, you'll see that they do not represent actual folders. This means that you can organize your project's groups without regard to where the files actually are on disk. (This is particularly important on multi-developer projects.) You can drag files around in the project navigator; you can move them in or out of groups as you see fit.

You can select multiple files in the project navigator and use Control-click to bring up the shortcut menu shown in Figure 2-22. Use the New Group from Selection command from that menu or choose File➔New➔Group from Selection to create a new group that contains your selected file. You can click the group name to change it. (Note that it's best to change filenames with the Edit➔Refactor command. It is described in Chapter 4, "Designing the Party Planner App.")

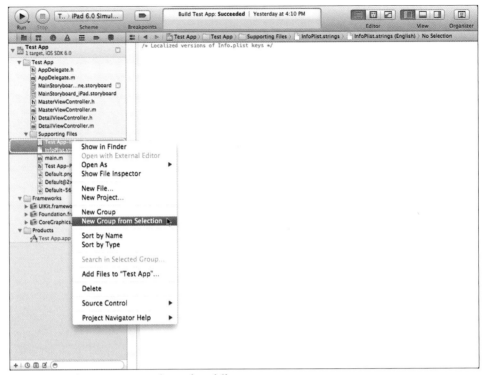

FIGURE 2-22 Create a new group from selected files.

Spotting Missing Files

Some of the filenames may appear in red. This indicates that the file is missing. When you first create a project from a template, the app file itself (Test App.app in the figure) is red: as soon as you successfully build it, the filename appears in black.

Using the Navigator Controls

At the bottom of the navigator, you find a row of controls. The one on the left lets you add new files to the project, as shown in Figure 2-23.

The first command lets you create a new file from a template (there is an Empty template in the Other category if you want a blank file). The interface is shown in Figure 2-24.

If you choose to create a new file, you can choose from the templates shown in Figure 2-24. The details of creating files from templates and setting options are shown in Chapter 4.

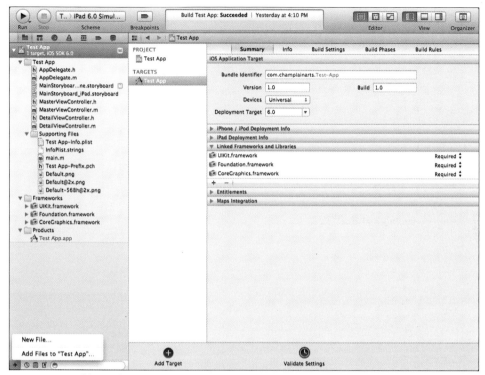

FIGURE 2-23 Add new files.

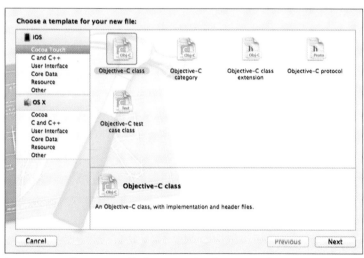

FIGURE 2-24 Create a new file for your project from a template.

You can name the file and give it a location on disk just as you would with any file. Once you have created it, you can move it around in the project navigator. You might want to group files with similar purposes in their own groups.

Rather than create a new file, you can add an existing file from your project, as shown in Figure 2-25.

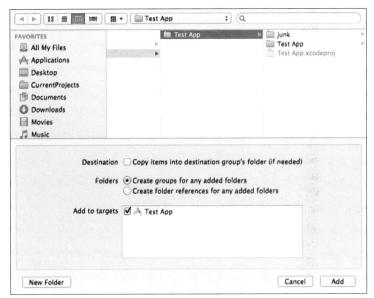

FIGURE 2-25 Add an existing file to your project.

As you can see in Figure 2-25, you have a choice of copying the added file into your project. Most of the time, that is the choice you want. Otherwise, you may wind up with project files all over your hard disk (and maybe on some network disks, too).

Make certain you have checked the target to which you want to add the file (at this point, most of your projects will probably only have one target, but make sure it's checked).

To the right of the + button in the bottom controls of the project navigator, there are three more buttons. They focus the project navigator on certain types of files. Click a second time, and the focus returns to all files. In order from left to right, here is what they do.

- You can choose to see recently modified files.

- You can see only files that are under source code control (that is an advanced topic not covered in this book).

- You can see only unmodified files.

Finally, to the right of the bottom of the project navigator is a filter. If you type text in there only those file whose names contain the text will be shown in the project navigator.

Using the Search Navigator

Part of the power of Xcode lies in its sophisticated finding and replacing tools. When you have a file open in the editor, you can use the Edit→Find command or the ⌘-F keyboard equivalent to open the find bar shown in Figure 2-26.

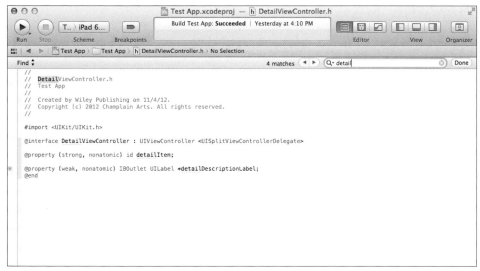

FIGURE 2-26 Use the find bar.

This is a traditional find. (There are many variations on it in the Edit menu.)

The search navigator is a multi-file tool. It is the third icon from the left at the top of the project navigator, as shown in Figure 2-27.

This command goes through your project files looking for the string you type in. The results are listed in the search navigator; you can click on any line to see it highlighted in the editor.

After you have performed a find, you can use the pop-up menu to switch to replace, as shown in Figure 2-28.

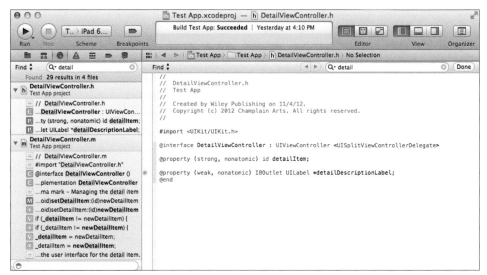

FIGURE 2-27 Use the search navigator.

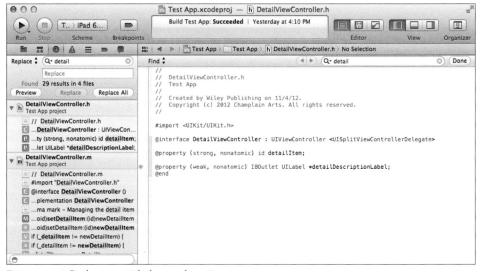

FIGURE 2-28 Replace text with the search navigator.

Using the Other Navigators

Most people use the other navigators less frequently than the project navigator. They are covered as needed later in this book.

Exploring the Utilities

Unlike the Navigator area, which simply shows one of the seven navigators at a time, the Utility area has two separate panes. The top pane is for inspectors, and the bottom pane is for libraries of reusable code, objects, and media.

You can resize either pane; in fact, as shown in Figure 2-29, you can drag the library pane all the way to the bottom so it disappears. Figure 2-29 shows only the inspectors.

FIGURE 2-29 Show only the inspectors.

Using the File Inspector

At the top of Figure 2-29 you see the File inspector on the left. It is always there when a file is shown in the Editor area (which is most of the time). As you can see, it shows you details about the file.

The most important setting here is the location pop-up menu. This describes how your project should deal with the selected file. The settings are:

- **Absolute path**—The path to this file is used exactly as-is. This may be correct for a shared file on a multi-developer project. On a simple, one-person project, this can prevent you from moving the project anywhere else without breaking the location path.

- **Relative to group**—The file is located relative to the group that it is in. This is a good setting to use if you are using shared groups, but it can cause problems when you move the project.

- **Relative to project**—This is a very commonly used setting. It means you can move your project folder anywhere you want and all the files within it will continue to function properly.

- **Relative to developer directory, relative to build products, relative to SDK**—Use this setting if you know what those phrases mean. Again, this is mostly a multi-developer setting or a setting for advanced single developers.

Using Quick Help

To the right of the File inspector is Quick Help. Highlight a word in the Editor area, and Xcode will attempt to find documentation for you. Figure 2-30 shows the display for the highlighted word UILabel. Some of the file references are hot: you can click on them to open the relevant file in the Organizer. Quick Help is smart enough to be able to provide you with information about methods and properties that you declare within your own project.

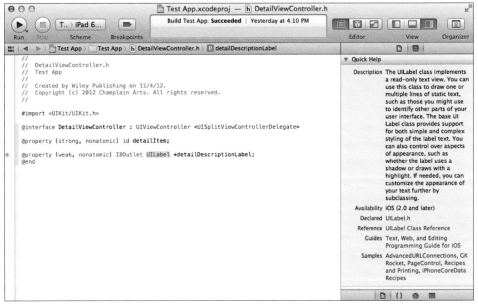

FIGURE 2-30 Use Quick Help.

Using Inspectors

When you are working with Interface Builder or the Core Data Model editor, you work in their graphical user interfaces. When you highlight an object (an interface element, for example, or a Core Data entity), additional inspectors appear next to Quick Help. The specific inspectors vary depending on the object you selected. They are discussed in the relevant chapters.

Using the Libraries

The lower pane of the Utility area contains libraries of reusable objects, code, and media. Choose which one you want with the four icons at the top of the pane. Just below the icons, a pop-up menu lets you quickly select from the items in the library you have selected. To the right of the pop-up menu, buttons let you choose to display the items in a list or as icons.

From the left, the icons represent:

- **Files**—These are the templates you see in the New File sheet.
- **Code Snippets**—You can drag these into a source code editor and modify them as you want. Common snippets such as `try/catch` blocks, `switch` statements, and even Objective-C `init` methods are available. You can add your own snippets.
- **Objects**—The Object library contains objects such as buttons, views, and labels that you can drag into Interface Builder documents.
- **Media**—These are the media files you have added to your project.

Summary

You learned how to work with Xcode, the integrated development environment (IDE) for iOS, as well as OS X and other Apple software. You saw how the workspace window can be adjusted to show the Navigator area, Utility area (with its libraries and inspectors), and the Editor area for editing text as well as editing data models and interfaces with graphical tools.

You saw how preferences can be configured so that mouse clicks and the modifier keys can work together to open files in preconfigured patterns. With the assistant editor, you can automatically open related files side by side to compare them.

In the chapters that follow you will find out more about inspectors as they are needed to work with the code that you write in traditional ways (that is, line after line of code). The Xcode environment integrates graphical and text code construction methods as you develop your apps.

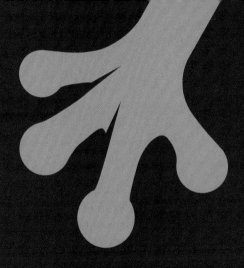

chapter three

Looking Ahead— Planning Your App

ARE YOU READY to start thinking about building your own app? By now, you should have looked at plenty of existing iOS software. You've been honing your developer's eye for what lies beneath the surface so that you can watch how people use apps and think about how you can improve on the user experience in your own app. You're ready to write your code.

Not yet.

Yes, you can sit down and write code for an app. But then what? What do you do with it? Do you submit it to the App Store? Do you chalk it up to a "learning experience" and then start over with a "real" app?

If you want to learn how to write apps and to actually write one, then that's what you should do: write an app. Writing a pretend app doesn't give you reusable experience. As a great teacher once said to a student, "If you don't take yourself seriously, how do you expect anyone else to?" Write a real app and take yourself seriously.

You may think that you just want to learn how to write an app, and you will be glad to work with someone else who will handle the business end (and someone else to handle the graphics, and someone else to...). You don't have to do everything yourself, and you don't have to be an expert in everything, but you do need to know how to plan your app. That's what this chapter is all about.

Answering the Money Question

When you tell your friends you're working on an app, many of them will be excited for you (and for themselves—they know an app developer!). They or you may dream of fame and fortune, but, alas, those are not terribly common among app developers. Even for the most financially successful apps, only a handful of people know who the developers are. And as for the fortune part, most apps make at most very modest profits.

Writing an app may not make you rich, but it very well may get you more work either as a writer of apps or in one of the many jobs that are being invented daily in the app ecosystem. An app that you write can even get you a totally unrelated job, as people see that you know new technologies and can adapt to them and use them successfully.

The "money question" about apps is one that you have to answer, at least for yourself. And in order to answer it, you need to think about the ways in which people make money from apps.

There are three cases in which the money you make from the app is a fixed (or nonexistent) amount. The number of people who buy the app doesn't affect your remuneration.

- You can give your app away for no purpose other than to entertain people or help them do something useful.
- You can give your app away in order to promote a cause or business.
- You can be paid to write an app to promote a cause or business that is given away by the cause or business.

In the following case, your remuneration is directly or indirectly dependent on the number of people who buy your app.

- You can sell your app and profit directly from the 70% of the price that Apple remits to the developer. The more people who buy your app, the more money you make.

In the last two cases, your remuneration is dependent both on the number of buyers but also on the number of users and what they do with the app.

- You can make money from paid advertisements.
- You can make money from in-app sales.

In both of these cases, Apple takes its usual 30 percent share and you get 70 percent or the revenue from ad revenue and in-app sales. Apple's Game Center is a powerful tool to help you get more users (and more repeat users) as well as to provide added benefits for gamers.

Think through where you see yourself and your app, and you should be able to organize your thoughts and your work. If your goal is to make money from in-app purchases or paid advertisements, remember that you are buying into a money flow that will be dependent on use and reuse of your app. Game Center can help you there, but you'll need to constantly replenish and retain your user base.

If your goal is to just sell your app, you don't need to retain your users, but you need to find new users on a constant basis.

In all of these app marketing models, you should consider using the modern tools—a website, social media (often Facebook and Twitter), as well as traditional media such as broadcast and print. Setting up a website today need not be a tremendous burden, and setting up Twitter and Facebook accounts is similarly easy. But as you approach the moment when your app is approved for sale in the App Store, you will not need those extra tasks. You (or a colleague) can work on them while you're developing the app.

> Deciding how you will address the money question is important, but it's not an irrevocable decision. Many apps have morphed from one model to another. The one point that you have to remember is that you must never make promises to your users that you can't fulfill.

Preparing Version 2

Things do move at warp speed in today's app world, but preparing version 2 before you've even laid out version 1 may seem a bit extreme, but it's a very good idea. Using a piece of paper, Reminders, Bento, or your favorite note-taking tool, start a list of features for version 2 as well as possible other versions such as Lite or Pro. As things come to mind, jot them down on the right list. At the beginning of app development, you (and friends) will often bounce a number of ideas around. Some won't pan out, but others will be useful. Just add them to the appropriate list and refer back to them as needed. Just don't let the ideas get lost.

Submitting the App to the App Store

Submitting the app to the App Store—isn't this jumping the gun a bit?

Many experienced developers do start by planning how they will submit their app to the App Store. As development proceeds, they bounce back and forth between the developing app and the plans for submitting it to the App Store. As you work on the app, you may discover that one feature or another is going to be more complicated than you thought. Will you stretch out the development cycle or put the feature into an update or new version? Conversely, you may see how to do something interesting very simply, and you may put it into your app's description that will be submitted to the App Store.

Keeping the developing app in sync with the developing App Store description will benefit both the app and its description. As an important added benefit, as both description and app mature, you'll have them to show to friends, colleagues, and testers. One particular problem facing many new app developers is that they may have developed an app that they can't easily describe. If you've lived with it night and day for months (even years!), you know what it does and what it's for. When someone sees it for the first time, they may be mystified.

Practice what some advisers call an "elevator speech." In the amount of time you spend between floors in an elevator, describe your app (or yourself if you're job hunting) to a prospective buyer (or employer) who is standing next to you in the elevator. You may be comfortable describing your app in 20 pages of documentation or a thousand lines of code, but most people who will want to know about it (even close friends or relatives) want to hear something much more concise—what does it do? And after that, the basic question is why should I use it? You'd better have answers for those questions—answers that are relevant not only to close friends and relatives but also to strangers.

If you look at the information in the App Store, you'll see that for each app, basic information is shown as you see in Figure 3-1.

FIGURE 3-1 Look at the App Store listings.
Source: Apple App Store.

There is more information behind the scenes that you need to provide to the App Store. This section shows you the data that you need to provide and that you should be thinking about from the beginning. As you'll see, all of the data is intertwined, and most of it directly affects the app that you will write. Changes you make now will be much simpler than changes you make later.

Identifying Your App and Yourself

You already began to identify your app and yourself when you first created it in Xcode, as you can see in Figure 3-2.

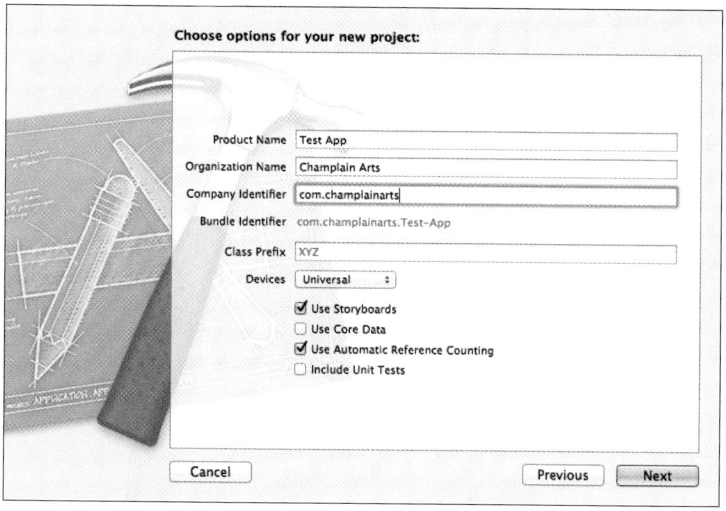

FIGURE 3-2 Identification starts when you create your app.

Bundle Settings

Most of the settings in Figure 3-2 can be changed as you work on your app, but most of them are much, much easier to set properly at the beginning. Perhaps the most important settings are the product name and company identifier. As you can see, they are combined by Xcode to create your app's bundle identifier. You can change the bundle identifier, but if you do so you often wind up getting involved with changing entitlements and permissions—the settings that let you use iOS features such as mapping, iCloud, and the App Store itself.

The good news is that, although the bundle identifier is critical, it is not seen by users in the normal course of events. This means that the product name and company identifier can be changed easily, but the bundle identifier is not easily changed. Many developers use codes for the product name. This means that when the product is finally named for distribution, it can still be referred to internally by the product name, and you won't be confused. Using Fall 2013 as a product name is not a great choice.

The organization name shown in Figure 3-2 defaults to the last organization name that you used in Xcode. You can change it as you go forward with Xcode, but you should use the search navigator to find and replace all the occurrences.

Settings for the App Store

The App Store settings that identify your app are related to the settings shown in Figure 3-2, but all of them are set (or overridden) when you submit the app to the App Store.

The ultimate reference for these settings is the iTunes Connect Developer Guide available to developers at `http://developer.apple.com/library/mac/documentation/ LanguagesUtilities/Conceptual/iTunesConnect_Guide/iTunesConnect_ Guide.pdf`.

- **Name**—This is the full app name. It will be rejected if it suggests that this is an official Apple product, and it can be rejected for other reasons, such as if it violates Apple's rules for developers (see `developer.apple.com` if you are a registered developer to get the current rules). This name appears on the App Store listing shown previously in Figure 1-1.

  Browse the App Store and look at the names of apps—The best names describe the app; they also often provide additional information such as the author or sponsor if that is a known brand name. Some apps include the word "free" in their title; if you do so, make sure you want to keep that pricing policy. Other words that are sometimes added to titles are "Lite" and "Pro" to distinguish among variations of the same app. You don't have to implement all of these—just knowing what you would put in a Lite or Pro version can help you organize your thoughts and plans.

- **Short name**—This is the name that appears below the icon on the home screen when your app is installed. Space is limited there, so you may need to shorten the name. If you do shorten the name, it should make sense. For example, the popular Disney app, "Where's My Water?" is installed as "Water."

- **Seller**—The seller is identified in the App Store. This one can be a bit tricky. If you are registered as an individual developer, the seller will be you: your name will appear here. If you are registered as a company, your company name will appear here (XYZ Company, Inc., for example).

  One of the reasons for thinking ahead to the App Store is to make certain that the seller name is what you want. If you are registered as a company, chances are that's the name you want to use. A common situation arises if you are registered as an individual and want your app to be sold by a company that you own or that you will set up.

  It is possible to change an individual developer registration to a company registration, but it is not an online click. You will have to submit appropriate documentation. This is not particularly burdensome, but it means that you have to budget time for it. (There is no fee for this.) If you set aside a week for this process, that is often enough. If your legal documents are not readily available (or if you need to go through the legal process of forming a corporation or partnership), you should add the time for that process.

  By the way, those documentation requirements apply not only to changing a developer registration but also to registering for the first time as a corporation. The time frames involved vary by country and jurisdiction within countries. In New York State, creating a corporation and registering it as a company developer with Apple can take a month, much of which involves waiting for processing the corporate paperwork. (Expedited options are available for the corporate paperwork.)

- **Copyright name and date**—This is the name of the copyright holder and the date of copyright. Because laws differ from country to country, you should consult a legal advisor if you have any questions about the copyright notice. Most people use a line such as

  ©Champlain Arts Corp, 2013.

- **Version**—This is the version of your app. You normally start with version 1.0. As you work through this section, you can jot down items for a version 2.0 and even 3.0 along with suggestions for 1.1 and 1.2. Minor versions (1.1, for example) can be free updates to correct bugs and to accommodate new features and new hardware. (Note that during development, you may start with a version 0.1 and subsequent versions such as 0.2 and 0.3. However, once you are ready to submit your app to the App Store, you should change the version to 1.0.)

Setting Marketing Data (Discoverability)

As of this writing, there are over 700,000 apps in the Apple App Store. (And there have been 35 billion downloads of them.). People find apps in various ways, including word of mouth, advertising or publicity in traditional media or on the web, and also by searching the App Store. You control a great deal of the search process in the App Store (technically, it's called *discovery*). The data in this section helps you fine-tune your discoverability. If you want to be serious about developing apps, work through this section carefully. The old saying about a tree falling in a forest causing no sound applies to undiscoverable apps in the App Store.

A lot of the data in this section is entered with checkboxes. Other information is submitted as text or as files that you upload. One of the reasons for thinking through your discovery features at the beginning of the development process is that now, before you have written any code, you can implement changes to your app's design. For example, a conversation now about how you might support various languages in the future even if you don't support them now is useful. There are consequences in the code that you'll write, as you'll see in Chapter 15, "Telling Users the News: Alerts and NSError."

- **Price tier**—You choose the price tier for your product. It can be free, or it can be in any of a number of price tiers. The tiers are based on US dollar values—Tier 1, for example, is $0.99, and Tier 2 is $1.99. After Tier 50 ($49.99), the prices go up in larger increments. Apple shows your product price on the App Store based on the tier you select and the store in which it is being viewed (see the following item). When you get around to actually submitting your app to the App Store, you'll see that you can set date ranges for your prices.

- **Store(s)**—You can choose in which store(s) your app appears. There are online App Stores for many countries in the world, and more are added over time. As stores in countries or regions are added, they are removed from the special region—ROW (rest of world).

- **Languages**—You can specify the languages in which your app is available.

- **Keywords**—You can supply keywords to describe your app. Many developers choose a mixture of very specific keywords and more general ones. This strategy may work well if you want experts as well as non-experts to find your app. If you are marketing your app to experts, the very specific (even jargon-y) keywords may work best, and if you want to appeal to a broader audience, specific and jargon-y keywords may not work. Look at other apps and try out searches on the App Store for yourself. Remember not to use names of products or other apps as keywords unless you have the right to use them.

- **Category**—People can browse the App Store by category. You can select a primary and secondary category. As of this writing, the categories are:

Books	Navigation
Business	News
Catalogs	Newsstand
Education	Photo & Video
Entertainment	Productivity
Finance	Reference
Food & Drink	Social Networking
Games	Sports
Health & Fitness	Travel
Lifestyle	Utilities
Medical	Weather
Music	

- **Icons**—Icons are a key part of your discoverability. Although people can't search on icons, when your app comes up as the result of an App Store search, the icon is displayed. Icon design is a very specialized skill. Some graphic artists specialize in icons, whereas others simply will not touch them. In a limited space, the icon must convey something about the nature of the app (is it geared to children, for example) as well as something compelling about the app itself.

  If you want to know what that phrase, "something compelling about the app itself" means, that's exactly the expertise of a skilled icon designer. Sometimes, an app icon includes graphics from the app itself (this is particularly true of games), but other times the icon uses none of the app's graphics or visual conventions. You will need a variety of icons for various purposes; they are outlined at `developer.apple.com`.

- **Description**—This is your chance to describe your app and convert people who are browsing to people who will download the app. There are many references about how to write good advertising copy on the web and in bookstores and libraries. One of the most repeated suggestions is to provide the information your user wants rather than what you want to tell. As you write and refine the description, you may go back to your app itself and change some of its features.

In writing the description, you may discover that you need to name elements of your user interface for the first time. For example, a common button in toolbars is a gear wheel, which brings up choices of actions the user can take. You can put that button there and implement it; many users will just try it out without knowing precisely what their choices will be. Because it's so easy to just click somewhere else, it's a great interface. But now that you're writing a description, you may have to tell people what that is. Do you call it a gear wheel? Do you call it the Actions button? Or do you follow the lead that you see in Apple's documentation. In the Apple documentation for user interface, objects such as this are often not named. Instead, a small image of the object in question is inserted directly into the text.

- **Screenshots**—You'll find details on `developer.apple.com` for the screenshots you should provide. They will appear next to your description, so making certain that they are coordinated will make your app's listing better. If it's not immediately clear what the objects in the screenshots do (a gear wheel for example), consider adding a few words in your description to explain them.

- **Rating**—Ratings are based on age. You choose the one that fits your app. Note that choosing an inappropriate rating can result in rejection of your app from the App Store. These are the current ratings.

  4+. Suitable for everyone.

  9+. Suitable for ages nine and over. Occasional realistic, fantasy, or cartoon violence as well as mild mature, suggestive, or horror-themed content is allowed along with simulated gambling. (Note the use of "occasional" and "mild.")

  17+. Replace "occasional" and "mild" in the previous section with "frequent" and "intense." Add sexual content, nudity, alcohol, tobacco, and drugs.

Describing Your App's Requirements

The app you submit will provide the information required in this section.

- **Devices**—iPad, iPhone, iPod touch, or iPad mini.

- **Version**—These are the versions of the OS you support. This book is relative to iOS 6. When you build the project in Xcode, you can test it in the simulator under iOS 5, which may also work for you. Previous versions are unlikely to work.

Specifying Integration Features

For the sake of completeness, here are the integration features that your app can provide; they will be listed in the App Store. You will set them up with entitlements as you set up your app with iTunes Connect, but unfortunately, there isn't room in this book to cover the details.

- In-app purchases
- iAd advertisements
- Game Center

Celebrating Learning iOS with Your App!

You've thought about how you will manage your app and how you will describe it in the App Store. There's just one thing missing: the app itself.

You may have your own idea that you're itching to get started with. That's great, but you need a framework to build your first app. If you have your own app idea, just put it aside for a little time while you work through this app. And if you don't have an idea for your own app yet, you can use the one described here to get started.

It's really quite simple. By the end of this book, you'll have learned the basics of iOS 6 app programming. That will be a time to celebrate. It will be a time to invite friends and colleagues to join you in a party (maybe friends and colleagues have also been working through the book and deserve their own party). You'll need to make a guest list and set the date and time for your party. Should there be food—light snacks or a meal? What about beverages? Particularly if several of you are celebrating your new-found familiarity with iOS 6, maybe you need some music.

That's a lot to keep track of. As one of the original App Store advertisements said, "there's an app for that."

Actually, there are several, but your very own party-planning app will be up and running by the end of this book.

Summary

This chapter helped you plan for your app's App Store listing. The development of the app and the development of the App Store listing often go hand-in-hand. New ideas for the app may emerge as you write the description for the App Store, and you may need to change the description as you get deep into coding the app.

You see the issues you have to reckon with about pricing apps and how to use the various tools of the App Store to help people discover your app. And, if you've followed the suggestions in this chapter, you have a to-do list for future enhancements to your app once version 1.0 ships.

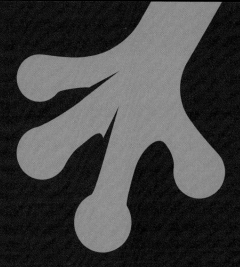

chapter four

Designing the Party Planner App

YOU HAVE A basic idea of what your party planner app should do. It was spelled out in the previous chapter—"You'll need to make a guest list and set the date and time for your party. Should there be food—light snacks or a meal? What about beverages? What about music?" That's not enough for you to start coding. You can apply the methodology described in the last chapter to categorize your app for the App Store, but you need to flesh out the details so that you know what you're coding.

This chapter walks you through the process of getting to a more complete specification of your app. Most developers find that the process of development is iterative: as you write more, your to-do list for the current and future versions gets longer. After the app goes live in the App Store, with luck, the list will get longer still as users ask for new features.

So it's time to do some concrete planning.

Planning thc App: The Choices

Based on the methodology described in the last chapter, here are the basic choices that you should consider for this app. The first choice is the money question. You might want to make this a paid app. Alternatively, you may want to make it a free app to promote your own (or a friend's) catering business. You can also use it to promote your own app-development skills.

As for the App Store settings, here are the choices at the moment.

Identifying Your App and Yourself

These settings identify the app and the seller:

- **Name**—Party Planner.
- **Short name**—Party.
- **Seller**—In the screenshots and in the App Store, the seller is Champlain Arts Corp. Your version will be yourself.
- **Copyright name and date**—© Champlain Arts Corp, 2013. Note that this is what you will see in the screenshots in this book. You should use your own name (either individual or organization).
- **Version**—1.0

Setting Marketing Data (Discoverability)

Here is where you describe the app and its requirements:

- **Price tier**—Free.
- **Store(s)**—All.
- **Languages**—English (for now).
- **Keywords**—Party, entertaining, planning, and celebration.
- **Category**—Primary—Entertainment. Secondary—Food & Drink.
- **Icons**—You will need to upload your own icons as described on `developer.apple.com`.
- **Description**—Party Planner helps you plan a terrific party. You can make a guest list and set the date, time, and location of the party. If there's a theme or a dress code, you can easily add a note to that effect.
- **Screenshots**—You will be able to capture your own.
- **Rating**—4+.

Describing Your App's Requirements

These settings let potential buyers know if they will be able to run the app on their devices:

- **Devices**—Universal (iPhone, iPad, iPod touch, and iPad mini).
- **Version**—iOS 6.

Specifying Integration Features

This app doesn't use Game Center, iAd, or in-app purchases.

Designing the App: The Conversation

Whenever I start a project to build an app of any kind, a database, or any kind of design, I start with a conversation so that I begin to understand the problem to be solved and so that the owner or client can fill me in on any terminology or processes I don't know. Here are the kinds of questions I'll ask about this app, and here are the answers that I'll receive. This "conversation" should give you an idea of the kind of process you'll go through in building an app.

If you are both client and developer, as is often the case, make sure you cover these points mentally.

What Kind of Data Do You Need to Track?

Parties, guests, and menus.

How Persistent Is the Data?

Some apps exist only in the moment. A calculator, for example, lets you enter numbers, operators, and functions. When you press the equals key, you see the result. Many calculators let you store these results in memory. After a formula is entered, the only data that may need to persist is a result if you store it in memory. You usually can add a result to memory (in the sense of addition) or replace the current memory value. The only persistent data is whatever is in memory, and, possibly, the last result on the screen.

You can build a party planner like that, but you probably want the data to persist so that when you go back to it next week, all the data is still there.

How Much Data Is There?

If your party data persists, how many parties do you want to keep? For a given party, how many guests do you want to be allowed to have; how many dishes on a menu?

The answer that I like to give is a fairly standard one: as much data can be stored as there is room in memory or on disk. From a practical point of view, when people are managing more than a handful of objects (guests, dishes, parties), they need a sophisticated interface so that they can keep track of it all. If you're a professional party planner and you use this app to keep track of parties, guest lists, and dishes for all of your jobs over the last (or next) 10 years, that's a lot of data. Is it reasonable to assume that you could fit all of that on an iOS device? The answer is yes, provided that the parties themselves are manageable. If you are planning embassy parties for guest lists of over 1,000 every night, an app just might not be the right tool.

So, this example assumes a moderate amount of data and a basic interface that uses existing iOS tools.

Is There Anything Else You Need to Consider?

If you're working for someone else, always ask this question—repeatedly—during the design conversation. As for sample data from any existing reports or records. I always tell clients, "Data doesn't lie." You (or a client) may think that some data condition never happens, but when you look at the data, there it is.

The anomaly may come about because there was some strange outside event such as a flood, or because the circumstances were unusual (a no-refund policy is often waived if the customer has died). By the same token, it is human nature to remember unusual events, so you'll find that clients often ask you to prepare for a circumstance that happened once 45 years ago.

There are some other issues you should consider when you're thinking about (or talking about) an app. They're not relevant to the example in this book, but here are some other questions to consider.

- Is the data shared among a user's devices? (Consider iCloud for this.)
- Is the data shared with other people? (You might look at the FileMaker products. FileMaker is a wholly owned subsidiary of Apple, and its database tools run on Windows, OS X, and iOS.)

Believe it or not, that's enough information to get started designing the app. There are three basic steps to designing the app:

- **Create the app from an Xcode template, sample code, or an existing app you've worked on**—Depending on the specific app you're building one or another strategy may be the simplest. The objective should be to start from whatever you can find that requires the least amount of modification.
- **Design the data**—This carries on where the conversation described above ends off. You will need to flesh out more details and refine the general statements you've made and listened to.
- **Design the interface**—Discover how people will get to the data and manipulate it.

From this point on, it's a matter of iterating forward and implementing finer and finer parts of the app until it's all done.

Getting Started with the Template

You saw a brief overview of creating a new project in Chapter 1, "Getting Started with iOS 6." Now, you'll start over to build your Party Planner app using those steps with a few variations. As described in Chapter 1, you start in Xcode with File➔New➔Project or from the Welcome to Xcode window. Both options let you proceed to select a template.

Choosing the Right Template

The Master-Detail Application template is a great template for working with a list of items, each of which can have details to which you can drill down. It comes in a universal flavor for both iPhone and iPad. On iPad it uses a split view controller. The data described in the conversation has at least three levels:

- The top level will be a list of parties. You'll be able to create new ones. (Nothing has been said yet about deleting old ones, but that's built into the template. Rearranging the items in the list is not part of the template.) The list is implemented with a UITableView and the data source protocol, which are discussed in Part IV, "Using Table and Collection Views."

- The next level will let you drill down to the details of a single party. That's part of the template.

- From the details for a single party, you'll be able to drill down to the list of guests and the menu of food. The menu list may be empty, and the guest list, too might be empty—particularly at the beginning. Drilling down to the next level needs to be programmed.

For a multi-level data structure that lets you drill down, the Master-Detail Application template is a good start for both iPhone and iPad.

Exploring Other Templates

The other template choices for iOS are suited to other needs.

- **Single View Application** is just that. There is no navigation and no drilling down, but of course, you can add it.

- **Utility Application** has two views. On iPhone they are configured as a front and back; on iPad they are a full-screen display and a popover.

- **Tabbed Application** can have two or more views. A tab bar lets the user choose one view or another. Note that the navigation in the Master-Detail Application is hierarchical—that is, drilling down from an item in a list to its details. With a tab bar (or a front/back application like Utility Application), all of the views are at the same logical level. Instead of drilling down, the user is choosing a different view at the same level.

- **Page-Based Application** provides a template for showing views that appear to be pages in a book. It's easy to swipe to go to the next or previous page. The interface is built in; you just have to provide the views for the next and previous page using a data source much as is the case with a `UITableView`.

- **OpenGL Game** is the best template to start a game.

- **Empty Application** just gives you enough to get started.

Creating the Project

Once you have selected a template, create your project. There are several differences in these steps from the steps shown in Chapter 1. That is because these will be used to build a real app.

1. Click the Xcode icon if it's in the Dock or double-click Xcode in the Applications folder to launch Xcode. Then choose to create a new project from a template (the first choice in Figure 4-1). You can also use File➜New➜Project.

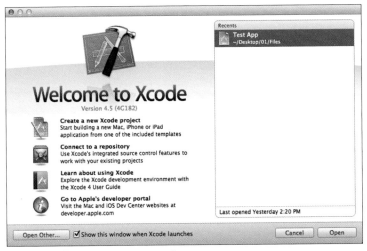

FIGURE 4-1 Begin to create a new project.

2. Select Master-Detail Application, as shown in Figure 4-2. Click Next.

3. Set the options as shown in Figure 4-3. Use your own organization name and company identifier. Set Devices to Universal and check the checkboxes for storyboards, Core Data, and Automatic Reference Counting (ARC).

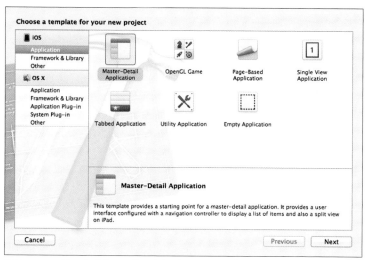

FIGURE 4-2 Use the Master-Detail Application template.

FIGURE 4-3 Set the project options.

4. Find a location for your project on your disk as shown in Figure 4-4. You'll be using this project frequently, so choose a location you can easily access. If you're using a Mac, you might want to store it locally rather than on a shared server that may not always be available.

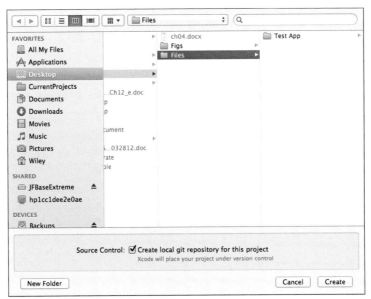

FIGURE 4-4 Create the project as well as a Git repository.

Use the option to create a local Git repository. (See the sidebar for a discussion of Git.) Then, click Create. (*Git* is pronounced with a hard G.)

5. Your newly created project will open in Xcode, as shown in Figure 4-5. Remember that you can change the configuration of the Xcode window, so it may not look precisely like this. Also, the bundle identifier will incorporate your company identifier that you set in Step 3. If the project is not open, use the disclosure triangle in the project navigator at the left to open it.

6. At the top right of the toolbar, open the Organizer. Show the Repositories tab, as shown in Figure 4-6. You should see all your files added to the repository. (If you have other projects in your repository, you may need to select this one from the sidebar at the left of the window.) At the bottom of Figure 4-6, you see the commit comment "Initial Commit." From now on, when you commit changes, you will provide the comment.

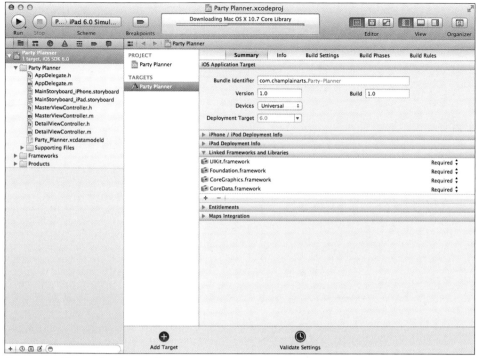

FIGURE 4-5 Your project is created.

FIGURE 4-6 Your files have been added to the repository.

Using a Git Repository

Git is a source code version-control system. It consists of a database to which you can add your code as you modify it. When you reach a point at which you want to freeze the code, you *commit* the code. Thereafter, you can restore your project back to that point. Git is tightly integrated into Xcode so that you can use it to keep track of modifications. In this book, I suggest you get in the habit of using Git. With Xcode, there's very little extra work for you to do. Git provides a definitive history of your project, and the comments you add as you commit files (they're required) keep track of the ways your app evolves. By relying on Git, you can get rid of those extra copies of your project in folders labeled "Friday before restructuring," "New Interface test," and so forth.

If you don't want to use Git, the code samples in this book will still work, but you will lose the security of the repository. If you want, you can use `github.com` so that your repository is available remotely. There is a small fee for private users, but Open Source projects with open repositories are free.

Getting Started with the Data

As noted, you're going to need to keep track of some data. For the purpose of the initial conversation, this was sufficient: "Parties, guests, and menus."

Now you need to get a bit more specific. Fortunately, Xcode has a sophisticated and easy-to-use data model editor. It is integrated with Core Data, a key framework of iOS (and OS X). Core Data is designed to manage persistent data—data that needs to be managed over time. In a game, the individual moves represent data, and they often do not need to persist (at least not once the game is over). What do need to persist are the final score, and, perhaps, the names of the players.

With Party Planner, you need to manage parties, guests, and menus before the party, and, perhaps, even afterward when you look back on the party. You need persistent data, and, on iOS, that typically means *Core Data*.

Introducing Core Data

You can certainly manage your own data with your own code. Keeping the data over time is a matter of usually writing it out to your app's sandbox on iOS or to a website. All of this you can do.

However, most people find that Core Data is much easier. Core Data is designed to be somewhat agnostic about exactly how the data is stored. Commonly, it uses the built-in SQLite library, which implements data management functionality. There is something about the thought of databases that sometimes makes people worry about complexity (in some ways, it's similar to the fear some people have of mathematics). Fortunately, not only is Core Data easy to use for a project like Party Planner; it also is actually easier and less work than using other techniques. As you'll see, it can be the same type of analysis that you would do on the back of an envelope, but with Core Data and its modeling tools, your data model will look much nicer than scribbles on the back of an envelope.

The Master-Detail Application template keeps track of the master list. Each item in the list contains a simple piece of data—the timestamp of its creation. You can see this if you run the app.

You can also look at things from the inside by looking at the data model. You'll find it in the project navigator: it's called `Party_Planner.xcdatamodeld`. If you select it, you'll see the data model as in Figure 4-7.

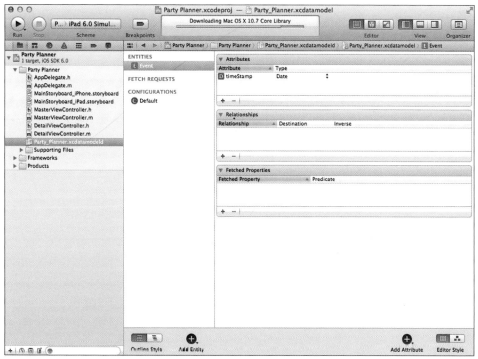

FIGURE 4-7 Look at the data model.

In the lower right of the window, you'll see a control for editor styles. This is the *table style*. At the left of the data model is a sidebar with three sections:

- **Entities**—These are the main items you will be following. In the template, there is one: `Event`. You will have three: `Party`, `Guest`, and `Menu`. (By convention, entities start with a capital letter.)

- **Fetch Requests**—These will be requests for data. There are none now, and you may not need any.

- **Configurations**—There is only a default configuration. You don't need to worry about configurations for a simple app such as this one.

There are three tables to the right:

- **Attributes**—These are values for the selected entity (`Event` in this case). They are comparable to properties in classes.

- **Relationships**—These are just what the word means in English. You have a relationship between guests and a party just as you have a relationship between menu dishes and the party.

- **Fetched Properties**—You don't need to worry about these.

If you select an attribute and open the Utility area as shown in Figure 4-8, you can see information about the data model file if you select the File inspector (the one on the left, shown in Figure 4-8).

When you have a data model open, the Core Data Model inspector (third from the left at the top of the Utility area in Figures 4-8 and 4-9 is available). In Figure 4-9, it has been chosen to inspect the `Event` entity, which is selected in the sidebar of the data model. You could change its name in the inspector.

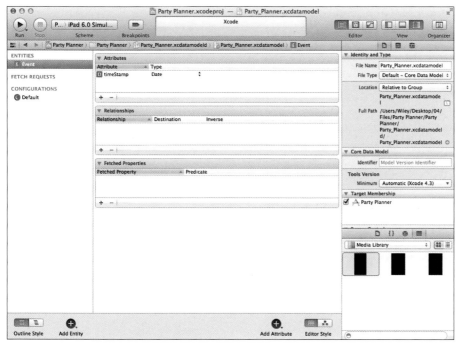

FIGURE 4-8 Look at the data model File inspector.

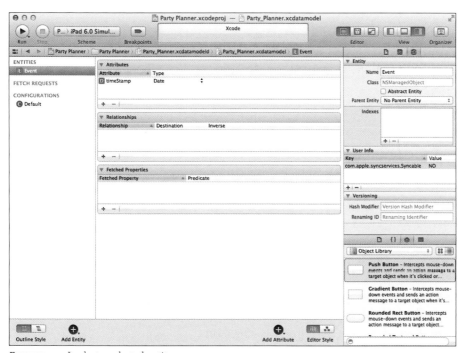

FIGURE 4-9 Look at a selected entity.

If you select an attribute, as in Figure 4-10, you see its data in the Core Data Model inspector. You can change its name or type either in the inspector or by clicking in the main window.

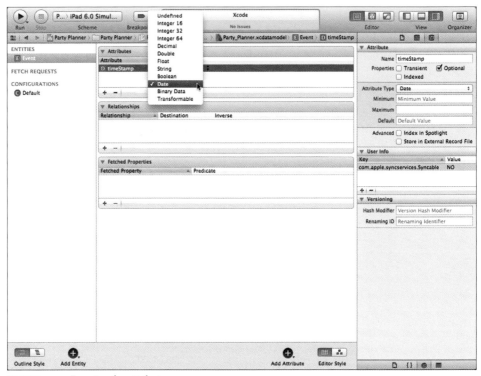

FIGURE 4-10 Examine the attributes.

At the bottom of the Core Data Model inspector, you'll see that you can add new entities. You can add new attributes to a selected entity by using the + at the bottom of the attributes table. You can also add them with the small + on the Add Entity button. You can delete a selected attribute with the minus sign at the bottom of the Attributes table.

Building Your Data Model

For now, you can make a few changes that will let you get started with your own data model. You can start from the template's data model. Here are the changes to make.

1. Select Event in the entity list.

2. Double-click its name in the entity list and change it to Party (that capital letter matters). Alternatively, with it selected, open the Core Data Model inspector and change its name there.

Note that either of these methods can be used to change an attribute or entity name. The details of changing a name are not spelled out each time.

3. Similarly change the `timeStamp` attribute to `partyName`. For the moment, leave its data type as `date`; later on you'll change it to `string`.

4. In the search navigator, search for `Event` as shown in Figure 4-11. If you select the found line of code, you'll see it in the file in the Editor area.

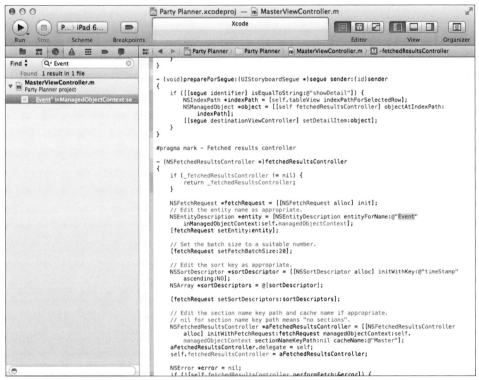

FIGURE 4-11 Search for "Event."

5. Using the pop-up menu, change Find to Replace, and enter `Party` as shown in Figure 4-12. When you click Replace, you will be asked if you want to take a snapshot of the project. It's a good idea to do so.

6. Similarly, replace `timeStamp` with `partyName`. (There should be five occurrences.) Make sure you use the Replace All button.

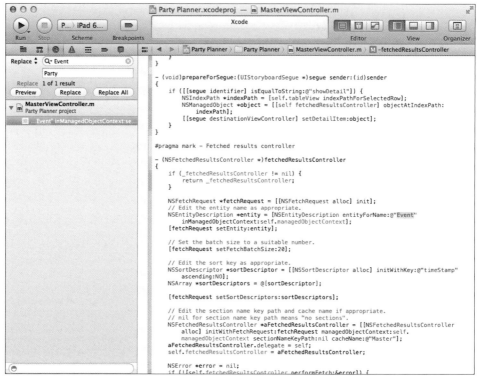

FIGURE 4-12 Replace "Event" with "Party."

7. Build and run the app. Because the `partyName` field is still a date, the app should run and show the date. It's okay to leave it like this for now so that you have something running with the new data model.

Summary

This chapter shows you how to start from a serious conversation about your app (focusing on the questions to ask), and then how to move on to creating the project from a template and building your data model (or, as in this case, modifying the template data model). Most of your work in this chapter has consisted of filling in forms for the template and using the Core Data Model editor's graphical user interface.

In the next part of the book, you'll move on to use yet another graphical user interface—storyboards—to create your app's interface. If you're itching to write code, have no fear. You'll be typing away in the third part of the book.

part 2

Storyboards: The Building Blocks of iOS Apps

chapter five
Walking Through the iPhone Storyboard

THE MASTER-DETAIL APPLICATION template gives you a solid basis for the Party Planner app (as well as many others). With the universal setting for your project, the template gives you both an iPhone and an iPad interface. They are similar and even share much of the same code; however, there are a few minor differences that mostly reflect the different screen sizes and interfaces on the two devices.

With the option to use storyboards, you have the latest and most powerful interface design tool that the engineers at Apple have produced. Many developers still swear by the old way of doing things—typing code out by hand. You'll soon find that graphical tools such as storyboards and the Core Data Model editor in Xcode save you time and make your design process faster.

An added benefit of the graphical tools is that you can share them with managers, clients, and other people who are not comfortable with reading code. Even if you are developer, manager, client, and user all rolled into one, being able to look at an overview of the interface (or data model, for that matter) can help you improve your app.

Introducing Storyboards

Storyboards in Xcode are basically the same as storyboards used in any other type of project. They have been used for decades to sketch out scenes that may appear in a commercial or film; they also are frequently used to sketch out computer games. The difference between those two types of storyboards is that in films or commercials, the scenes are sequential. In a game, the scenes typically require user intervention to go from one to the next.

 Since the days of mainframe computers, programmers have often used *flowcharts* to sketch out the logical flow of a program or app. There is a great deal of similarity between storyboards and flowcharts, but the most significant difference is that with storyboards, there is a sketch of what the screen will look like at each step of the way. With a flowchart, each component is code, pseudo-code, or a textual description of processing. The graphical representation of the screen is rarely a part of a flowchart.

Looking at the Storyboarding Process

In the normal scheme of things, you sketch out your app's interface using simple storyboarding techniques. Most of the time, developers work from the basic app design and then sketch out at least the key components with paper and pencil or a white board. As you progress from the general descriptions in your app design to the interface elements in your storyboard, you often wind up changing and adding details to both the app design and the storyboard. (The same process occurs as you sketch out your data model.)

Switching back and forth among overall app design, interface design, and data model design often is very productive and efficient. In the past, it was common to work on each component separately and finish each one before proceeding to the next. Unfortunately, this process often turns out to waste time because the needs of each component often require adjustment as the interface and data model are built and integrated.

Looking at Storyboarding for the Template

Storyboarding lets you develop your interface. Learning how to use the storyboard tools and terminology to create and describe your interface isn't hard. In this chapter, you have an opportunity to look at storyboards in a way that you don't look at them as you develop an app. In the Master-Detail Application template, you have a working app on which you can build. Among the files that are included in the template are two storyboard files—one for iPhone and one for iPad (if you have chosen to create a universal app as suggested previously).

This means that rather than create the storyboard first and then test it, you have an opportunity to run the template app and see what the interface is and then go back to the storyboard to see how it has been created. This process is outlined in this chapter.

Introducing the iOS Simulator

The iOS simulator is a critical component of the iOS development process. You launch it from Xcode with the Run button, which is located at the left of the toolbar at the top of workspace window. When set to simulate the iPhone, the simulator shows a basic configuration, as shown in Figure 5-1.

FIGURE 5-1 The iOS simulator shows you a basic device.

The built-in apps on the simulator display varying degrees of functionality. For example, you can adjust settings as you see in Figure 5-2, but you won't be able to make telephone calls with the simulator.

FIGURE 5-2 Built-in apps are available in the simulator.

When you are working with an iOS project in Xcode, you can choose to run it using any of the schemes that you (or, more often, the template) have prepared, as you see in Figure 5-3.

The specific choices of scheme for your project are often generated using your project settings, including which version(s) of the operating system you are targeting. For a universal project, you are, at least, given the choice of the current iPad and iPhone OS along with a choice for a connected device—that is, an iPhone or iPad connected by a cable to your Mac.

Xcode will take charge of running the app on the device. Among other things, this will enable you to debug the app as it runs on a device. (See Chapter 11, "Testing the App with the Debugger," for more information.)

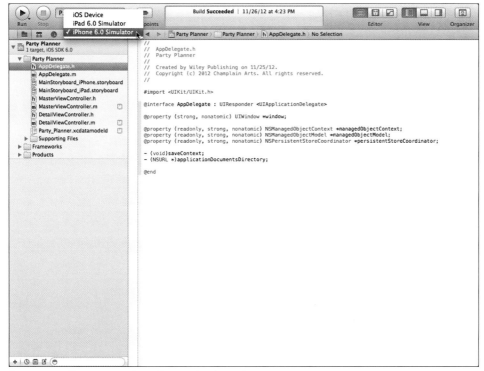

FIGURE 5-3 Choose your scheme for running the project.

Until very recently, the iOS Simulator was referred to as the iPhone simulator because that is how it started.

When you click Run in Xcode, the simulator will launch and show you a representation of the device that you have chosen with your app running inside it. Figure 5-4 shows the Party Planner app as it appears if you have followed the steps in this book.

FIGURE 5-4 Launch the Party Planner app in the simulator.

A variety of commands in the Hardware menu let you simulate rotation, shaking, and other events, as you can see in Figure 5-5.

You will probably use the rotation commands frequently. As you can see in Figure 5-6, when you first build the Master-Detail Application template (now the Party Planner project), rotation works properly.

FIGURE 5-5 Use the Hardware menu to simulate actions using the device.

FIGURE 5-6 Rotation is managed correctly in the template.

Walking Through the Template and the Storyboard

Now it's time to walk through the interface that you have in the template. As you will see, there is a great deal of functionality already built into it. This section provides parallel walk-throughs of the interface: a walkthrough of the interface that users see along with a walk-through of the storyboard that creates the interface. This is just the first exploration of the interface and storyboard—you will delve deeper into both in the other chapters in this part of the book.

Storyboards consist of *scenes* and *segues*. A scene is a view with its view controller, and a segue is a transition from one scene to another.

Looking at a Scene

Figure 5-4 shows you the initial scene in the Master-Detail Application template (it's now your Party Planner app). The + at the top right lets you add more items to the list in the scene, and the Edit button at the top left lets you edit the list.

The list is implemented using a *table view*. You'll find out more about table views in Part IV, "Using Table and Collection Views." For now, there's one important point to bear in mind with regard to the Edit button. When you are dealing with a list, the Edit button lets you edit the list—that means deleting items from the list (you add them with the +). In some apps, the Edit button also lets you rearrange the items in the list.

If you tap an item in the list, you move to the next scene, a *detail* view, as shown in Figure 5-7.

At the top of the scene shown in Figure 5-7, there's a *navigation bar* with a button that lets you move back to the list view shown previously in Figure 5-4.

Considering View Controllers

The scenes shown in Figures 5-4 and 5-7 are managed by *view controllers*. View controllers are instances of `UIViewController` or subclasses of it. View controllers are just that—controllers. They control other view controllers or views.

There are two types of view controllers:

- **Content view controllers** display content in one or more views.

- **Container view controllers** manage other view controllers (which usually, in turn, manage still more view controllers or content).

FIGURE 5-7 View a detail view, with a navigation bar.

The distinction between content and container view controllers was clearly specified in *View Controller Catalog for iOS* first published on `developer.apple.com` in January 2012. Older documentation is superseded by this document and its terminology.

Container view controllers must be used in a specified hierarchy. You have seen these view controllers in iOS apps, and they will be discussed throughout this book. The hierarchy is as follows.

• **Split view controllers** (if used) are the top-level view controller. In the Master-Detail Application template for iPad, there is a split view controller.

- **Tab bar controllers** (if used) can be placed within a split view controller or can be a top-level view controller.

- **Navigation controllers** (if used) can be placed within a tab bar or split view controller; a navigation controller can be also be a top-level view controller.

Subclasses of these controllers follow the same rules.

Non-standard containment (such as placing a split view controller within a tab bar controller) can be confusing to users. The containment order is specified in iOS 6 documentation. You will find examples of what is now non-standard containment in various examples on the web. You should stick to this containment order going forward.

Considering Views

View controllers can control views as well as other view controllers. In Figures 5-4 and 5-7, you see the views that are managed by the relevant view controller. Each scene has a view controller, and that view controller may contain one or more views.

Looking at a Segue

Segues are the transitions between scenes. Tapping an item in the list shown in Figure 5-4 launches a segue that takes you to the appropriate detail scene, as shown in Figure 5-7. In Figure 5-7, tapping the Master button takes you back to the master list shown in Figure 5-4.

Looking at the Storyboard

Figure 5-8 shows you the storyboard behind Figures 5-4 and 5-7. In Figure 5-8, the project navigator at the left of the workspace window is shown along with the storyboard editor. The storyboard editor has a *canvas* on which you can draw your interface. Within the storyboard editor, you have the option to show or hide the *document outline* at the left of the canvas. In Figure 5-8, the document outline is not shown.

The document outline is shown in Figure 5-9.

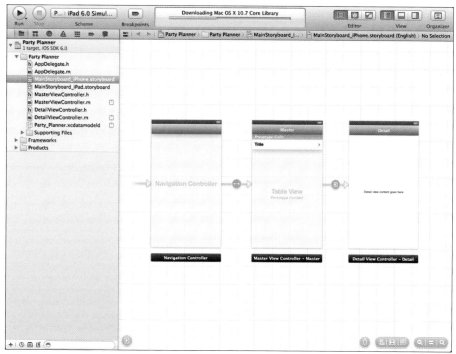

FIGURE 5-8 Look at the storyboard without the document outline.

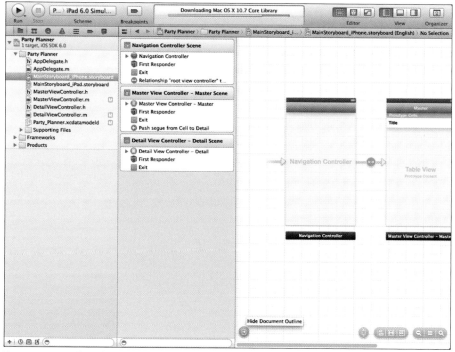

FIGURE 5-9 Look at the storyboard with the document outline.

Looking at the Scenes in the Storyboard

If you compare Figures 5-8 and 5-9, you'll see that the storyboard has three scenes. In the main section of the storyboard editor, they are labeled:

- Navigation Controller
- Master View Controller—Master
- Detail View Controller—Detail

If the document outline is shown, they are labeled as scenes. In the document outline, each scene has a root view controller at the top of its section in the document outline. Within the document outline, disclosure triangles let you open or close the objects within the scenes. Figure 5-10 shows you the document outline with all of the disclosure triangles opened.

FIGURE 5-10 Open all the disclosure triangles.

By working with the document outline as well as the canvas, you can switch back and forth between the hierarchical structure of the view controller in the document outline and the visual representation of the views on the canvas. When you select a view in either the document outline or on the canvas, it is selected and highlighted in both the document outline and the canvas. (When working with some views, sometimes it is necessary to select them in the document outline because they are not easily visible on the canvas—either because of their size or because they are behind another object.)

Looking at Segues and Relationships in the Storyboard

In Figure 5-10, you can see the three scenes of the storyboard. The segues link scenes together on the canvas and in the document outline. In the document outline, the main view controller is at the top of a scene; at the bottom of the scene, the segue manages the transition to the next scene and its view controller.

In addition to segues, you sometimes see another type of connection between two scenes. For example, in Figure 5-10, in the first scene, you see a *relationship* from a view controller to the master scene and its view controller. In the third scene, instead of a segue or a relationship, you see an exit from the storyboard. In Figure 5-8, notice at the left of the canvas that there is an arrow pointing to the first scene. Each storyboard has its own entry point.

Exploring the Navigation Controller

Navigation controllers are a critical part of the iOS interface. They manage a stack of list controllers. The navigation controller provides the functionality that lets you drill down through a hierarchy of view controllers and pop back up. (This is the behavior shown previously in Figures 5-4 and 5-7.)

When you look at Figure 5-10, you will see that the navigation controller is the first controller for this storyboard (note the incoming arrow at the left of the navigation controller). The navigation controller is a container view controller, and it contains the master view controller. The master view controller has a segue to the detail view controller, which displays data for a specific item in the master list.

In some older documentation both from Apple and third parties, the master view controller in a navigation controller was sometimes referred to as a *root view* controller. In usage today, a root view controller is the root (or top-level) view controller in a containment structure. A master view controller, as in the Master-Detail Application template, is a specific example of a root view controller.

If you look closely at Figure 5-10, you'll see that the navigation bar at the top of the scenes is part of the navigation controller. When you are using a container view controller, part of the container view controller is displayed along with the other view controllers in the hierarchy.

Creating Your Own View Controllers

There is a certain degree of complexity in using container view controllers. Before you worry too much, this section walks through the actual process you'll use to create container view controllers, and you'll see that much of the work is already done for you. If you're using an Xcode template such as the Master-Detail Application template, everything is set up for you. But if you are starting from scratch, here's how easy it is to add a container view controller hierarchy.

1. Create a new project using the Single View Application in the iOS templates.

2. Make certain that you choose the Universal devices setting, as shown in Figure 5-11.

FIGURE 5-11 Create a new application.

3. Select the iPhone storyboard in the project navigator.

4. Select the single view on the canvas and delete it with the Delete key.

5. Open the Utility area, as shown in Figure 5-12. At the bottom of the library (the lower pane of the Utility area), make certain that you have selected Objects in the pop-up menu.

6. Drag a navigation controller into the canvas, as shown in Figure 5-12.

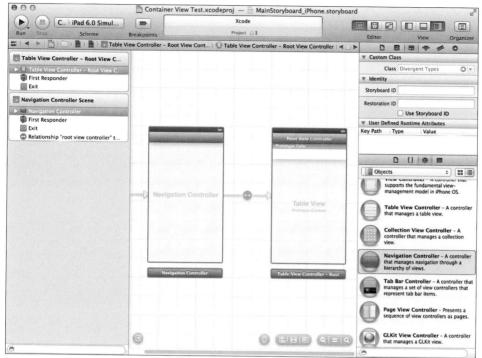

FIGURE 5-12 Add a navigation controller.

What you'll see is that the navigation controller object actually consists of two scenes—the navigation controller as well as a root view controller, which happens to be a table view controller. Together, they implement the basic navigation. (You can see the two scenes both on the canvas and in the document outline.)

Delete your scenes before continuing.

As you can see in Figure 5-13, something similar happens when you drag a tab bar controller into your now-empty canvas from the library. In this case, you get the tab bar controller as well as two view controllers that are already wired up to the tab bar. (You can add others if you want.)

Switch to the iPad storyboard. In that storyboard there is just one scene; delete it.

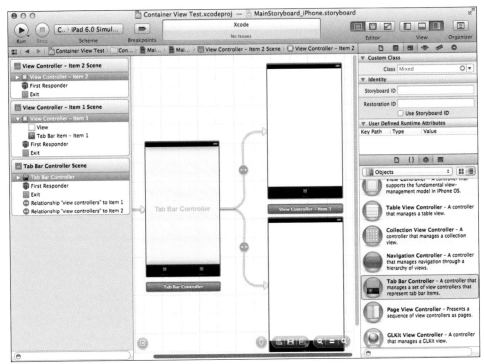

FIGURE 5-13 A tab bar controller gives you three scenes.

Chapter 9, "Building the Detail Data View," has more detail about the iPad storyboard.

If you want to create a split view controller (remember it will be the highest level of containment), drag the split view controller from the library into your empty iPad storyboard. This time, you get four views, as you can see in Figure 5-14.

Look at the document outline to see the containment. The highest level is the split view controller. Within it, you have a navigation controller and a root view controller. Separately, you have a detail view for the other part of the split view. (This is what you have in your Party Planner app).

Figure 5-15 shows the Party Planner app. Note that there are two relationships from the split view controller—one for each of the parts of the split view.

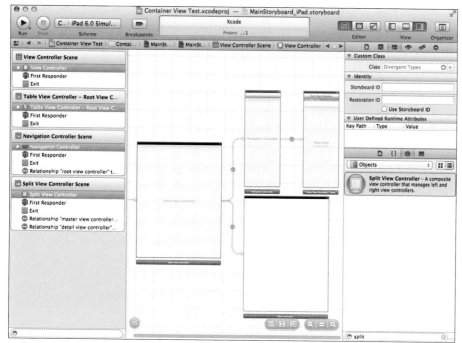

FIGURE 5-14 Create a split view controller.

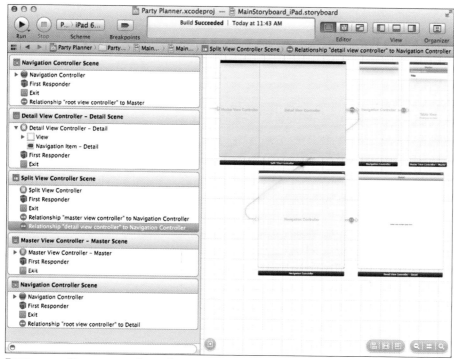

FIGURE 5-15 There are two relationships in the split view controller.

You can get rid of the project you have just created. Its only purpose was to show you how to add complex objects from the library to your storyboard. Now, you'll return to the Party Planner app.

Adding Objects from the Library

You've seen how to add objects from the library to your storyboard. The most frequent types of objects that you add are views to display content. Here is how you'll add them to the Party Planner app.

1. Locate the detail view controller either in the document outline or on the canvas of the iPad storyboard.

2. Inside the detail view controller, select the View object in the canvas or the document outline (it may be easier to do this in the document outline, as shown in Figure 5-16).

   You may want to experiment with selecting the view and the detail view controller in the document outline. Notice how the highlighting on the canvas changes depending on which is selected.

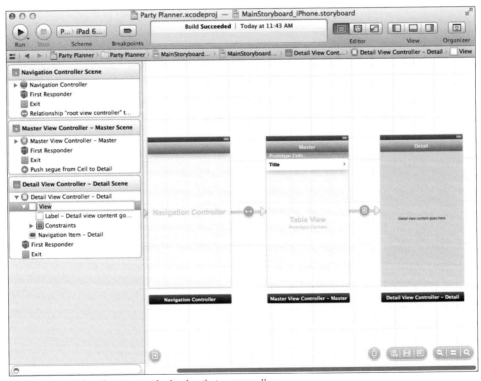

FIGURE 5-16 Select the view inside the detail view controller.

3. Show the Utility area.

4. Make certain that Objects is selected in the pop-up menu at the top of the library.

5. Scroll to find the text field in the library.

6. Drag the text field into the view, as shown in Figure 5-17. (If you can't drag it in, check that you have the view selected rather than the detail view controller.)

   You can rearrange the new text field and the existing label. You may need to select them in the document outline and then move the selected objects on the canvas.

   Guides are shown to help you align the object.

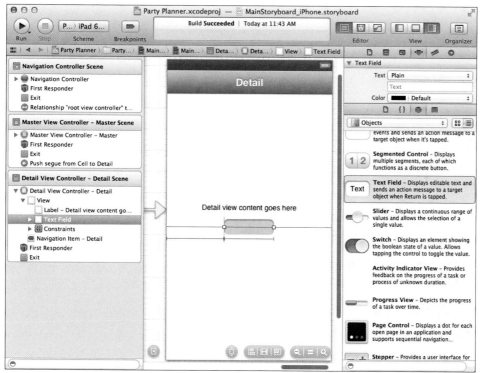

FIGURE 5-17 Add a text field.

7. You can add any other objects in the same way. For now, add a round rect button and notice how the guides appear, as shown in Figure 5-18. (Round rect buttons are the most commonly used kind of buttons—you see them often as OK and Cancel buttons.)

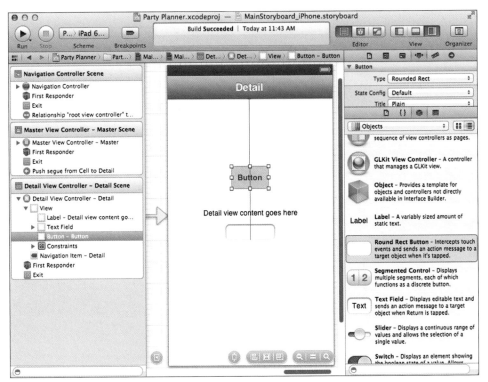

FIGURE 5-18 Add a round rect button.

Summary

This chapter introduces you to storyboards—the tools for developing your interface. The terminology of storyboards in Xcode is basically the same as it is in movies and other types of storyboards: scenes are sketched out and linked together with transitions called *segues* in Xcode.

For Xcode storyboards, the scenes are view controllers. There are two types of view controllers: container view controllers (they contain other view controllers) and content view controllers (they control views). There is a specified order of containment for container view controllers, but with Xcode 4 and later, you can fortunately drag containment view controller structures from the library to your canvas.

You've seen how to add objects to your storyboard. As you'll see in the following chapter, the Utility area provides you with inspectors that let you adjust and customize their settings.

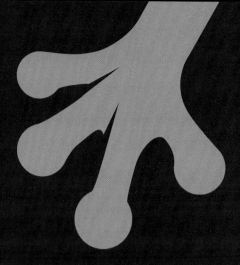

chapter six

Working with Storyboard Inspectors

YOU HAVE SEEN the interface of your Party Planner app (based on the Master-Detail Application template) from the perspective of the user as well as from your perspective as an interface designer using storyboards. There's another perspective to look at, and it is the perspective of code. In Chapter 5, "Walking Through the iPhone Storyboard," you saw how to add objects to your interface (a text field and a button served as examples).

In this chapter, you'll see how to work with code that is already part of the Cocoa Touch frameworks as well as code that you write. With storyboards, this is another set of graphical user interface tools. They let you connect the objects of the interface to the code in the frameworks.

The structure of the storyboard and the code that's behind it is basically simple, but it may take a little getting used to. Remember that if you're still thinking about programming as writing line after line of code, you have to adjust to the nonlinear development process of Objective-C and Cocoa Touch. Part of that adjustment is understanding the code that's already in the template. Once you grasp the basics of storyboard design, you'll find that implementing new functionality is often a matter of just using a few checkboxes and Control-dragging in the Interface Builder editor. There may be a few lines of code to be written at the end of the process, but that's the structure you're working with: a graphical user interface for app design.

Looking at the Party Planner App

You can now run the Party Planner app as it is at the end of Chapter 5, "Walking Through the iPhone Storyboard." As you can see in Figure 6-1, when you move from the master view controller to the detail view controller, the button and text field that you added are visible.

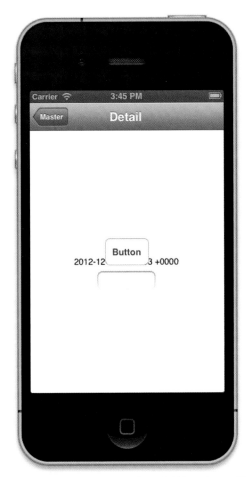

FIGURE 6-1 Your button and text field have been added to the detail view controller.

If you click the button, it flashes. If you click into the text field, the keyboard rises up, as shown in Figure 6-2.

Beyond the flashing of the button and the presence of the keyboard, nothing else happens. The flashing is part of the button object's built-in behavior as is the keyboard that is available when you click in the text field.

FIGURE 6-2 The keyboard is enabled.

When talking and writing about behavior on iOS devices, you *tap* a button or the text field. On OS X, you *click* a button or click in a text field. Because the iOS Simulator is an OS X app, many people use the OS X terminology and talk about clicks, but they are *taps* on the actual devices. This is an issue with the simulator. I have never heard anyone talk about clicking on an iOS device interface element.

In Chapter 5 you were able to compare the interface of the app with the storyboard. Now, you can compare both with the code that supports them. And to do that, you'll need to explore the storyboard inspectors in the Utility area.

Using Outlets and Actions

Several of the inspectors let you work with outlets and actions. They are key parts of the links between the graphical user interface of Interface Builder and the code you write (or that has been written for you in the template).

Looking at Outlets

Outlets are properties or instance variables that are flagged as being part of the interface. They are the link between code and interface.

You can declare a property for a class using code such as the following:

```
@property (weak, nonatomic) IBOutlet
  UILabel *detailDescriptionLabel;
```

The compiler directive `@property` introduces the property declaration. Following that, attributes of the property are placed in parentheses.

Next comes the part that matters: `IBOutlet` is used to indicate that this property is part of the interface and can be manipulated with Interface Builder.

Then, the type—`UILabel`—appears as it does in any C declaration. For objects, you always declare them as a reference with an asterisk. Finally, the name of the property appears.

If you are declaring *instance variables* instead of properties, the declaration is even simpler:

```
IBOutlet UILabel *detailDescriptionLabel;
```

`IBOutlet` has no purpose other than to let Xcode know that this will be part of the interface. In fact, the compiler never sees it. `IBOutlet` is a define that resolves to a blank. When you declare a property or variable using `IBOutlet`, Interface Builder will let you connect objects such as text fields to it. That is the link between object and code.

Behind every property there is an instance variable. Xcode can create them automatically with its default settings so you don't have to do anything. If you compare the property for `detailDescriptionLabel` with the instance variable declaration, you'll see that the instance variable declaration uses the name and the type (as well as the `IBOutlet` define) shown in the property. The property has additional information regarding how memory should be managed for the underlying instance variable. The only thing you do have to know if you use automatically created instance variables is that they are named from a variation of the property name. The instance variable (sometimes called the *backing variable)* for the `detailDescriptionLabel` property is `_detailDecriptionLabel`.

Looking at Actions

Actions are methods that have a common signature. They are flagged with `IBAction` to let Interface Builder know that they can be connected to items such as buttons that will trigger the action. They are the functional side of the link between interface and code.

An action has the following signature:

```
- (IBAction)myAction:(id)sender;
```

The keyword `IBAction` is used as the return type of the method. In fact, as is the case with `IBOutlet`, the compiler never sees `IBAction`. It is processed by Interface Builder, but it is a define that resolves to `void` by the time the compiler sees it.

An action has a single argument. It is of type `id`, which means that it can be any object whatsoever. The name of the action is up to you.

Exploring the Storyboard Inspectors

Depending on what is selected in the current editor of the workspace window, different inspectors are available. This section provides an overview of the storyboard inspectors; it also provides highlights of some of the more commonly used settings.

Remember, that inspectors are a key part of the integration of storyboards with code. In fact, that is their primary task. Just about every inspector setting can also be set programmatically by writing code. However, many people (including the author) find the use of the graphical user interface of inspectors to be faster and easier than writing line after line of code. Perhaps the most convincing argument for using inspectors is that it's harder to introduce typos into your code. When you are writing code manually, you can misspell anything you want. Although Fix-It in Xcode does catch many typos, there are many others that can't be caught. When your options are limited to choices in a pop-up menu or a set of radio buttons, as is frequently the case with inspectors, you can choose the wrong value, but you can't type in an unknown value.

When you are editing a storyboard, there are six inspectors at the top of the Utility area. Here is a summary of each of them; details are included in the sections that follow. From left to right, the inspectors are:

- **File inspector**—This is always the left-most inspector. It provides information about the file you are editing.

- **Quick Help**—This provides information about the selected text in the editor. Because the storyboard editor isn't text-based, the Quick Help icon appears, but there is no content for it.

- **Identity inspector**—This provides an answer to the question, "What is the selected object in the storyboard?"

- **Attributes inspector**—This inspector lets you set and inspect attributes of the selected object. Perhaps the most important attribute is the name of the class that implements the code for the selected object. This single attribute is the heart of the link between the code and the storyboard object.

- **Size inspector**—This is where you specify the size and layout behavior of the selected object.

- **Connections inspector**—Every interface object is an instance of a class that is set in the Identity inspector. Depending on what that class is, one or more *connections* may be available to be set. A connection is declared and implemented in the code for the class (with Cocoa Touch framework code or your subclass of a Cocoa Touch class). That connection is drawn graphically in the storyboard editor to an object on the canvas or in the document outline.

Using the File Inspector

No matter what type of file you're editing, the File inspector is at the left of the inspectors in the Utility area, as shown in Figure 6-3.

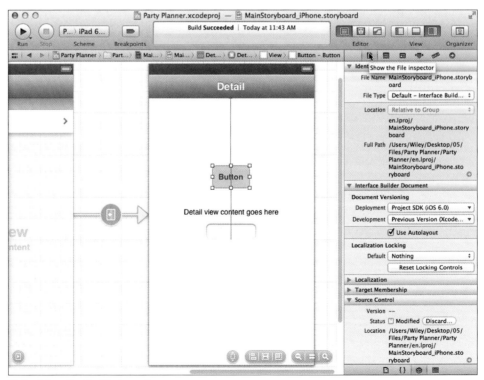

FIGURE 6-3 Use the File inspector.

Most of the time you don't need to change any of the settings in the File inspector. The settings that you may need to check or adjust most often are:

- Filename

- Location

- Auto Layout

Renaming Files and Classes

If you need to rename a file, you should use Edit➔Refactor➔Rename to do so. That command properly renames files and the references to them. The most common way of doing this is to open a file that contains the declaration of a class. Select the class name, and then choose Edit➔Refactor➔Rename. You'll be asked to approve the process, and then Xcode will rename the file and all references to it in your project.

Changing File Location

You can specify the location for each file in your project. The full path to the file you are editing is shown in the full path section. That path is what you are looking at. The small arrow next to the full path reveals the file in the Finder.

Your choices for location let you manage how Xcode handles files when they move. The pop-up menu has the following choices:

- Absolute path

- Relative to group

- Relative to project

- Relative to developer directory

- Relative to build products

- Relative to SDK

The first three are most commonly used.

The absolute path is exactly that. When you add a file to a project and set its location to absolute path in the File inspector, that file will be used at all times. If you move the project to another directory, the original file will continue to be used. Sometimes this setting is used on multi-person projects whereby a certain file is used at a given path by all of the developers (there are other, more elegant ways of doing this such as using a multi-project workspace).

More common is the relative to group setting (it's the default in many Xcode templates). Files are located based on the group in which they are placed. If the group is moved elsewhere, all of the files in it are located based on the group. This setting lets you move your project from one directory to another without breaking the links to the files within the project: they all will move.

Finally, the relative to project setting keeps all of your project's files together. You can safely move the entire project folder to another directory without breaking any links.

Using Auto Layout

The last setting is Auto Layout. This is a new (Xcode 4 and iOS 6) tool that enables you to specify your view layouts in ways that automatically adapt not only to rotation but also to various-sized screens. Auto Layout is described in Chapter 7, "Laying Out Your Scenes and Views."

Using the Identity Inspector

The Identity inspector is available when you have selected an interface element in Interface Builder. It doesn't matter whether you select the object in the canvas or in the document outline: wherever it is selected, its identity will be shown, as you see in Figure 6-4.

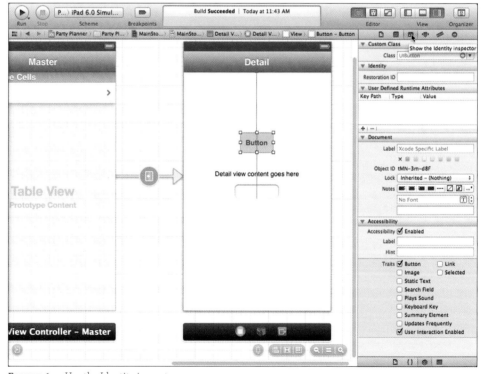

FIGURE 6-4 Use the Identity inspector.

The two most frequently used settings in the Identity inspector are the *class* and the *label*.

Setting the Class

As you can see in Figure 6-4, when you select a button on the canvas, the class is initially set to UIButton—the framework class that implements the button. For many cases, that's all you need to do.

However, as you can see in Figure 6-5, if you select an interface element such as the detail view controller, its initial value is DetailViewController. If you use the drop-down menu, you can change the class to any of the subclasses of DetailViewController. And the critical point here is that those subclasses can be in the Cocoa Touch framework or they can be in your own code in your project. Just declare a subclass of DetailViewController, and you'll be able to link it to a specific object on the interface.

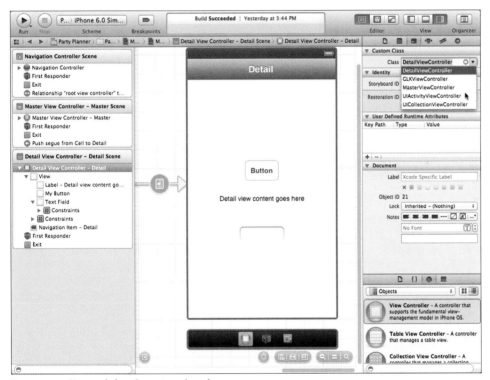

FIGURE 6-5 Use a subclass for an interface element.

Setting the Label

Xcode automatically generates the names of the interface elements shown in the document outline. You can add your own labels in the document section of the Identity inspector, as you can see in Figure 6-6. By entering **My Button** in the label field, you can see it identified that way in the document outline.

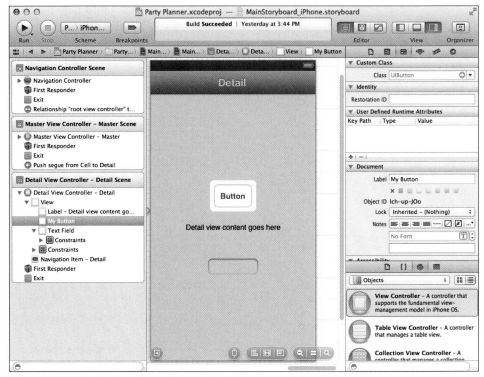

FIGURE 6-6 Use labels to make your document outline more readable.

 As is the case with all data entry fields in iOS, the data is updated when you click out of a field. If you just type in a new label name, it will not show up immediately.

Using the Attributes Inspector

The Attributes inspector lets you customize your interface elements, as shown in Figure 6-7.

 In Figure 6-7 you may notice that the title of the view controller (shown in a bar below the view controller) is sometimes replaced by three icons. An unselected view controller displays its name; the three icons appear when the view controller is selected. You'll find out how they are used in "Using the Connections Inspector" later in this section.

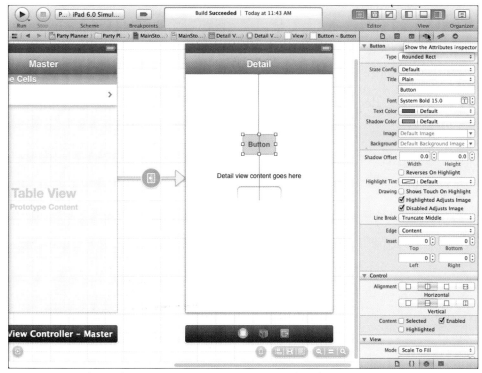

FIGURE 6-7 Use the Attributes inspector to customize your interface elements.

The Attributes inspector's settings vary depending on the object that you have selected. When you drag an object from the library into your canvas (or document outline), it arrives with the default settings. The number of attributes available for the variety of interface objects is remarkable. Chances are that any interface customization you're thinking of can be accomplished with existing attributes. The best way to familiarize yourself with the built-in attributes is to create a new project and experiment with the interface elements you're interested in and their attributes.

Using the Size Inspector

The Size inspector lets you adjust the size of the selected element, as seen in Figure 6-8. As you are drawing and moving objects on the canvas, guides appear to help you align them, but for absolute precision, nothing beats the use of actual measurements.

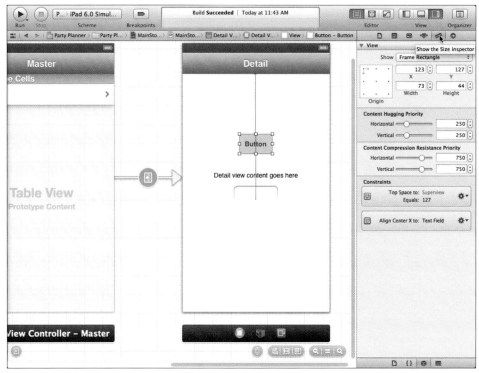

FIGURE 6-8 Use the Size inspector to adjust the size of a selected element.

Using Points for Units of Measurement

The units shown in the Size inspector are *points*. A point is ¹⁄₇₂ of an inch; it has been used in desktop publishing as a standard unit of measurement.

Many computer monitors were built with 72 pixels per inch. As a result, in common usage, *pixel* and *point* were interchangeable. However, only the point is an actual unit of measurement.

With the advent of high-resolution displays, far more than 72 pixels can be used per inch. Thus, the interchangeability of the two terms no longer applies on high-resolution displays such as Apple's Retina Display. You will still find many people who use the two terms interchangeably, but for measurement (and the Size inspector), only *point* is the correct term.

If you are designing an interface, you want the elements to appear in certain places on the screen, and those places are expressed in points. If you are designing a graphic to be displayed in a certain place on the screen, you may very well want to talk about pixels. A graphic designed for use on a Retina Display may need to have many more pixels in it than one designed for an older display.

If this is confusing, here's a summary that works for many people: If you're using Xcode, work with points, and if you're using Photoshop, use pixels.

As you see in Figure 6-8, you can specify the X and Y coordinates for the top-left corner of a selected element as well as its total width and height. These coordinates are in the units of the object in which it is contained.

In Figure 6-8, you can see settings for content hugging and compression as well as for constraints. These are part of the Auto Layout mechanism introduced with iOS 6. It is discussed in Chapter 7.

Using the Connections Inspector

Shown in Figure 6-9, the Connections inspector is where you connect outlet and actions in your code to the interface elements.

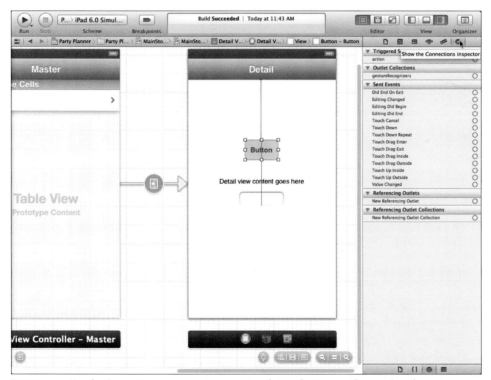

FIGURE 6-9 Use the Connections inspector to connect outlets and actions to the interface elements.

Connecting a Button (Overview)

With the button selected in Figure 6-9, you can see the events that it can send out. The general paradigm for managing these events as follows:

1. Select an interface element such as a button.

2. Find the action that you want to use. For example, Touch Up Inside is the usual action for a tap (the tap consists of two gestures—down and then up).

3. Control-drag from the circle of the action in the Connections inspector to the object that you want to affect, such as a text field in the canvas or in the document outline.

4. When you are over the object, you will see the possible actions that can be triggered.

As the interface is built in Chapter 8, "Building on the Data Model," you'll see how to implement these steps.

Exploring the Three Icons Below a View Controller

As noted previously, when a scene or view controller is selected, its name is replaced by three icons, as you see in Figure 6-9. In Figure 6-10, you can see the document outline for the detail view controller. You can tell by the position of the pointer, that the left-most of the three icons has been selected for the detail view controller scene.

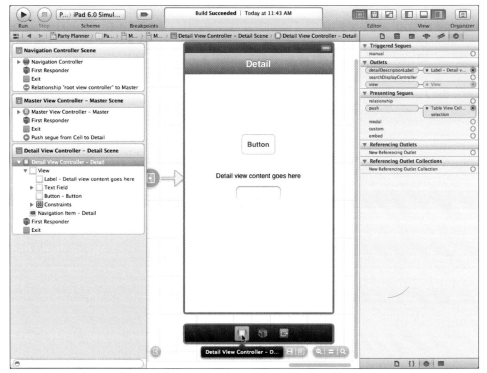

FIGURE 6-10 Select the file's owner.

File's Owner

That left-most icon below a scene is what used to be called *file's owner*. It is the root level view controller of the scene, and clicking on the icon below the scene also selects it in the document outline. It also selects the view controller on the canvas. (You can experiment with the document outline to see the difference in highlighting of a view controller and the main view within it.)

In Figure 6-10, look at the Connections inspector for the view controller. You'll see that now you have several groups of connections. You can connect them by Control-dragging from one of them to another interface element.

- Triggered Segues

- Outlets

- Presenting Segues

- Referencing Outlets

- Referencing Outlet Collections

There really are only three types of connections, although there are five items in this list. This reflects the fact that there are two sides to a connection in many cases. Figure 6-10 shows the Detail View Controller - Detail Scene. Notice that the presenting segue for this scene is a push segue from the Table View Cell selection.

Select the Master View Controller - Master Scene, as shown in Figure 6-11, and you'll see the connection from the other end. The same connection from the point of view of the Master View Controller - Master Scene is shown as a triggered segue. It's the same segue in both cases, but whether it's triggered or presenting depends on which way you look at it. Are you looking at what is happening when an object is selected (that's the selection in Master View Controller - Master Scene) or are you looking at how a view controller was presented (that's the view from the Detail View Controller - Detail Scene)?

Similarly, in Figure 6-12, you can see that from the viewpoint of the Master View Controller - Master Scene, the presenting segue for itself comes from the navigation controller.

In much the same way, outlets and referencing outlets are two sides of the same connection. As you can see in Figure 6-10, `detailDescriptionLabel` and `view` are connected respectively to `Label - Detail view content goes here` and `View`. Property and variable names start with lowercase, so you can see that the actual connection is between a property or instance variable and a label in Interface Builder where initial capital letters are allowed. (Also, labels for objects in Interface Builder can contain spaces, which cannot appear in property and variable names.)

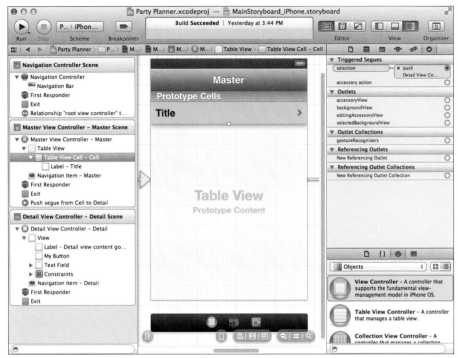

FIGURE 6-11 Compare triggered and presenting segues.

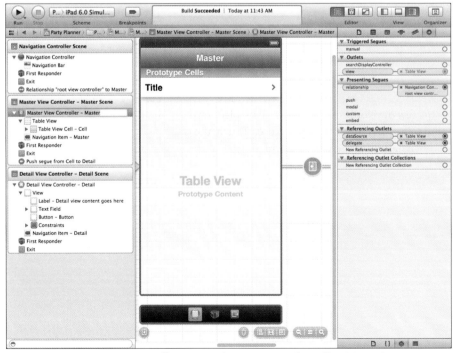

FIGURE 6-12 The navigation controller presents the Master View Controller - Master Scene.

Referencing outlet collections is an advanced topic that is not covered in this book.

First Responder

The middle of the three icons underneath a selected scene is a list of first responders. The first responder is the action that is at the front of the target chain—that is, the actions for the hierarchy of selected objects. The first responder might be a button, and if it can't handle an action, its view gets a chance to handle the action. Because actions all have the same structure using `IBAction` and a single `id` parameter, Xcode can collect all of the possible first responders so that you can Control-drag from an action to something that will receive it. You'll see more about first responders in Chapter 8.

Exit

Finally, the Exit icon at the right of the selected scene may contain additional connections to exit the storyboard.

Summary

Storyboards have a series of inspectors for you to adjust their settings and parameters. Together with the Interface Builder canvas, this gives you a graphical user interface with which to build your app's interface.

The storyboards that are part of the built-in Xcode templates are already set up for you. This means that you're not starting from scratch to build your own storyboards. However, this also means that your first step with storyboards (and with the code of the templates) is the relatively more difficult task of analyzing code that's been written by other people.

Some developers find it difficult (or just annoying) to work on code written by other people. In practice, few developers start from a blank piece of paper or an empty file. Between templates and robust frameworks such as Cocoa Touch, the challenge is understanding what you have and making your concepts fit in with it.

Now that you've seen the basic structure of storyboards, it's time to build the interface for your app where you will—finally—start from a blank slate.

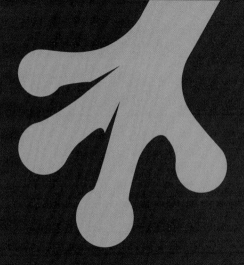

chapter seven

Laying Out Your Scenes and Views

INTERFACE BUILDER LETS you draw your interface easily. As noted, you can avoid Interface Builder if you want: you can create and manage all of your interface elements programmatically. There are many drawbacks to that approach—a significant one of them is that, when you use Interface Builder to build your interface, the files that you build—xib files—are actually composed of XML (you normally don't see it, but it's there). Because your interface files are text-based, you can search them using the Search navigator in some cases. Also you can use the Edit➜Refactor command to rename some of the elements just as you would rename a method or class.

Yet another significant benefit of using Interface Builder to build your interface is that, as you use a graphical interface, you are going to experience some of the same joys and frustrations that your users will experience. You can become the usability test lab and keep track of what works for you and what doesn't.

Laying out your scenes and views with a graphical user interface makes a great deal of sense: you can place interface elements just where you want them to be shown. Alignment guides prompt you to easily align the elements. The system by which this has been accomplished is very powerful, but it does have some limitations. In OS X 10.7 and iOS 6, *Auto Layout* was introduced to make things easier.

The layout tools that have been used in the past mostly let you manage the size and position of interface elements within their containers (on a personal computer, the most common container is a resizable window). iOS and mobile devices introduced a new issue into the picture: not only can containers be resized, but they also can be rotated as the mobile device itself is rotated. Then, in 2011, further sizing issues entered the picture with the advent of iPhone 4 and its Retina display, along with the iPad mini. See "Using Points for Units of Measurement" in Chapter 6, "Working with Storyboard Inspectors."

To further complicate the issue, Apple is more an international company than ever before. In the past, products including the operating systems were often released first in the US and then were rolled out across other countries and regions. Although that still happens, new products from Apple are increasingly released around the world at almost the same time. This means that it's important for software to be released in as many supported languages as possible.

And that's not all by any means. Each year at the Worldwide Developers Conference (WWDC), Apple presents design awards to outstanding apps for Mac, iPhone, and iPad. A separate category for student apps is also awarded. (`https://developer.apple.com/wwdc/awards/`). It's well worth your time to review these winning apps. They are not necessarily the most financially successful apps, but Apple has singled them out for their innovative use of the technologies. Perhaps most valuable to developers such as yourself, on the website Apple describes exactly what of each app makes it stand out as an example to other developers. In 2012, the two winners in the student category were:

- daWindci from Reality Twist GmbH, Mimimi Productions at Mediadesign Highschool of Applied Sciences, Germany
- Little Star from BiBoBox Studio at Dalian Nationalities University, China

International support is important to Apple, Apple developers around the world, and to the users of devices.

Auto Layout helps developers cope with resizing and rotation of devices and containers as well as with multiple screen sizes. In this chapter, you'll see how to use both the old and new versions of sizing tools. First, you'll find a high-level overview of the old techniques (*springs* and *struts*), and then you'll delve into Auto Layout.

In this book, most chapters build on previous chapters and provide groundwork for chapters that follow. If you have been working through the examples in this book, make a copy of your Chapter 6 project and work on it. In part because this chapter covers both the old and new ways of laying out interfaces, your experimentation may provide a hybrid interface that is useful for learning the tools but is not desirable for a finished app.

Using Springs and Struts

The springs and struts approach to managing a changing interface has been part of Interface Builder since the days of NeXT. It's very simple, and, once you get the hang of it, very quick to use.

Working with a copy of your project, you can enable springs and struts. Figure 7-1 shows the project as it is at the end of Chapter 6. As you can see, in the File inspector there is a setting for Auto Layout. If it's on, turn it off so you can use springs and struts.

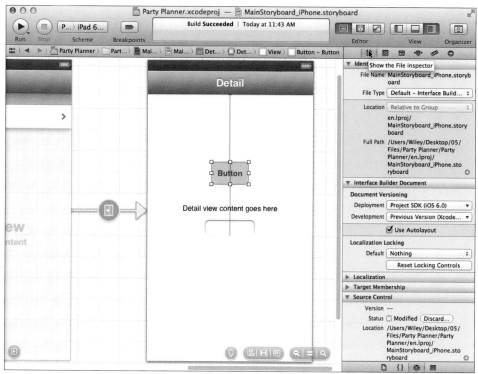

FIGURE 7-1 Turn off Auto Layout in order to use springs and struts.

Delete the button and the text (select them and press Delete), leaving only the text field. Select it and use the Size inspector as shown in Figure 7-2. (It's the next-to-last button at the right of the inspectors list).

The autosizing control is where you do your work. In the center, a rectangle stands in for your selected view (no matter what its shape). On each of the outer four sides of the rectangle, you can click to enable or disable the strut. When enabled, that side of your view is pinned to its container. A common setting is to enable struts for a button or text field so that it is always in the top left or bottom right of its containing view.

In Figure 7-2, the view is pinned to the right and left sides of its container. What do you think will happen?

If you run the app on the iOS simulator, you'll see that the left side of the text field is pinned to the left edge of the screen. As you rotate the device on the simulator, that pinning will be preserved. The right side isn't pinned.

Inside the rectangle, the *springs* let you control resizing. For example, in Figure 7-3 you see that the horizontal spring within the rectangle is enabled, allowing it to grow and shrink.

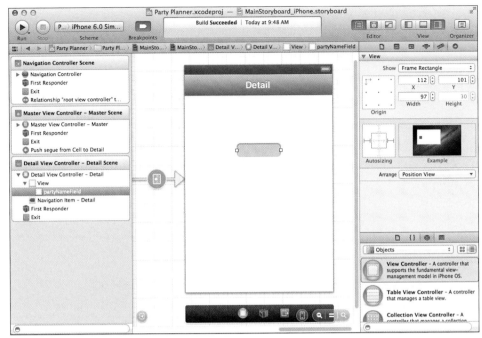

FIGURE 7-2 Use the Size inspector.

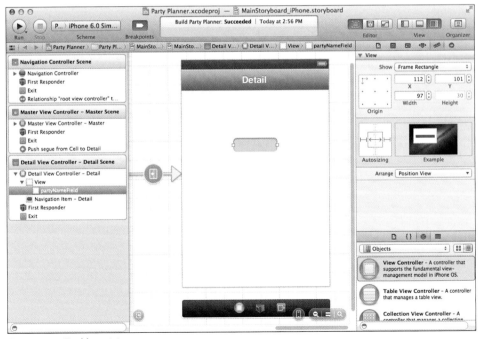

FIGURE 7-3 Enable resizing.

Now, if you run the app and rotate it, you'll see that the text field is pinned to each side of the screen, and in addition, the text field grows and shrinks as shown in Figure 7-4.

FIGURE 7-4 The text field grows and shrinks.

This works very well, but it is not hard to come up with examples where the behavior is counterintuitive.

Using Auto Layout

Auto Layout takes a different approach to layout. Instead of having to specify the relationship between a view and its container, you specify the relationship between two views. In addition, Auto Layout lets you move beyond simple yes/no choices for springs and struts. You can allow ranges of values, and, most important, you can prioritize your settings. As the view is laid out at runtime, the sizes and locations of views may not match any specific values you have set. Instead, they will reflect the best possible arrangement by taking into account your preferred settings based on their priorities.

Don't worry: iOS 6 does most of the work. You just have to define and prioritize your settings. There are three areas that you have to focus on to get the most out of Auto Layout:

- Content Hugging
- Content Compression Resistance
- Constraints

To begin with, turn Auto Layout on (refer to Figure 7-1 to see the control in the File inspector).

Understanding Intrinsic Content

As is the case with springs and struts, as you move or resize a view in Interface Builder, guides appear to help you position the view in any of several possible locations relative to another view (or views) and the superview (or container). These guides are sensitive to the edges and centers of views. The basic function of guides is still available with Auto Layout, but now they are full-fledged objects: they appear in the document outline. They are *constraints*. For an example, look at Figure 7-5.

In Figure 7-5, you see a text field (it's the one you worked with in Chapter 6). Now that you're using Auto Layout, there's a new way to talk about views.

In the Size inspector in the Utility area, you see its X and Y coordinates as well as its width and height. (Note that height is dimmed at this point: you'll see why later.) The width and height of the selected view make up its *intrinsic content* size. You specify the intrinsic content size of a view at the top of the Size inspector just as you always have done. Intrinsic content size is an attribute of the view.

Related to the intrinsic content is the *alignment rect* of a view. This is the rect that you use for aligning a view; it does not include a frame for the view. (And don't worry—you just specify the alignment in most cases and you don't have to worry about how iOS and Xcode implement it.)

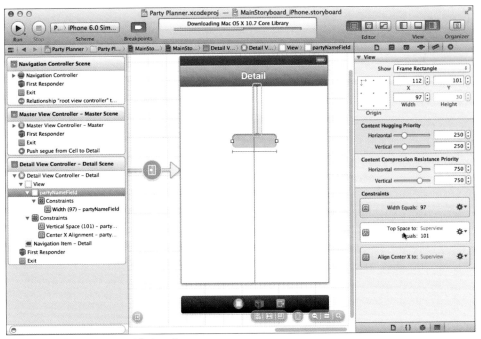

FIGURE 7-5 Position views with Auto Layout.

Using Constraints

In Interface Builder, remember that you're drawing views for the view controller to manage. The view controller uses constraints to determine how the intrinsic size of a view will be used or changed at runtime.

In Figure 7-5, there are three constraints shown. As you can see in the document outline, the `partyNameField` is selected. Within it, there's a section of constraints in the document outline, and within constraints, there is a width constraint set to 97—it is specified at the top of the Size inspector. You can click on it in the document outline to see how it is shown on the canvas (it's the line just below the text field with two vertical endpoints).

The constraints are shown on the canvas and they also are listed under Constraints in the Size inspector in the Utility area. Note that this width constraint is the first one shown under Constraints. Note, too, that it is a constraint on `partyNameField` (you can tell that because it is shown under Constraints, which is part of `partyNameField` in the document outline).

The other two constraints shown in the Size inspector are constraints on the `View` object itself. You can see them on the canvas: the Vertical Space constraint is the highlighted constraint from the top of the view to the top of the text field, and the Center X Alignment constraint appears exactly as the centering guide has always appeared. (Notice that the wording of the constraints is slightly different in the document outline and in the inspector, but this just reflects the formatting of the two sections in Xcode.)

Although things look a bit different from previous implementations, your work is much the same when you are using Auto Layout and constraints rather than guides.

The following sections show you the differences.

Working with Content Hugging

You can set a *content hugging priority* for the text field in both horizontal and vertical directions. This means that in both directions, when the view is resized, it stays as close as possible to its intrinsic content size. (Remember that views are often resized when a mobile device is rotated; they can also be resized when they are shown on a device with an unanticipated screen size.)

Using Content Compression Resistance

The *content compression resistance priority* is the priority that controls the shrinking of a view in either direction.

Setting and Editing Priorities

Neither priority matters by itself. What matters is which one is higher. For example, in Figure 7-5, the text field can grow in either direction. You can select any constraint in the document outline or on the canvas. In the Size inspector, the selected constraint is highlighted as you see in Figure 7-5. You can then use the gear wheel to edit it, as shown in Figure 7-6.

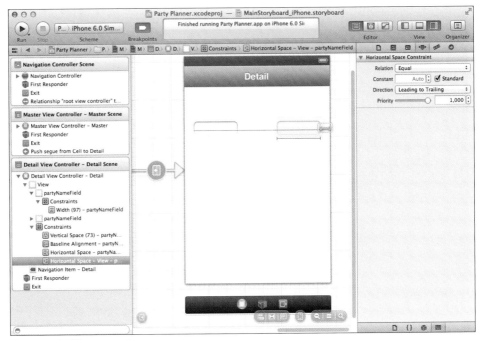

FIGURE 7-6 Edit a constraint.

As you can see, you have a great deal of control over your constraints and views. The best way to become more familiar with the options is to experiment. And in case the issue of constraints is a bit daunting, rest assured that for many purposes you can just position your views where you want them. The default settings may not be optimal, but they will get you well on your way.

Working with Menus

For selected views, there are also menu commands you can use with Auto Layout. For example, when you have two or more views selected, you can use the Editor➔Align menu shown in Figure 7-7 just as you can in many drawing programs.

As you see in Figure 7-8, you can pin a selected view in a variety of ways. *Pinning* is a commonly used term for making an object's position relate to another object. Try out the pin menu, and you'll see that it's a quick way to create the constraints you learned about in the previous section.

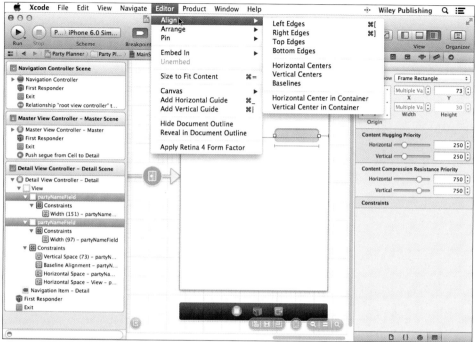

FIGURE 7-7 Align objects.

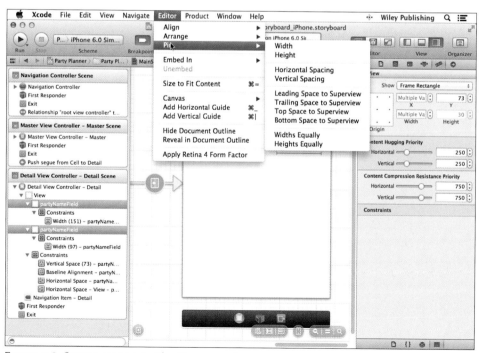

FIGURE 7-8 Create a constraint with a Pin command.

Summary

This chapter shows you the basics of the two layout technologies for iOS: Auto Layout as well as springs and struts. They can be used together, but the advice from Apple's engineers is to use Auto Layout. It accommodates device rotation easily, and, as we have seen with iPhone 5 and iPad mini in 2012, it can make the transition to new device screen sizes easy.

Now it's time to move on to build the app itself. There's more to do with the data model, and there's work to be done on the detail view controller as well as the master view controller.

part 3

Building the Party Planner App

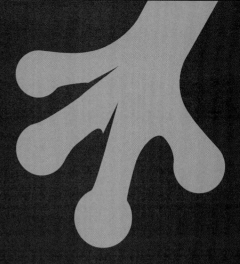

chapter eight
Building on the
Data Model

AT THE END of Chapter 4, "Designing the Party Planner App," you set up the data model to begin to work with your party data. At the end of Chapter 5, "Walking Through the iPhone Storyboard," you experimented with adding a button and a text field to the storyboard. These are small steps on the road to building your app. In this chapter, you expand the basic data model and the storyboard and begin to create the interface for your app.

For some people, the idea of databases and data models seems dauntingly complicated. There's no reason to worry. The concepts you work with in building the data model for Party Planner are exactly the same concepts you work with in organizing a party in real life. You'll deal with guests, the menu, and details of the party. In the world of relational databases (including Core Data), the words you use to describe these are everyday words that you could use to organize your party.

By the end of this chapter, what you will have are:

- An instantiated object from the data model—a *party*. It might be called something such as `party`.

- A view to display the instantiated object. It might be called something such as `partyView`.

You'll be able to drill down to the next layer of detail. Within the party object, you'll have a number of attributes (in database-speak) or properties (in Objective-C-speak). Each one of them will be displayed in a view. (Most of them will be text field views.) Similar naming might identify them as `partyName` (for the object from the data model) and `partyNameView` (for the interface element).

Expanding the Data Model

Some developers like to build the data model first and then design an interface to allow for user interaction with it. Other developers like to design the interface and then determine what the data model needs to look like. Still others do it both ways. In general, no matter how complete your interface design or your data model is, when you actually start to put the pieces together, you'll find a few gaps and a few areas where you may need to make adjustments to one or the other.

In this chapter, you'll see how to expand the data model and then build the interface around it, but keep in mind that in real life, this nice sequential process is likely to involve some back-and-forth work on both the data model and the interface at the same time. Fortunately, Xcode makes such back-and-forth work easy.

Expanding the Interface with Entities

As you can see in Figure 8-1, at the end of Chapter 4 your data model had one entity (called `Party`). The `Party` entity had a single attribute (called `partyName`), which remained as a date from the Master-Detail Application template.

In planning your app in Chapter 4, you need two additional entities: `Guest` and `Food`. The simplest way to add them is to use the pop-up menu below the left side of the data model. Click and hold over the pop-up menu and choose Add Entity. You'll create a new entity, and you can immediately change its name from `Entity` or `Entity1` (the default names) to `Guest` and `Food` (see Figure 8-2).

 You can also use commands in the Editor menu to add entities.

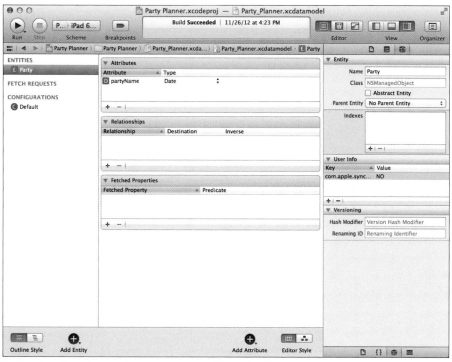

FIGURE 8-1 The data model you've created, as of the end of Chapter 4.

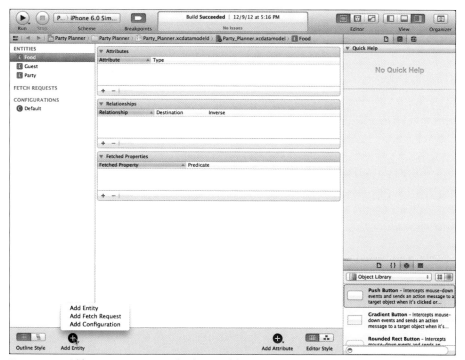

FIGURE 8-2 Add two new entities to the data model.

Filling in the Attributes for the Entities

You can add attributes for the entities as you go (that is, the attributes for the first entity) or you can add all the entities and then go back to add attributes to each one. In either case, the process is the same:

1. Select the entity.

2.a. Using the pop-up menu in the center of the editor at the bottom, choose Add Attribute.

2.b. Use the + under the attributes pane to add an attribute.

3. In either case, the new attribute will be named `Attribute` (or `Attribute1`, `Attribute2`, and so on). Select it in the attributes pane and immediately change its name.

4. Select the appropriate type, discussed in Chapter 4.

Figure 8-3 shows the `Party` entity with three attributes. In Chapter 4 you renamed `timeStamp` to `partyName`; now add `date` and `location`. `location` and `partyName` should be strings, and `date` should be a date.

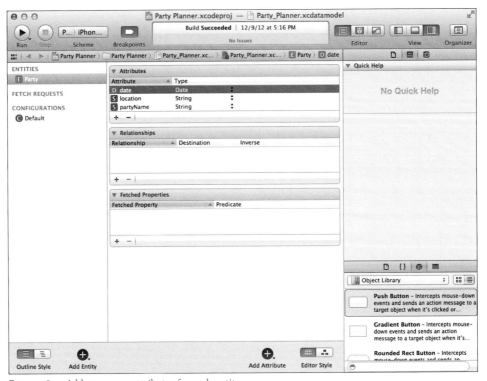

FIGURE 8-3 Add or rename attributes for each entity.

Follow these steps again to add an attribute to Food and to Guest. Names must be unique within an entity, but you can have a name attribute for Food and a separate name attribute for Guest. Create them and set them both to be strings.

The table view shown in the figures of this chapter so far lets you select an entity and work with it. The Editor Style control in the bottom right of the data model editor lets you switch between the table view and a graph view, as shown in Figure 8-4. As you can see, you see all of the attributes for each of the entities in your data model and not just a single selected entity.

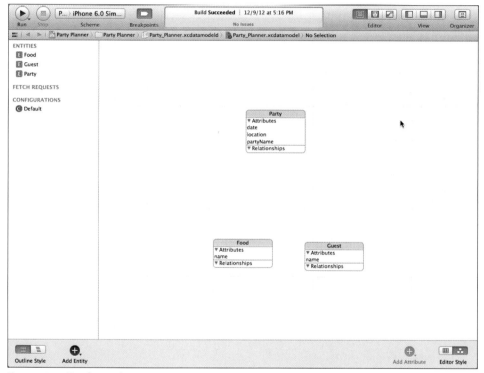

FIGURE 8-4 Use the graph view.

You can also use commands in the Editor menu to add attributes.

Building Relationships

The heart of a relational database is its relations (not surprisingly). In the context of databases, the word *relation* has exactly the same meanings it has in real life. It can mean a relative (such as a parent or spouse), but it also more generally describes any kind of connection.

Database relationships are the connections between two tables (in Core Data, *entities*) in the database. They can represent real-world objects such as students and classes, or they can represent concepts such as plans and implementations. In some implementations of relational databases, relationships are *bidirectional*. In Core Data, however, a relationship describes the connection between an entity and another entity, which is referred to as the *destination* of the relationship.

Creating a Basic Relationship

You can build a relationship in your data model by following these steps.

1. Select an entity in your data model, as shown in Figure 8-5 where `Party` is selected.

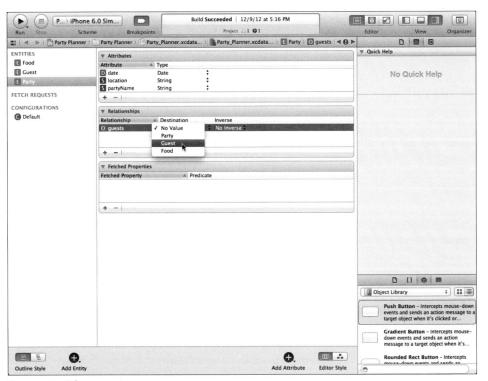

FIGURE 8-5 Select an entity.

2. In the relationships pane, create a new relationship by clicking + at the bottom left.

3. Using the Destination pop-up menu as shown in Figure 8-5, choose the destination of the relationship—that is, the entity to which the selected entity will be related. As you can see in Figure 8-5, your choices include the selected entity itself (Party in this case). That is called a *self-join*. It's an advanced topic in data management. (In Step 7, you will see another way of setting the destination. If you want to follow along, change the destination to No Value before you move on.

4. Next, name the relationship. (Relationship names start with lowercase letters in part to distinguish them from entities, which are always capitalized.) The relationship name will start out as relationship, relationship1, or the like. Give it a meaningful name. Often, the name of the relationship is a plural form of the entity involved in the relationship. Thus, in Figure 8-5, the relationship from Party to Guest is called guests, because the relationship can encompass many guests.

5. Select the Core Data Model inspector in the Utility area, as shown in Figure 8-6. As you can see, you can name (rename) the relationship using the Core Data Model inspector, and you can also set its destination there (as opposed to the method shown in Step 3).

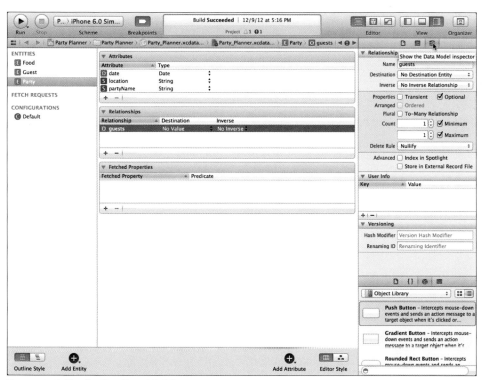

FIGURE 8-6 Use the Core Data Model inspector.

6. Once you have created a relationship between two entities, you'll find that you can select it as an *inverse relationship*. Thus—either in the Relationships pane or in the Core Data Model inspector—at this point you can create a new relationship from the `Guest` entity to the `Party` entity. As shown in Figure 8-7, you now can set the inverse relationship to the `guests` relationship you created in Steps 1 through 5.

7. In the Core Data Model inspector, you can further define the relationship as you see in Figure 8-8. Once again, it is important to point out that these settings aren't particularly database-specific: they are real-life issues. They are described in the following section.

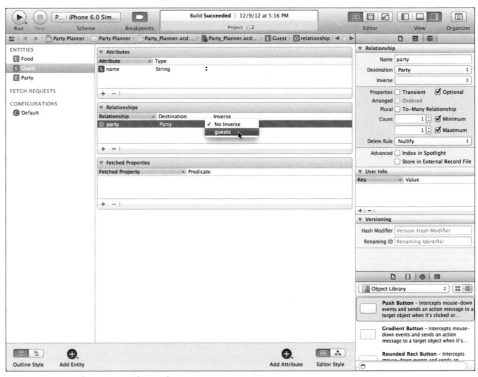

FIGURE 8-7 Set the inverse relationship.

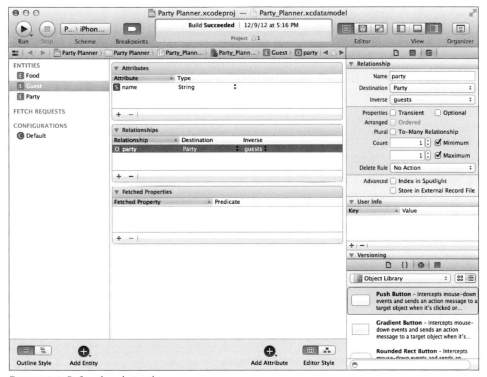

FIGURE 8-8 Refine the relationship.

Refining a Relationship

As you can see in Figure 8-8, there are a number of settings you can apply to a relationship. These are the settings you use most often. (Note that these can only be set in the Core Data Model inspector—they are not available in the Relationships pane in the center of the editor.)

These settings are an important part of the database because once you have set them, Core Data will enforce the rules you set. That means that you don't have to write code to manage these refinements to your database: it's done for you.

- **Optional**—This checkbox means just what it says: is the relationship optional or required. In the data model being built here, the party relationship from Guest to Party, is not optional. You cannot have a guest without a party. You could construct a different data model that keeps track of people even if they are not invited to a party, but that is a more complex model.

  Note that this is a case in which the direction of the relationship matters. The guests relationship from Party to Guest is optional because you can have a party without any guests, as would be the case when you are setting up a party and before you have invited anyone.

- **To-Many Relationship**—There is a database term for this concept: *cardinality*. It simply expresses the concept that for one party there can be many guests (that's a to-many relationship). In the data structure being built here, for the guests relationship you will want to set the to-many relationship checkbox. For its inverse, party (the relationship from Guest to Party), you do not want a to-many relationship because in this data model, a guest can only be invited to one party. (As noted, allowing multiple guests to be invited to multiple parties is a bit more complex.)

- **Delete Rule**—This pop-up menu gives you four choices of the behavior for Core Data to take when an object is deleted. The delete rule defines what happens to the related objects when the main object is deleted. The choices are:

  - **No action**—This is just what it says: if an object is deleted, the related objects are not affected. This can cause internal database problems, so be certain that you know that you want to use it. If you delete a party, for example, and if there is an inverse relationship from a guest to the party, once the party has been deleted, the guest has a reference to a non-existent object, and that can cause difficulties and even crashes.

  - **Nullify**—Continuing with the previous scenario, if you choose the nullify delete action, the reference to the now-deleted party in the guest data is set to null. That's a valid value, and it doesn't cause a crash.

  - **Cascade**—The cascade delete rule in this case would mean that when a party is deleted, all of its guests are deleted. That is the behavior you want to use with Party Planner.

  - **Deny**—Finally, the deny delete rule says that you cannot delete something that is required. Instead of using the cascade delete rule, you might want to set up a deny rule for a party so that you have to manually delete each guest before you can delete the party.

Next Steps

Follow the steps in this section to create relationships from Party to Food and vice versa. If you assume that the Food entity represents various types of food, the relationship from Party to Food is a to-many relationship (in most cases). It might be optional if you want to allow for parties with no food. As is the case with guests, the inverse relationship from Food to Party is required: you cannot have food in this data model without having a party at which to serve it.

Table 8-1 shows the relationships that should be created at this time.

Table 8-1 Relationships for the Party Planner App

Relationship Name	Entity (Source)	Destination	Inverse	Optional	To-Many
guests	Party	Guest	party	✓	✓
menu	Party	Food	party	✓	✓
party	Guest	Party	guests		
party	Food	Party	menu		

Figure 8-9 shows the process in action. The menu relationship is the relationship from Party to Food. Once it is created as shown in Figure 8-9, you can use it as an inverse relationship for a new relationship from Food to Party that you might want to call party. (You already have a party relationship from Guest to Party, but because they are based on different entities, the duplicate names don't cause problems.)

FIGURE 8-9 Review the data model.

Building the Detail View Controller

Now that the data model is expanded, you'll see how to connect your interface elements to your code and to one another. If you're thinking, "There's a lot of connecting to be done," you are right. In a sense, you have parallel interface elements with the objects representing data working with interface objects in the frameworks as well as those you have created (and will create). They have to be connected so that, at runtime, they function together as a single entity.

To the users, there is no distinction: a text field displays the name of the party and lets you modify it. However, from your point of view, you need to remember that these are two distinct objects. The text field displays and lets the user edit the data; you are responsible for moving the actual data in the data object to and from the text field.

Because the master view controller functions in the template without changes (at least not at this time), this chapter and the following one focuses on the work you do in the detail view controller to display the selected party's details. The steps you'll need to take are:

1. Convert your data model to a `Party` class in your project.

2. Modify the app to use your `Party` class instead of what is already there.

3. Add a text field to display the `partyName` attribute of the `Party` class in the detail view controller.

The first step is described in this chapter. The second and third are described in Chapter 9, "Building the Detail Data View."

In Chapter 10, "Saving and Restoring Data," you see how to move between the interface fields and the persistent store.

Creating and Removing the Database

The data model you have built with Xcode and the Core Data Model editor and its inspectors defines your database. In the Master-Detail Application template, the first time you run the app, a new database is created based on your data model. You don't have to do anything: the code is already in the template.

However, you may encounter an issue as you continue to build your app. The data model for your database is incorporated into the database that is created by the template. If you make changes to the data model and attempt to re-open a database created from a previous version of the data model, you are likely to get an error. There are ways to manage this in production apps, but during development, it is often easiest simply to remove an old database file. The template won't find it when you launch the app for the first time, and so it will create a new database from your current data model. That code is built into the template.

Not every change to a data model invalidates existing data files. Furthermore, Core Data contains migration code that you can use to modify existing data files. This is an advanced topic, so you might want to look at the relevant documentation on developer.apple.com. For many developers, it's easiest to handle data model changes that happen during the development cycle by just removing the old database. For apps that are in production, the migration tools make database changes easy for users to handle (because they don't see the issue at all).

1. In the Finder, select your Home directory.

2. While holding down the Option key, choose Go➔Library. (Unless the Option key is pressed, the library is not in the Go menu.)

3. Select Application Support, iPhone Simulator, and then the iOS version number as shown in Figure 8-10.

FIGURE 8-10 Open the library.

4. Continue drilling down to the Applications subfolder.

5. You'll find a folder for each of the apps you've used on the simulator. The folder names are strings of letters and numbers. You may have to open several folders to find the one with your Party Planner app.

6. Inside the same folder as your Party Planner app, open the Documents folder as shown in Figure 8-11. Inside it you'll see the database called Party_Planner.sqlite. Delete it.

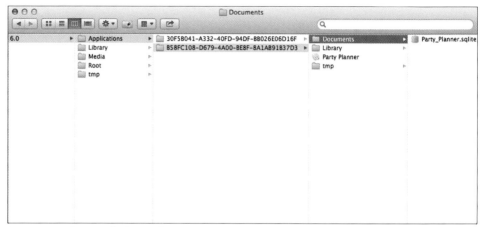

FIGURE 8-11 Remove the SQLite file.

7. The next time you run the app, a new database will automatically be created with the new data model.

Creating the Party Class from the Data Model

Once you have built your data model, you can easily convert it to classes for your project using Xcode. Remember that the data model is used to construct your data file, so, as noted in the sidebar called "Creating and Removing the Database," when you make a change to the data model, you must regenerate the classes.

Looking at the Existing KVC Code

The classes that you work with in Core Data are `NSManagedObject` or subclasses of it. The Master-Detail Application template uses `NSManagedObject` classes. This is the simplest way of handling the data. The template uses key-value coding (KVC) to access the attributes of the data model entities. In the `insertNewObject` method of `MasterView Controller.m`, a new object is created as an `NSManagedObject`, and its attribute is set with KVC.

Key-value coding is a mechanism for accessing the properties of an object (which are the attributes of an entity) by using the name. You pass in the name to KVC, and you get the value back. Search for key-value coding on `developer.apple.com` if you want more information. It's not essential at this point because the template uses KVC, and you're about to replace it with another technique.

Here is the code that sets the attribute:

```
[newManagedObject setValue:[NSDate date] forKey:@"partyName"];
```

You pass in the value for the object (a date, in this case), and you specify the key (that is, the attribute name) using a string. Compare this to the way you set a property on a class, as shown in the following section. That code would be written like this:

```
self.newManagedObject.partyName = [[NSDate date] description];
```

Setting the attribute directly using dot syntax is more efficient than asking the framework to use a string to find the necessary attribute at runtime. By creating classes for your data model entities, you can improve the performance of your app; you also can make your code easier to write. You'll notice that the KVC version is slightly longer than the dot syntax version.

Creating the Classes from the Data Model

If you have followed the steps in this chapter, your data model now contains three entities—Party, Food, and Guest—along with the relevant relationships. The simplest way to convert them to classes is to make a class out of each one. Here are the steps to follow:

1. Open the data model.

2. Select the Party entity from the list of top-level components at the left of the data model editor, as shown in Figure 8-12.

FIGURE 8-12 Select the Party entity.

3. Choose Editor➔Create NSManagedObject Subclass, as shown in Figure 8-12.

4. If you have selected an attribute for the entity, you are asked which entities to create, as shown in Figure 8-13. In this case, you can select only Party or all of them. If you have made changes to any of the subclasses created previously, don't recreate them unless it's absolutely necessary—your changes will be lost. However, in a case such as this where you have no changes to the previously generated subclasses, your choice doesn't matter. Click Next.

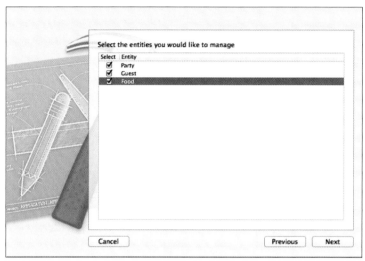

Select the entities you would like to manage

Select	Entity
☑	Party
☑	Guest
☑	Food

Cancel   Previous   Next

FIGURE 8-13 Select the entities to subclass.

5. Choose the location for the new files that will be created, as shown in Figure 8-14.

The scalar option lets you use simple C scalar types rather than Objective-C object types where possible. This can have a very marginal improvement in performance, but many developers prefer to stick with the Objective-C types (that means, do not check the box). You can specify a group into which to place the new files, and you must select the target (there is only one choice in your app at this point). In this sequence, the new files will be placed in the basic group of files; that enables you to see how to create a new group from them in the next step.

6. Xcode will create a pair of files for each class—Party.h, Party.m, Guest.h, Guest.m, Food.h, and Food.m. You can see them in the project navigator at the left of Figure 8-15.

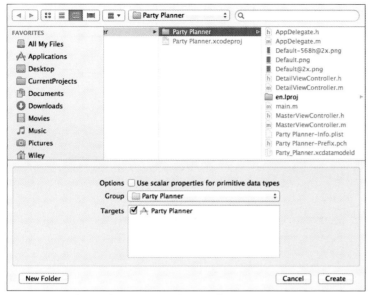

FIGURE 8-14 Choose the location for the new files.

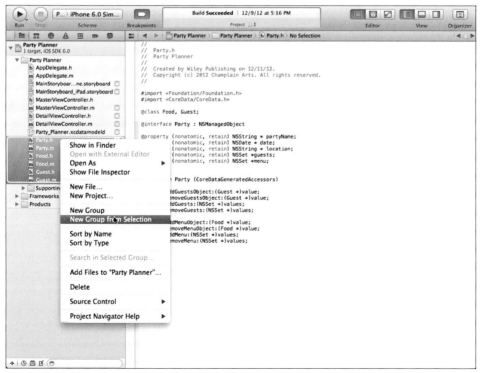

FIGURE 8-15 Select the new files and make them a group.

7. Select the new files and use the shortcut menu (Control-click or right-click if your mouse is set up for two buttons) to choose New Group from Selection, as shown in Figure 8-15.

8. A new group will be created from the selected files. Click in the new group name and edit it, as shown in Figure 8-16. **Data Model** is a good name.

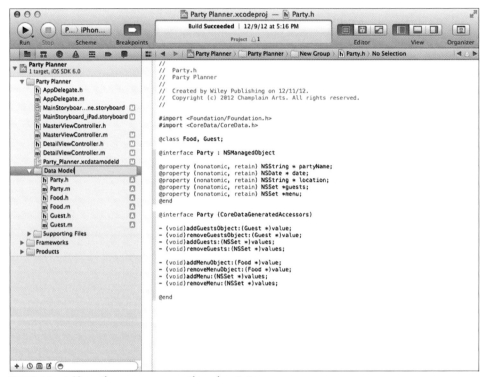

FIGURE 8-16 Name the new group something descriptive.

Looking at the Code

The three classes that have been created for you let you access the data directly with properties. You don't have to do anything with the code that's generated, but it's a good idea to know what's going on.

The Party class is the heart of your data model. Listing 8-1 shows the Party.h file.

Listing 8-1   The Party.h File

```objc
#import <Foundation/Foundation.h>
#import <CoreData/CoreData.h>

@class Food, Guest;

@interface Party : NSManagedObject

@property (nonatomic, retain) NSDate * date;
@property (nonatomic, retain) NSString * location;
@property (nonatomic, retain) NSString * partyName;
@property (nonatomic, retain) NSSet *guests;
@property (nonatomic, retain) NSSet *menu;
@end

@interface Party (CoreDataGeneratedAccessors)

- (void)addGuestsObject:(Guest *)value;
- (void)removeGuestsObject:(Guest *)value;
- (void)addGuests:(NSSet *)values;
- (void)removeGuests:(NSSet *)values;

- (void)addMenuObject:(Food *)value;
- (void)removeMenuObject:(Food *)value;
- (void)addMenu:(NSSet *)values;
- (void)removeMenu:(NSSet *)values;

@end
```

The code begins by importing two Cocoa Touch frameworks. Then, you see a forward reference to Food and Guest, which will be used by Party. The interface for Party shows that it is a subclass of NSManagedObject. Following that you see that the Party attributes from the data model have been changed into properties that you can use in your code.

That's all that you care about on the data side.

There is a second interface for Party just below the first one. Technically, this is a *category* called CoreDataGeneratedAccessors. These are methods that you can call to manipulate the class. As you can see, you can add and remove Guest and Menu (Food) objects. You also can add and remove NSSet objects: these represent relationships.

The corresponding .m file (shown in Listing 8-2) imports the three main data model files (Party.h, Food.h, and Guest.h). Its implementation consists of promises to deliver the Core Data properties at runtime. (That's code you never see.)

Listing 8-2   The Party.m File

```
#import "Party.h"
#import "Food.h"
#import "Guest.h"


@implementation Party

@dynamic date;
@dynamic location;
@dynamic partyName;
@dynamic guests;
@dynamic menu;

@end
```

Listing 8-3 shows you the Food.h file. It is comparable to Guest.h and is much simpler than Party.h. What is important to note is that you add and remove related objects such as Guest and Food using the methods in Party. Thus, the main object controls all of the related objects.

Listing 8-3   The Food.h File

```
#import <Foundation/Foundation.h>
#import <CoreData/CoreData.h>

@class Party;

@interface Food : NSManagedObject

@property (nonatomic, retain) NSString * name;
@property (nonatomic, retain) Party *party;

@end
```

Listing 8-4 is comparable to both Guest.m and Party.m.

Listing 8-4   The Food.m File

```
#import "Food.h"
#import "Party.h"


@implementation Food

@dynamic name;
@dynamic party;

@end
```

Summary

This chapter shows you how to build on your initial data model. In particular, you learned how to build relationships among the model entities. You also learned how to convert your data model into code using Xcode.

Much of your work up to this point has been with Xcode and its graphical development tools, including Core Data Model editor and Interface Builder. Now, you're venturing into writing code. For some people, that is actually more comfortable than drawing relationships among entities or drawing interface elements. For others, it's a bit daunting. No matter which camp you're in (or if you're in neither or both), you'll see that the Apple engineers have brought the same ease-of-use standards to the developer tools that they have brought to apps for music, word processing, and all the other wonderful iOS apps they've created.

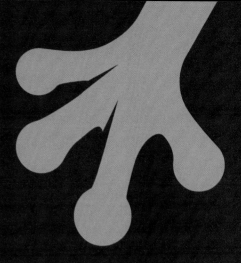

chapter nine

Building the Detail
Data View

IN CHAPTER 8, "Building on the Data Model," you expanded the model and converted it to a `Party` class in your project. As noted, there are two additional steps to take with your expanded data model:

- Modify the app to use your `Party` class instead of what is already there.

- Add a text field to display the `partyName` attribute of the `Party` class in the detail view controller.

Once the text field is added, you'll be able to add fields for the other data elements of `Party`. That will go a long way to completing the iPhone interface. At that point, you'll learn how to lay out the iPad interface.

These steps are somewhat different from the steps you have previously taken to build the Party Planner app. Unlike building your data model with the Core Data Model editor or designing your user interface with storyboards, you'll have to get out your keyboard and start dealing with code—yes, typed-in code in the great tradition of programmers for over half a century.

Actually, "typed-in" is not quite accurate. Yes, there's some typing to do, but much of the code is pasted in; other sections of code are in the template and they need a little tweaking. And even when you're typing in code, Xcode's Fix-It and code completion will let you press the Return key or click an option to have Xcode do the work for you.

Nevertheless, you're now in the world of text-based code for a while, but you'll return to the graphical user interface of storyboards to develop the actual interface of the detail view for both iPhone and iPad.

You'll see how the universal setting makes it easy for you to modify iPad and iPhone interfaces with the minimum of effort and the maximum amount of reused code.

 This chapter introduces you to the basics of creating a view and its supporting controller. In Part IV, "Using Table and Collection Views," you'll learn another way of moving data to and from a view. Many apps use both techniques. The techniques described in this chapter are often used for relatively small amounts of data, whereas the techniques described in Part IV are often used for larger amounts of data. The data for an individual party falls in the middle ground, whereby either technique is valid.

Using the Party Class

In Chapter 8, you used Xcode to create subclasses of NSManagedObject for Party, Food, and Guest. Now it's time to use them. In the section called "Looking at the Existing KVC Code" in Chapter 8, you saw the way in which new NSManagedObject instances are created and how the initial data is set using KVC. Now it's time to review that code in detail and convert it to use the new Party class directly rather than with KVC.

You may want to review "Introducing Core Data" in Chapter 4, "Designing the Party Planner App." In that section, you modified the template so that it uses your data model with the Party class and the partyName attribute rather than the Event class and the timeStamp attribute of the template.

Listing 9-1 shows the code for insertNewObject as it is in the Party Planner app as it exists at the end of Chapter 8. It incorporates the changes previously mentioned from Chapter 4. (As is the case with many of the listings in this book, they have been reformatted in some places to accommodate printed page layouts. In addition, some comments—marked JF—have been added.)

Listing 9-1   insertNewObject in MasterViewController.m

```
- (void)insertNewObject:(id)sender
{
  // Get the Core Data stack info JF
  NSManagedObjectContext *context =
    [self.fetchedResultsController managedObjectContext];
  NSEntityDescription *entity =
    [[self.fetchedResultsController fetchRequest] entity];
```

```
// Create the new managed object JF
NSManagedObject *newManagedObject =
  [NSEntityDescription insertNewObjectForEntityForName:
    [entity name]
  inManagedObjectContext:context];

// If appropriate, configure the new managed object.

// Normally you should use accessor methods, but
// using KVC here avoids the need to add a custom class
// to the template.
[newManagedObject setValue:
  [[NSDate date] description] forKey:@"partyName"];

// Save the context.
NSError *error = nil;
if (![context save:&error]) {
  // Replace this implementation with code to
  // handle the error appropriately.
  // abort() causes the application to generate a
  // crash log and terminate. You should not use this
  // function in a shipping application, although it
  // may be useful during development.
  NSLog(@"Unresolved error %@, %@", error, [error userInfo]);
  abort();
}
}
```

As you can see, the code that creates a new managed object has four main sections:

- Getting the Core Data stack info
- Creating the new managed object
- Setting attributes of the new managed object
- Saving the managed object context

This code is generally the same for any managed objects that you use (you'll see why in the sections that follow). The only difference is typically in the attributes that you set.

Getting the Core Data Stack Info

This section provides you with information about how the Core Data stack is set up and what it does. If you are building your app from a template, everything that is described in this section will be done for you automatically, so, if you want, you can skip over this section and come back to it at your leisure. If you want a good understanding of what is happening, read it now.

In the Master-Detail Application, the Core Data stack is set up in `AppDelegate.m`; it consists of three properties. The properties are:

```
@property (readonly, strong, nonatomic)
  NSManagedObjectModel *managedObjectModel;
@property (readonly, strong, nonatomic)
  NSManagedObjectContext *managedObjectContext;
@property (readonly, strong, nonatomic)
  NSPersistentStoreCoordinator *persistentStoreCoordinator;
```

These components of the Core Data stack do most of the work. You saw how to build the managed object model in Chapters 4 and 8. The persistent store coordinator works with your persistent stores. In many cases—including this template and the Party Planner App derived from it—there is one persistent store and the persistent store coordinator serves as a pass-through to that one persistent store—which is the SQLite database. The managed object context sits between the managed object model and the persistent store(s). What matters to you is that when data is retrieved, it is retrieved into a managed object context, and when it comes time to save data, you actually save the managed object model.

You may also notice references to fetch requests. You can create fetch requests—specific data elements you want to retrieve—with the Core Data Model editor. In the template so far, the template code handles fetching the data, so you don't have to worry about fetch requests in the Core Data Model editor.

As long as you have properly set up the Core Data stack in `AppDelegate.m`, as described in the following sections, you use them as you work with your managed objects. (The template sets them up, but as noted in the section entitled "Building Your Data Model" in Chapter 4, you may have to make customizations for the name of your entity.) That is why there is very little customization needed as you use the code discussed in this section—you've already done it in `AppDelegate.m`. Assuming you have followed the steps in Chapter 4, here is how you have set up the core data stack.

In the Master-Detail Application template, the Core Data stack is set up in `AppDelegate.m`, but, as you can see in Listing 9-1, the stack is accessed via the `fetchedResults Controller` property inside `MasterViewController.h`. Here is the property declaration:

```
@property (strong, nonatomic)
  NSFetchedResultsController *fetchedResultsController;
```

And here are the first two lines of Listing 9-1 that use that property to retrieve the stack objects.

```
NSManagedObjectContext *context =
  [self.fetchedResultsController managedObjectContext];
NSEntityDescription *entity =
  [[self.fetchedResultsController fetchRequest] entity];
```

And where does the fetched results controller come from? See "Adding the Managed Object Context to the `MasterViewController`," later in this section.

Setting Up the Managed Object Model

Your managed object model file has the extension `xcdatamodeld`. In the templates, it is automatically moved into the app bundle as the app is built. Thus for the Party Planner app, it is `Party_Planner.xcdatamodeld`, as you can see in Figure 9-1—look at the window title. (Spaces in the app name are replaced by underscores automatically.)

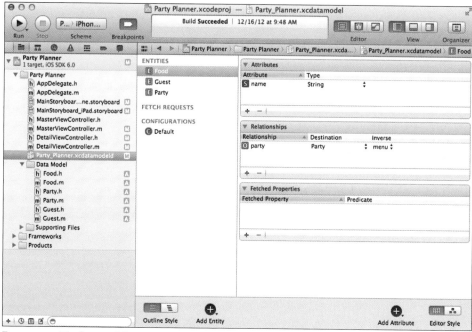

FIGURE 9-1 The data model is in your project.

If you create a new project from a template that supports Core Data, Xcode does this as you create your app from the template. You don't need to make any modifications.

You work with the `xcdatamodeld` in Xcode. During the build process, it is automatically converted to a `momd` file (thus, the extension in the code that follows). The `momd` is a runtime version of the Xcode data model file. The `xcdatamodeld` file contains information such as how you have arranged the graph editor of your data model in the editor. That information is not needed at runtime.

```
// Returns the managed object model for the application.
// If the model doesn't already exist, it is created
// from the application's model.
```

```
- (NSManagedObjectModel *)managedObjectModel
{
  if (_managedObjectModel != nil) {
    return _managedObjectModel;
  }
  NSURL *modelURL = [[NSBundle mainBundle]
    // name of the data model JF
    URLForResource:@"Party_Planner" withExtension:@"momd"];
  _managedObjectModel = [[NSManagedObjectModel alloc]
    initWithContentsOfURL:modelURL];
  return _managedObjectModel;
}
```

Setting Up the Persistent Store Coordinator

The persistent store coordinator handles one or more persistent stores—in this app, there is one (a very common situation). The persistent store coordinator needs to know about the file(s) that are used to store your data along with the data model that defines their structure. In AppDelegate.h, this is the code that performs that task. As with the data model, there is one important line that identifies the file (this time it's the SQLite file and not the data model file). As is also the case with the data model, this is created for you automatically when you create the project from the template.

```
// Returns the persistent store coordinator for the application.
// If the coordinator doesn't already exist, it is created and the
// application's store added to it.
- (NSPersistentStoreCoordinator *)persistentStoreCoordinator
{
  if (_persistentStoreCoordinator != nil) {
    return _persistentStoreCoordinator;
  }

  NSURL *storeURL = [[self applicationDocumentsDirectory]
    // here is the data store name JF
    URLByAppendingPathComponent:@"Party_Planner.sqlite"];

  NSError *error = nil;
  _persistentStoreCoordinator = [[NSPersistentStoreCoordinator
    alloc] initWithManagedObjectModel:[self managedObjectModel]];
  if (![_persistentStoreCoordinator
    addPersistentStoreWithType:NSSQLiteStoreType
    configuration:nil URL:storeURL options:nil error:&error]) {
    /*
    lengthy comment omitted JF

    NSLog(@"Unresolved error %@, %@", error, [error userInfo]);
```

```
    abort();
  }

  return _persistentStoreCoordinator;
}
```

Setting Up the Managed Object Context

This is done for you using the persistent store coordinator and the data model. As noted previously, it uses those two objects, but you don't have to provide specific setups for the managed object context.

Adding the Managed Object Context to the MasterViewController

Fetch requests work with the Core Data stack to retrieve data. In the Master-Detail Application template, you have a single fetch request in the `MasterViewController` class. It retrieves all of the `Party` entities when the app starts to run. (In fact, it retrieves *parts* of all the `Party` entities. When Core Data encounters a partially retrieved entity [known as a *fault*], you can use them directly. When necessary, Core Data will retrieve the necessary parts of the full entity. Faults are not errors; they are an efficiency mechanism.) Listing 9-2 shows you the code. You can also create fetch requests with the Core Data Model editor.

Listing 9-2   fetchedResultsController in MasterViewController.m

```
- (NSFetchedResultsController *)fetchedResultsController
{
  if (_fetchedResultsController != nil) {
    return _fetchedResultsController;
  }

  NSFetchRequest *fetchRequest = [[NSFetchRequest alloc] init];
  // Edit the entity name as appropriate.
  NSEntityDescription *entity = [NSEntityDescription
    // you changed entityForName in Chapter 4 JF
    entityForName:@"Party"
    // use the managed object context of this object JF
    inManagedObjectContext:self.managedObjectContext];
  [fetchRequest setEntity:entity];

  // Set the batch size to a suitable number.
  [fetchRequest setFetchBatchSize:20];

  // Edit the sort key as appropriate.
  NSSortDescriptor *sortDescriptor = [[NSSortDescriptor alloc]
    //you set the sort key in Chapter 4 JF
```

```
     initWithKey:@"partyName" ascending:NO];
  NSArray *sortDescriptors = @[sortDescriptor];

  [fetchRequest setSortDescriptors:sortDescriptors];

  // Edit the section name key path and cache name if appropriate.
  // nil for section name key path means "no sections".
  NSFetchedResultsController *aFetchedResultsController =
    [[NSFetchedResultsController alloc]
    initWithFetchRequest:fetchRequest
    managedObjectContext:self.managedObjectContext
    sectionNameKeyPath:nil cacheName:@"Master"];
  aFetchedResultsController.delegate = self;
  self.fetchedResultsController = aFetchedResultsController;

  NSError *error = nil;
  if (![self.fetchedResultsController performFetch:&error]) {
    // Replace this implementation with code to handle the
    //  error appropriately.
    // abort() causes the application to generate a crash
    // log and terminate. You should not use this function
    // in a shipping application, although it may be useful
    // during development.
    NSLog(@"Unresolved error %@, %@", error, [error userInfo]);
    abort();
  }

  return _fetchedResultsController;
}
```

When you are reusing this code, there are two changes you may need to make:

- You need to supply the name of your entity in entityForName as noted.

- You need to supply the sort order for the fetch request results. This involves identify-
  ing the sort key and the sort order.

If you are not using a template but are implementing the Core Data stack for yourself, you
will typically have code such as Listing 9-2 in one or more of your controller objects. You may
have multiple sets of fetch requests in different controllers to manage different data and different contexts. If you do that, you can follow the structure of the Master-Detail Application.
That means:

1. Set up the Core Data stack in the app delegate as described in this section.

2. Typically, the app delegate creates one or more view controllers in application:
   DidFinishLaunchingWithOptions: as shown in Listing 9-3.

Listing 9-3   application:didFinishLaunchingWithOptions: in MasterViewController.m

```
- (BOOL)application:(UIApplication *)application
    didFinishLaunchingWithOptions:(NSDictionary *)launchOptions
{
  // Override point for customization after application launch.
  if ([[UIDevice currentDevice]
      userInterfaceIdiom] == UIUserInterfaceIdiomPad) {
        UISplitViewController *splitViewController =
          (UISplitViewController *)self.window.rootViewController;
      UINavigationController *navigationController =
        [splitViewController.viewControllers lastObject];
      splitViewController.delegate =
        (id)navigationController.topViewController;

      UINavigationController *masterNavigationController =
        splitViewController.viewControllers[0];
      MasterViewController *controller = (MasterViewController *)
        masterNavigationController.topViewController;
      // set the managedObjectContext for the new controller JF
      controller.managedObjectContext = self.managedObjectContext;
  } else {
      UINavigationController *navigationController =
        (UINavigationController *)self.window.rootViewController;
      MasterViewController *controller = (MasterViewController *)
        navigationController.topViewController;
      // set the managedObjectContext for the new controller JF
      controller.managedObjectContext = self.managedObjectContext;
  }
  return YES;
}
```

3. Declare a managedObjectContext property in each of the new view controllers that will need it. Note that this will need to be in the `.h` file rather than the `.m` file so that you can use it in Step 4.

```
@property (strong, nonatomic)
  NSManagedObjectContext *managedObjectContext;
```

4. After each view controller is created, you set its managedObjectContext to the managedObjectContext in the app delegate. Two view controllers are created in Listing 9-3, and each has its managedObjectContext set. Comments highlight those lines.

```
// set the managedObjectContext for the new controller JF
controller.managedObjectContext = self.managedObjectContext;
```

If you do not see where view controllers are created in `application:DidFinishLaunching WithOptions:`, they may be created directly from your storyboard. You can use `self.window` to access the `window` property of the app delegate. Then use the `rootViewController` property to get to the top-level view. This was an important change in iOS 4.0, so you will still find code around that does not recognize that there is a way to find the root (or top-level or content) view. The code to use is `self.window.rootViewController`. In many templates, the root view controller is a controller created in the template, and you can modify its code—for example to add and set a property for the managed object context.

Creating the New Managed Object

Now you need to create your new `Party` object. As described in the previous section, the Core Data stack and the fetch request identify the `Party` object. Thus, the code at the beginning of Listing 9-1 has already been set up with the data that is needed. That is why no customization is needed to use the new `Party` object.

However, if you're going to want to access attributes of the new `Party` object, you'll need to make the following change. As it stands now, the code in `insertNewObject:` in `MasterViewController.m` creates a new `NSManagedObject`. Because of the settings in the Core Data stack, it will be a `Party` object, but the code only identifies it as an `NSManagedObject` rather than as the specific subclass that it now is.

The code to create the new object is as follows:

```
// Create the new managed object JF
NSManagedObject *newManagedObject =
  [NSEntityDescription insertNewObjectForEntityForName:
    [entity name]
    inManagedObjectContext:context];
```

Simply change `MasterViewController.m` so `newManagedObject` is an instance of `Party`.

In order not to get a compile error, import the header file to the top of `Master ViewController.m`:

```
#import "Party.h"
```

Here is what the code inside `newManagedObject:` should look like now:

```
// Create the new managed object JF
Party *newManagedObject =
  [NSEntityDescription insertNewObjectForEntityForName:
    [entity name]
    inManagedObjectContext:context];
```

Setting Attributes of the New Managed Object

You usually do need to set the attributes of the new object. Because `newManagedObject` is now an instance of `Party`, you can use this code in `insertNewObject:` in Master `ViewController.m`:

```
newManagedObject.partyName = [[NSDate date] description];
```

Note that the `partyName` attribute is now an `NSString`, so you need to convert the `NSDate` to an `NSString`. `description` provides an `NSString` version of an object, so that will do for now (eventually you'll not use a date—you'll make the party name editable).

> You may want to rename `newManagedObject` to `newParty` because that is what it is. The argument for not renaming it is so that you can trace back the code to the template's code. Perhaps until you are comfortable with the templates and the frameworks, you may want to do minimal renaming. Once you're comfortable, however, objects should be clearly named.

Here is what `insertNewObject:` should look like now:

```
- (void)insertNewObject:(id)sender
{
  NSManagedObjectContext *context =
    [self.fetchedResultsController managedObjectContext];
  NSEntityDescription *entity =
    [[self.fetchedResultsController fetchRequest] entity];
  Party *newManagedObject = [NSEntityDescription
    insertNewObjectForEntityForName:[entity name]
    inManagedObjectContext:context];

  // If appropriate, configure the new managed object.
  // Normally you should use accessor methods, but using KVC here
  // avoids the need to add a custom class to the template.
  // Old code - JF
  //   [newManagedObject setValue:[NSDate date]
  forKey:@"partyName"];
  newManagedObject.partyName = [[NSDate date] description];
  // Save the context.
  NSError *error = nil;
  if (![context save:&error]) {
    // Replace this implementation with code to handle the error
    // appropriately.
    // abort() causes the application to generate a crash log and
    // terminate. You should not use this function in a shipping
    // application, although it may be useful during development.
```

```
    NSLog(@"Unresolved error %@, %@", error, [error userInfo]);
    abort();
  }
}
```

Saving the Managed Object Context

Finally, you save the managed object context. As the code in Listing 9-1 shows, this is just a matter of asking the managed object context to save itself. You do check for errors, and that will be discussed in Chapter 15, "Telling Users the News: Alerts and NSError." The mechanics of saving data are discussed in Chapter 10, "Saving and Restoring Data."

Connecting Interface Elements to Properties

In previous chapters you have experimented with connecting interface elements to your code. You may have a property connected to your text field as a result of your experiments. Here is how to check existing connections, how to remove them, change them, and create them.

Checking Existing Connections

You can check existing connections from either end—that is, from the code side or from the Interface Builder side.

Checking a Connection from the .h File

A connected property has a filled-in circle to its left in the .h file, as shown in Figure 9-2.

Click in the circle to see the interface element to which the property is connected, as you see in Figure 9-3. You will see the storyboard filename and the name of the interface element. This can be a default name as shown in Figure 9-3, or a name you have specified in the label attribute.

This can be a good way of tracking down problems. In Figure 9-3, you can see that this property is connected to the iPad storyboard. If you have followed the steps in this book, you have worked on the iPhone storyboard. That means that any connections to the iPad storyboard are just experiments. In the next section, you'll see how to remove this connection.

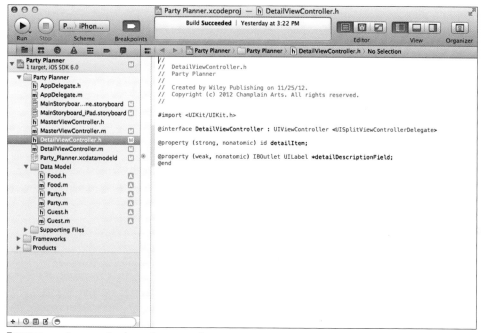

FIGURE 9-2 A connection has a dot next to its property.

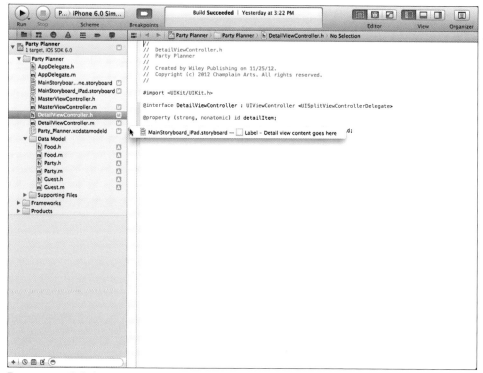

FIGURE 9-3 Click the connection symbol to see its destination.

Checking a Connection from the Storyboard

Control-click an interface element to see what it is connected to, as shown in Figure 9-4.

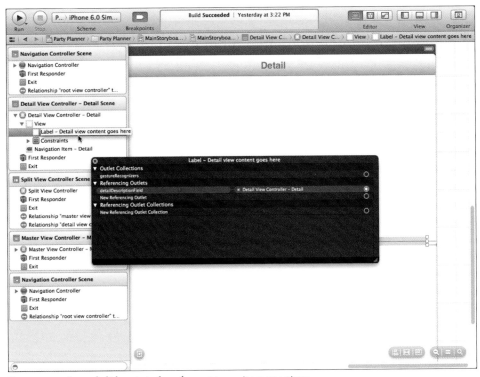

FIGURE 9-4 Control-click an interface element to see its connections.

As you are experimenting or even working for real it is quite easy to get incomplete and incorrect connections as is the case here. Avoid this by providing your own Xcode-specific labels in the Attributes inspector, as described in Chapter 8. If you wind up with bad connections, your app will crash, and these crashes are often in places you don't expect (that's because the connection goes somewhere you don't think it should go).

Removing Existing Connections

Sometimes you have to remove connections from the storyboard file. Figure 9-5 shows a .h file with an unconnected IBOutlet. The circle to the left of the property is not filled in. This means either that it was never connected or the connection has been removed.

To remove a connection from the storyboard, control click on the interface element as shown in Figure 9-4. The name of the interface element is shown at the left. At the right, is its property destination. The destination has a small x that you can use to delete it.

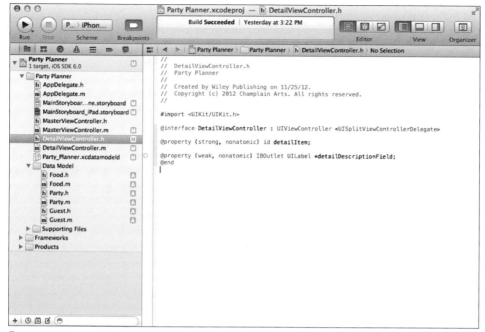

FIGURE 9-5 An unconnected IBOutlet has an empty circle.

Changing Existing Connections

If you have an existing connection you must remove it and draw the new connection.

Creating New Connections

Use the assistant to open the .h file and the storyboard. If either is open, the Automatic setting in the jump bar will open the other. Control-drag from the canvas or document outline in a storyboard to an IBOutlet property to connect it. Figure 9-6 shows a label object in the document outline being connected to an IBOutlet property called detailDescription Field.

Using the Assistant

The assistant editor lets you open two or more files at the same time. This is useful when you want to compare two files, but it's essential when you want to connect an object in a storyboard to code in a source code file. Open the assistant editor using the center button in the Editors group at the right of the toolbar or choose View➔Assistant Editor➔Show Assistant Editor. The file you have been working with is shown at the left or top of the assistant editor (you can control the configuration with View➔Assistant Editor). The jump bar in the assistant editor pane will let you choose a related file such as the .h file for a storyboard or the .h file for a .m file, or manually choose a file. There is more on the assistant editor in Chapter 2, "Getting Up to Speed with Xcode."

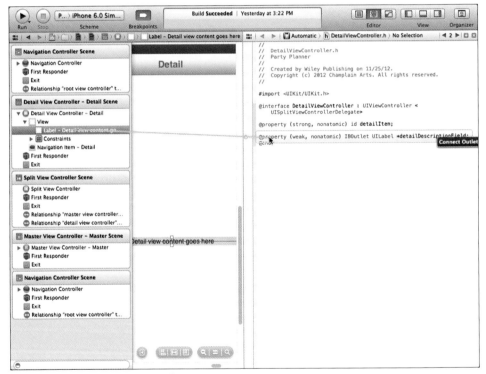

FIGURE 9-6 Connecting to an IBOutlet.

If you drag to any other place in the class header, you will be prompted to create a new IBOutlet, as shown in Figure 9-7.

You can then name it as shown in Figure 9-8.

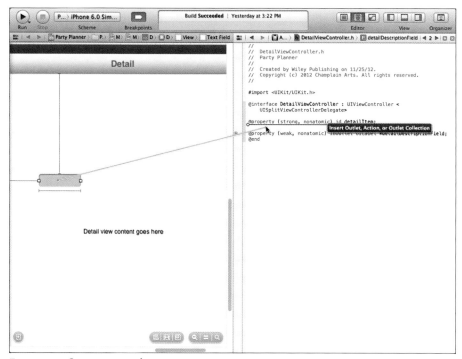

FIGURE 9-7 Create a new outlet.

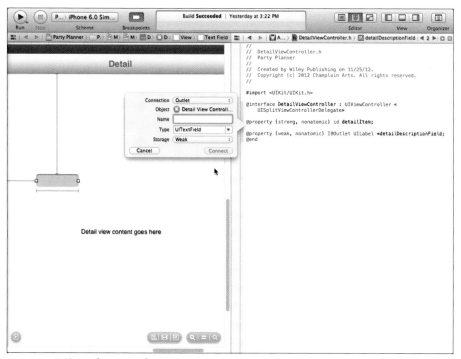

FIGURE 9-8 Name the new outlet.

You'll find out more about creating actions in Part V, "Interacting with Users."

Laying Out the Detail View

Now it's time to lay out the detail view. As noted previously, you'll do this here, and then you'll learn how to do it in a different way (using table views) in Part IV.

Cleaning Up the Experiments

Begin by getting rid of any experiments in the interface. Depending on what you have done, your interface may look different from the one shown here. These steps assume that you have worked only on the detailViewController. (If you have worked on mainViewController, the app will probably not work so you might want to revert to the version from Chapter 8.)

Here are the steps to take.

1. Open the iPhone storyboard.

2. Select the Detail scene as shown in Figure 9-9. It is probably easiest to work in the document outline. Delete anything other than the views shown in Figure 9-9. (If party NameField is not there, don't worry. You'll find a step in the following section to create it.)

3. Open DetailViewController.h as shown in Figure 9-10.

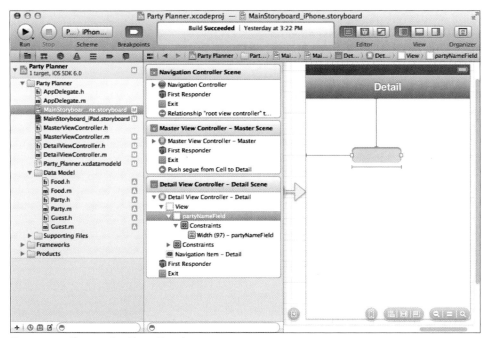

FIGURE 9-9 Clean up the iPhone Detail scene.

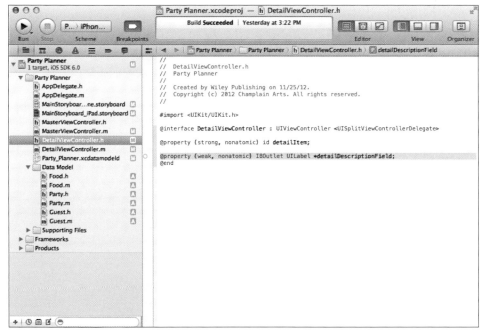

FIGURE 9-10 Open DetailViewController.h.

4. Delete any properties other than `detailItem`.

5. Open the iPad storyboard.

6. Select the Detail scene as shown in Figure 9-11.

7. Do not delete the top-level `View` object, which is the second line in the document outline shown in Figure 9-11.

8. Delete any other fields, labels, or views from within the top-level `View` object.

9. You cannot directly delete the constraints. They are automatically deleted as their views are deleted. For example, Figure 9-12 shows that the width constraint of the text field is within the text field object (not the position of the disclosure triangles).

10. Some constraints involving the top-level `View` object are related to specific fields within it, as you see in Figure 9-13. Deleting the subviews will delete the constraints.

FIGURE 9-11 Clean up the iPad Detail scene.

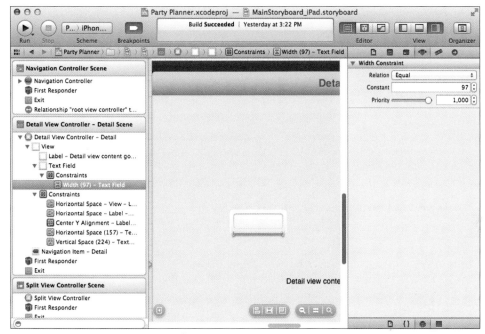

FIGURE 9-12 Some constraints are within views.

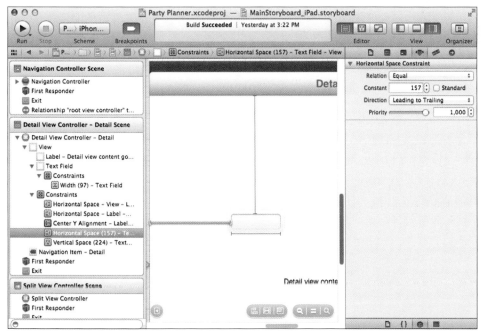

FIGURE 9-13 Some constraints involve two views.

11. Figure 9-14 shows the Detail scene as it should be now in the iPad storyboard.

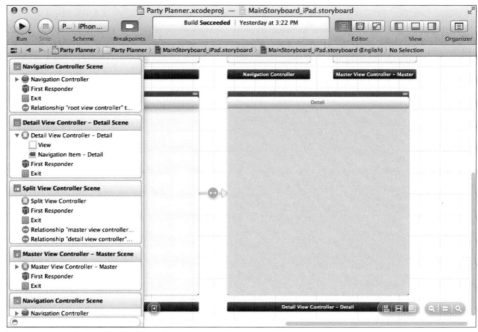

FIGURE 9-14 Review the iPad Detail scene.

Adding a Field to the Storyboard

These are the steps to use to add a field to the storyboard. If the `partyNameField` is not present, use these steps to create it.

1. If necessary, select View➜Utilities➜Show Object Library to show the Object library. (Note that this is an alternate way of showing the Object library from showing the Utilities area and then selecting the Object library in the bottom pane.)

2. If necessary, open the iPhone storyboard and locate the Detail scene.

3. Drag a text field from the Object library into the Detail scene.

4. Immediately provide a label in the Identity inspector. Figure 9-15 shows the entry of `partyNameField` for the selected field.

5. Widen the field so that it is as wide as the iPhone screen with the recommended insets at left and right, and so that it is centered, as shown in Figure 9-16.

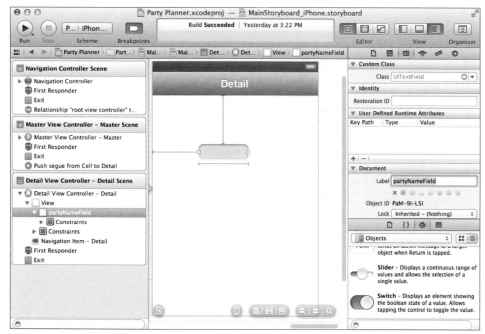

FIGURE 9-15 Label the new field.

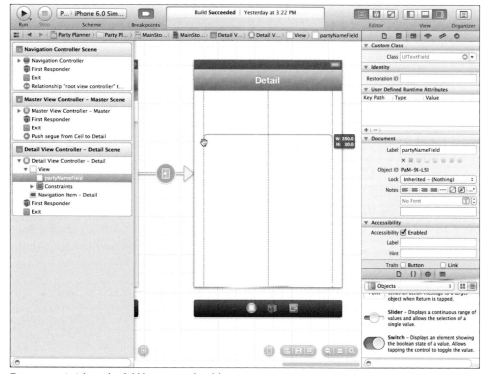

FIGURE 9-16 Adjust the field location and width.

6. Set the placeholder text to **Party Name**, as shown in Figure 9-17. That text will appear if nothing has been typed into the field. It is a common standard to provide the field content rather than a phrase such as "Enter Party Name Here."

7. You can experiment with other settings in the Attributes inspector, but the defaults shown in Figure 9-17 are a good place to start.

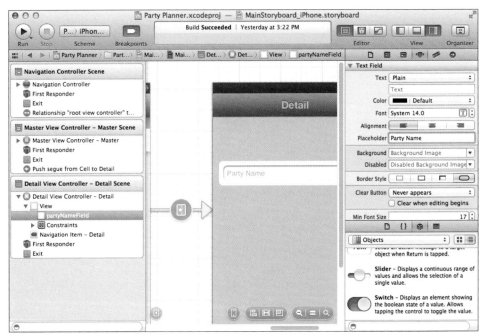

FIGURE 9-17 Set the placeholder text.

Adding More Fields to the Storyboard

Refer to the Party.h file that you created from the data model to see the list of properties that need to be entered.

```
@interface Party : NSManagedObject

@property (nonatomic, retain) NSDate * date;
@property (nonatomic, retain) NSString * location;
@property (nonatomic, retain) NSString * partyName;
@property (nonatomic, retain) NSSet *guests;
@property (nonatomic, retain) NSSet *menu;
@end
```

In addition to partyName, you need fields for date and location. The related records (guests and menu) will be entered separately. Because the data model shows them as optional, you will have no difficulty coming back to them later on (in Part IV).

Here are the steps to follow.

1. Select the partyNameField and duplicate it twice using Edit→Duplicate as shown in Figure 9-18.

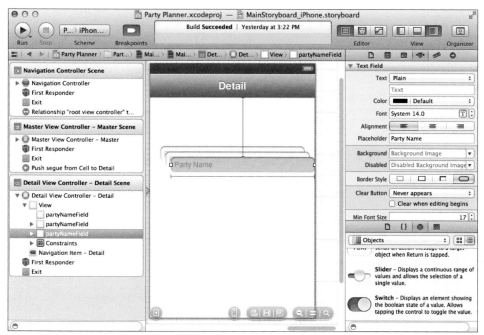

FIGURE 9-18 Duplicate partyNameField twice.

2. Select all three fields.

3. Choose Editor→Align→Left Edges.

4. Drag one field to the top of the screen until the guide appears.

5. Drag the next field up to just beneath the first field until the guide appears.

6. Repeat with the third field.

7. As you can see from Figure 9-19, constraints are automatically added for the spacing. (The constraint is just to the left of the pointer in Figure 9-19.)

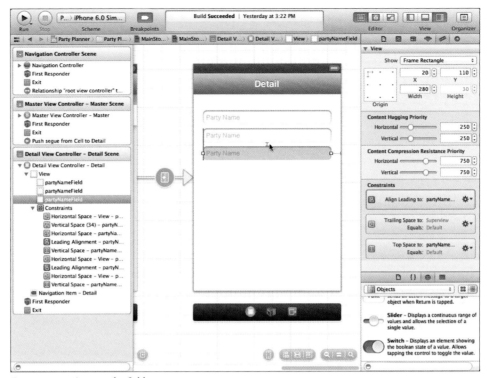

FIGURE 9-19 Arrange the fields.

8. Before moving on, set the label for each field appropriately (`dateField`, `location Field`).

9. Set the placeholder text (Date, Location).

Creating and Connecting the Properties

The final step is creating and connecting the properties. Even if you had a `partyNameField`, you deleted its property and connection when you cleaned up `detailViewController.h`, so you need to follow the steps for all three fields. They are outlined in "Creating New Connections" earlier in this chapter.

Using the assistant editor, Control-drag from one of the fields to the `DetailView Controller.h` file, as shown in Figure 9-20. If you see Connect Field rather than Create Outlet or Connection, try again—you may have dragged to an unconnected existing outlet rather than the list of properties (they can be very close together).

As you see in Figure 9-21, you just need to name the property. The other settings are fine.

If you see different values for any of the entries other than the name, click Cancel and try again. You may have accidentally Control-dragged from the background view or another object.

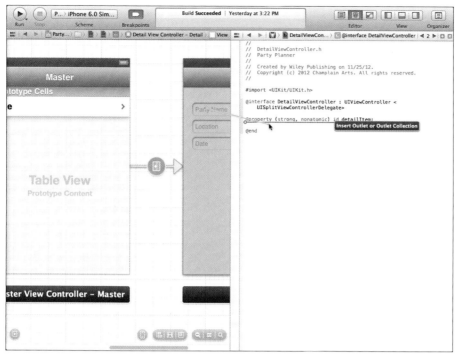

FIGURE 9-20 Begin to create a property and connection.

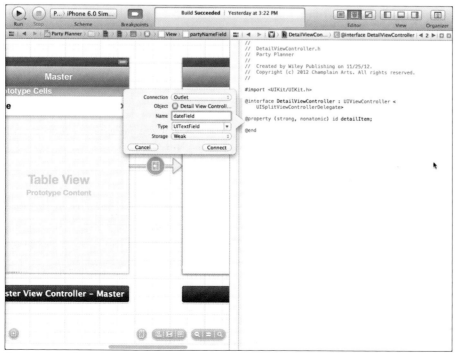

FIGURE 9-21 Name the property.

Displaying the Data

You may need to adjust the `configureView` method in `DetailViewController.m` to use the field name. Here is what `configureView` looks like at the end of Chapter 8:

```
- (void)configureView
{
  // Update the user interface for the detail item.

  if (self.detailItem) {
    self.detailDescriptionField.text =
      [[self.detailItem valueForKey:@"partyName"] description];
  }
}
```

This code uses the old label field (`detailDescriptionField`) from the template and sets it to the party name using KVC. Change it to use the newly created and named `party NameField`:

```
- (void)configureView
{
  // Update the user interface for the detail item.

  if (self.detailItem) {
    self.partyNameField.text =
      [[self.detailItem valueForKey:@"partyName"] description];
  }
}
```

Chapter 10 shows you how to clean up this code when you save and restore the data.

Creating the iPad Interface

Here are the steps to create the iPad interface.

1. In the iPhone storyboard, select all three fields in the Detail scene from the canvas (not from the document outline).

2. Copy them with Edit➜Copy or with the ⌘-C shortcut.

3. In the iPad storyboard, show the Detail scene.

4. Make sure View is selected in the document outline.

5. Paste the fields onto the canvas, as shown in Figure 9-22.

6. All three remain selected, so you can move them together if you want to rearrange them.

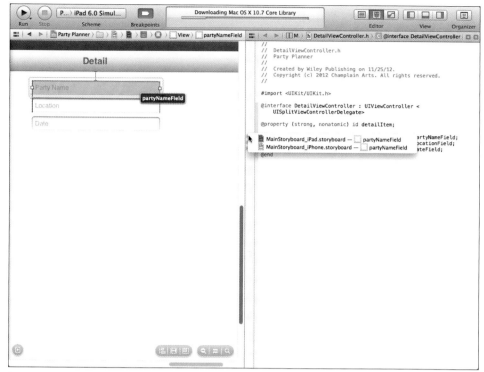

```
//
//  DetailViewController.h
//  Party Planner
//
//  Created by Wiley Publishing on 11/25/12.
//  Copyright (c) 2012 Champlain Arts. All rights reserved.
//

#import <UIKit/UIKit.h>

@interface DetailViewController : UIViewController <
    UISplitViewControllerDelegate>

@property (strong, nonatomic) id detailItem;
```

MainStoryboard_iPad.storyboard — partyNameField   artyNameField;
MainStoryboard_iPhone.storyboard — partyNameField   ocationField;
@end   ateField;

FIGURE 9-22 Paste the fields onto the iPad storyboard.

Finally, connect the iPad fields to the properties you created in detailViewController.h. This is a critical step; you have separate storyboards for iPad and iPhone, but you have one set of properties for both. Compare Figures 9-6 and 9-7 in "Creating New Connections" earlier in this chapter to see how the user interface is different when you create a new connection (Figure 9-7) or add to an existing outlet (Figure 9-6).

Now, when you hover the pointer over the circle to the left of an IBOutlet property, you'll see all of the connections. If possible, the connected object is highlighted in the assistant editor.

This technique of starting with the iPhone interface is the fastest way to build a universal application. Because of the difference in screen sizes, you'll have extra space on the iPad interface, but don't worry about that—you see how to use the larger iPad screen more effectively in Part IV.

Summary

In this chapter, you complete the work of expanding the data model and building the interfaces for both the iPhone and iPad storyboards. Because this is the first time you have been through the process, it may seem overly complex. However, after you have repeated the process of building the data model, converting it to a subclass of NSManagedObject, building a basic interface in a storyboard, and then using the assistant to create properties and connections, it will go faster and faster and seem very simple. The steps you have carried out are the heart of modern iOS app building.

(Some developers still swear by old-style .nib and .xib files, but the process shown here is faster once you get the hang of it.)

You should be able to run both the iPad and iPhone versions of the app. Just remember to set the Scheme pop-up menu in the top left of the workspace window to the iPad or iPhone simulator.

Unfortunately, you can't really test if the app is working because no matter what data you type in, nothing is stored. That will be corrected in Chapter 10, "Saving and Restoring Data."

chapter ten

Saving and Restoring Data

THE DETAIL DATA View, as developed through the end of Chapter 9, "Building the Detail Data View," provides editable fields for the main data elements of the party (the party name, location, and date), but it stops there. In this chapter, you continue on to save and restore data using both the interface and your data store. You'll see that there are three related aspects to this task:

- **Implementing Edit mode**—You can use an edit mode in which the fields are editable; when not in edit mode, the data fields are read-only. This is done using a special Edit button. When clicked, it sends you into edit mode, and the button name changes to Done.

- **Saving the data**—The click that changes the Edit button to a Done button not only has to modify the fields to make them editable; it also has to save the data in the database.

- **Retrieving data**—When the view is displayed, you want any data from the database to be shown in the fields.

Figure 10-1 shows the editing interface on iPad; Figure 10-2 shows the interface on iPhone. You will implement them in this chapter. (Note that the default data for a new party name is still a timestamp. You'll see how to change that in this chapter.)

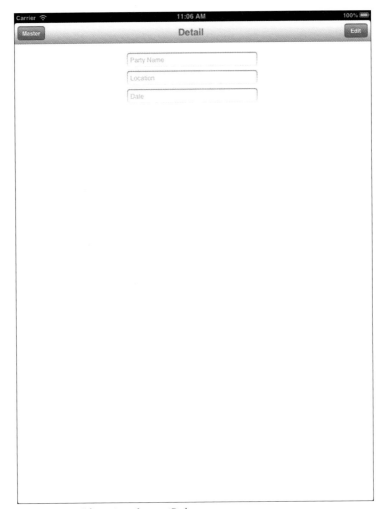

FIGURE 10-1 Editing interface on iPad.

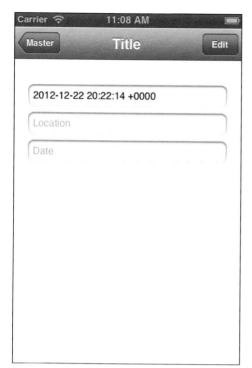

FIGURE 10-2 Editing interface on iPhone.

Understanding the Editing Interface

If you are coming to iOS from a background of personal computers, you may have implemented many editing functions in your time. On iOS, the process is somewhat different and simpler. You may be used to a process in which the user enters an edit mode, makes some changes (or not), and then clicks Save or Cancel. The editing is often done in a separate dialog.

On iOS, cancelling an operation is often achieved by simply performing another operation. If the user has unsaved data, it can be automatically discarded, although in some cases, it is appropriate to ask the user to confirm that the data should be discarded (the choice is usually made based on the amount of data to be discarded and its significance). Thus, the process frequently is to enter edit mode right on the current view, let the user make changes, and then have the user tap Done. Any other action discards the changes.

As you have seen in Chapter 6, "Working with Storyboard Inspectors," there are many settings available for you to use in customizing views and their interface elements. In-place editing takes advantage of these settings so that when the user taps an Edit button, the view becomes editable, and the fact that it is editable is reflected in slight changes to the interface.

You may be surprised at how subtle interface changes can be noticed by users. Even if they are not noticed, the user may not worry. Consider the scenario in which a user taps an Edit button. The user expects data fields to be editable at that point. The button changes to Done, and when the user taps Done the expectation is that the data is committed. The subtle changes to the interface just reinforce the behavior that the user expects. You may want to consider the degree to which you change the interface. For example, if some fields are editable and others are not, then the change in appearance of the editable fields definitely needs to be noticeable so that people do not attempt to edit fields that can't be edited. In any event, there is generally no need to create a separate view and view controller for editing.

Setting Up the Edit-Done Button

As you saw in Part II, "Storyboards—The Building Blocks of iOS Apps," you can design your interfaces graphically. There are separate storyboards for iPhone and iPad apps (if you are creating a universal application). Clearly, spacing and screen sizes influence the design of your interface.

Handling Universal Apps

It is also possible to build an interface at runtime using code. Many people (including the author) believe that using storyboards is more efficient than writing code. One major point is that with code, you can type anything you want—including syntax errors. When you are drawing the interface in Interface Builder, you can certainly put the wrong object in the wrong place, but, by and large, the internal code that is generated will not have typos in it.

However, if you are building a universal app, you do have to build two storyboard interfaces. Often, as is the case with the Master-Detail Application template, the two interfaces are basically similar. This means that you can use the storyboard to build them, and then, at runtime, you can modify them with code. You already saw this in Chapter 9 with Listing 9-3, `application:didFinishLaunchingWithOptions:`. In that code, you can see that a check is made for `userInterfaceIdiom`. If it is an iPad, it is assumed that there is a split view controller created from the storyboard; otherwise, it is assumed that you are on an iPhone and there is no split view controller.

If you examine the code carefully, you'll see that in both cases, an instance of `Master ViewController` is created. You'll find that class in the template, and you'll see that its code is basically the same whether it is used on iPhone or iPad. What is different is where that view controller and its view are placed.

The code shown in Listing 9-3 is used to set the `managedObjectContext` property of the `MasterViewController` to the `managedObjectContext` of the app delegate. (As noted, this is a common way of sharing the Core Data stack in the app delegate with the view controllers that need it.)

Setting Up the iPad Managed Object Context

In order to find the `MasterViewController` on iPad, here is the code that is used. It's in `application:didFinishLaunchingWithOptions:` and was shown in Listing 9-3. Here is the annotated code. You don't have to make changes to it, but it's worth understanding because you will be modifying it for iPhone in the next section.

1. First locate the `splitViewController`. Remember, this code is in `AppDelegate.m`, so the window property has been set.

```
UISplitViewController *splitViewController =
  (UISplitViewController *)self.window.rootViewController;
```

2. Using the `splitViewController`, locate the `navigationController`, which is the last object in the array of view controllers.

```
UINavigationController *navigationController =
  [splitViewController.viewControllers lastObject];
```

3. Set the `splitViewController` delegate to the `topViewController` of the `navigationController`:

```
splitViewController.delegate =
  (id)navigationController.topViewController;
```

4. Set the `masterNavigationController` to the zero-th element of the `splitViewController.viewControllers`. (Compare this to Step 2, which uses the last object of `splitViewController.viewControllers` rather than the zeroth object. In fact, there are only two in a split view controller.)

```
UINavigationController *masterNavigationController =
  splitViewController.viewControllers[0];
```

5. Set the local variable `controller` to the `topViewController` of the `navigationController` as a `MasterViewController`.

```
MasterViewController *controller = (MasterViewController *)
  masterNavigationController.topViewController;
```

6. Now that you have the `MasterViewController` in the local variable `controller`, you can set its `managedObjectContext` property to the `managedObject` property of the app delegate.

```
// set the managedObjectContext for the new controller JF
controller.managedObjectContext = self.managedObjectContext;
```

Setting Up the iPhone Managed Object Context

For iPhone, the `MasterViewController` is found in a different part of the storyboard's view hierarchy, but it's there, and the code you write for `MasterViewController` will work on both iPhone and iPad.

Here's what happens for iPhone in Listing 9-3. As is the case with the iPad code, this is just to orient you to the code you will add in the next section.

1. On iPhone, `navigationController` is the window's root view.

   ```
   UINavigationController *navigationController =
     (UINavigationController *)self.window.rootViewController;
   ```

2. Set the local variable `controller` to the top view controller of `navigation Controller`. This is analogous to Step 5 for iPad.

   ```
   MasterViewController *controller = (MasterViewController *)
     navigationController.topViewController;
   ```

3. Now that you have the `MasterViewController` in the local variable `controller`, you can set its `managedObjectContext` property to the `managedObjectContext` property of the app delegate. This is identical to Step 6 for iPad.

   ```
   // set the managedObjectContext for the new controller JF
   controller.managedObjectContext = self.managedObjectContext;
   ```

It's important to take away the fact that Step 6 (iPad) and Step 3 (iPhone) are identical. You'll add the Edit-Done button by writing code that will be executed on both iPhone and iPad.

Adding the Button

On both iPhone and iPad, `MasterViewController` is inside a navigation controller. (You'll find out more about navigation controllers in Chapter 17, "Back to the Storyboard: Enhancing the Interface.")

This button will be needed in `DetailViewController`. On both iPhone and iPad, `DetailViewController` is inside a navigation controller. For now, all that you need to know is that for any view that is inside a navigation controller, you can get that navigation controller using the view controller's `navigationItem` property. You also need to know that for every view controller, you have an `editButtonItem` (the Edit-Done button). You just have to put them together.

You do this in `viewDidLoad`, placing the new button at the right of the menu bar (this is where it is shown in Figures 10-1 and 10-2).

```
- (void)viewDidLoad
{
  [super viewDidLoad];
  // Do any additional setup after loading the view,
  // typically from a nib.

  // Add this line JF
  self.navigationItem.rightBarButtonItem =
    self.editButtonItem;

  [self configureView];

}
```

You should be able to run the app now and see the button's behavior.

Implementing setEditing

The button will automatically send a `setEditing: animated:` message to `DetailView Controller`. You'll need to implement that method. The bare-bones version of it is:

```
- (void)setEditing: (BOOL)flag animated: (BOOL)animated
{
    [super setEditing: flag animated:animated];
}
```

Add this code to `DetailViewController.m`. (Note that it doesn't need to be exposed in `DetailViewController.h` because it is only used within `DetailViewController`.)

Adjusting the Interface for Editing

Now you need to make whatever changes you want to the interface. Here is an example of the type of change you may want to make. In Figure 10-3 you see the fields in the app. They are displayed using a `borderStyle` of `UITextBorderStyleNone`. On the right, they are displayed using a `borderStyle` of `UITextBorderStyleRoundedRect`, which invites editing.

Here are the steps to take:

1. Check to see if flag (`setEditing`) is YES or NO.

2. If it is YES (that is, you are going to be editing), set the field's `borderStyle` to `UITextBorderStyleRoundedRect`.

3. If it is NO (that is, display only), set the field's `borderStyle` to `UITextBorder StyleNone`.

FIGURE 10-3 Adjust border styles.

You have to do this for all three fields, so here is what `setEditing: animated:` looks like now:

```
- (void)setEditing: (BOOL)flag animated: (BOOL)animated
{
  [super setEditing: flag animated:animated];

  if (flag == YES) {
    _partyNameField.borderStyle = UITextBorderStyleRoundedRect;
    _locationField.borderStyle = UITextBorderStyleRoundedRect;
    _dateField.borderStyle = UITextBorderStyleRoundedRect;

    _partyNameField.enabled = YES;
    _locationField.enabled = YES;
    _dateField.enabled = YES;
} else {
    _partyNameField.borderStyle = UITextBorderStyleNone;
    _locationField.borderStyle = UITextBorderStyleNone;
    _dateField.borderStyle = UITextBorderStyleNone;
```

```
    _partyNameField.enabled = NO;
    _locationField.enabled = NO;
    _dateField.enabled = NO;
  }
}
```

Remember that within `DetailViewController`, you can access the backing variables of the properties directly using the underscore notation. If you run the app now, you'll see that it looks correct, but there are two problems you should notice.

The first time you run it, you'll see that the fields are shown with `UITextBorder StyleRoundedRect`. Once you start to use the Edit-Done button, all is well, but the default set in the storyboards is now wrong. As shown in Figure 10-4, change the default for all three fields in both storyboards to no border style (the dotted border at the left of border styles).

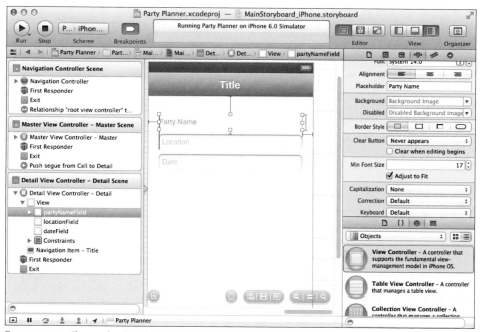

FIGURE 10-4 Change the default border style in the storyboards.

You'll also see that even with no border style, you can edit the field. Solve that by disabling the Content Enabled checkbox in the storyboard for each field, as shown in Figure 10-5.

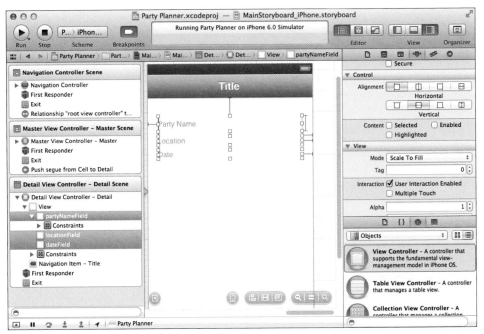

FIGURE 10-5 Disable the fields in the storyboard.

Saving the Data

Now that you've set up editing, you need to store the data in the data store. Once again, you can use `setEditing:` `animated:` for the task. As created from the template, the detail view controller has a `detailItem` property, which, in this case, will be an instance of `Party`. You can see it in the `DetailViewController.h` file.

```
#import <UIKit/UIKit.h>

@interface DetailViewController : UIViewController
  <UISplitViewControllerDelegate>

@property (strong, nonatomic) id detailItem;

@property (weak, nonatomic) IBOutlet UITextField *partyNameField;
@property (weak, nonatomic) IBOutlet UITextField *locationField;
@property (weak, nonatomic) IBOutlet UITextField *dateField;

@property (strong, nonatomic)
  NSManagedObjectContext *managedObjectContext;

@end
```

Moving the Data to the Party Instance

What you will need to do is to move the data from the fields into the Party object—that is detailItem. (As noted previously, you might change detailItem to be a Party object to avoid casting it, but leaving it as detailItem may make the code more readable as you compare it to other samples. It all depends on you and your level of comfort with the frameworks.)

To move the data into the detailItem object as a Party, you use variations on this syntax:

```
((Party*)_detailItem).partyName = _partyNameField.text;
```

Add that line and the following two to setEditing: animated: so that it now looks like this:

```
- (void)setEditing: (BOOL)flag animated: (BOOL)animated
{
  [super setEditing: flag animated:animated];

  if (flag == YES) {
    partyNameField.borderStyle = UITextBorderStyleRoundedRect;
    locationField.borderStyle = UITextBorderStyleRoundedRect;
    dateField.borderStyle = UITextBorderStyleRoundedRect;

    partyNameField.enabled = YES;
    locationField.enabled = YES;
    dateField.borderStyle enabled = YES;
} else {
    partyNameField.borderStyle = UITextBorderStyleNone;
    locationField.borderStyle = UITextBorderStyleNone;
    dateField.borderStyle = UITextBorderStyleNone;

    partyNameField.enabled = NO;
    locationField.enabled = NO;
    dateField.borderStyle enabled = NO;


    // move the data from the fields to the object - JF
    ((Party*)_detailItem).partyName = _partyNameField.text;
    ((Party*)_detailItem).location = _locationField.text;
    // we will come back to the date
    //_dateField.text = [((Party*)_detailItem).date description];

  }
}
```

For now the date will not be stored. It needs to be converted to a date, which you will do in Chapter 17.

The dot syntax for referencing properties in Party works with a Party instance. What you have is detailItem, which is of type id. Thus, you coerce it to a Party object. (To do this, you must be certain that it really is a Party object before you coerce it, which is true in this case.)

Dot syntax was described in Chapter 8, "Building on the Data Model," in the "Looking at the Existing KVC Code" section.

Thus, schematically, this is similar to

```
aParty.partyName = _partyNameField.text;
```

This code illustrates an instance of Party (called aParty). As an instance of Party, it has a partyName property. A text field object called partyNameField in the storyboard is an instance (in the code), and it has a text property. This code moves the NSString that is in the text property to the partyName property of aParty.

Saving the Data

Having moved the data to the Party instance, you now need to save the context. There is code in MasterViewController.m for insertNewObject: that does this. The relevant part of that code is:

```
// Save the context.
NSError *error = nil;
if (![context save:&error]) {
  // Replace this implementation with code to
  // handle the error appropriately.

  // abort() causes the application to generate a crash log
  // and terminate. You should not use this function in
  // a shipping application, although it may be useful
  // during development.
  NSLog(@"Unresolved error %@, %@", error, [error userInfo]);
  abort();
}
```

You'll see how to refine the error message in Chapter 15, "Telling Users the News: Alerts and NSError."

The only problem you have in using this code is that you need a reference to the managed object context. You've already seen how the Core Data stack is created in the app delegate.

The reference to the managed object context is passed through into `MasterViewController` from the app delegate.

At this point, you now need part of the Core Data stack (the managed object context) in `DetailViewController`, and at the moment, it's only in `MasterViewController`. The simplest way to handle this is to follow the same pattern by which it was passed from `AppDelegate` to `MasterViewController`. The app delegate created the Core Data stack. It then created `MasterViewController` and set a property in `MasterViewController` to the reference to the managed object context from the Core Data stack.

`MasterViewController` creates `DetailViewController`. So, following the pattern, modify `MasterViewController` to pass its reference to the managed object context through to `DetailViewController`. There is a difference here, though. When the iPad storyboard is loaded, `DetailViewController` exists. When the iPhone version is loaded, it does not. So you need two separate sections of code that do the same thing to the same detail view controller at different times. (There are other ways you could handle this, but this is simple at this point.)

Here is how you do that for iPad.

1. Add a managed object context property to `DetailViewController.h`:

```
@property (strong, nonatomic)
  NSManagedObjectContext *managedObjectContext;
```

2. In `MasterViewController`, locate `viewDidLoad`. It now looks like this:

```
- (void)viewDidLoad
{
  [super viewDidLoad];
  // Do any additional setup after loading the view,
  // typically from a nib.
  self.navigationItem.leftBarButtonItem = self.editButtonItem;

  UIBarButtonItem *addButton = [[UIBarButtonItem alloc]
    initWithBarButtonSystemItem:UIBarButtonSystemItemAdd
    target:self action:@selector(insertNewObject:)];
  self.navigationItem.rightBarButtonItem = addButton;

  if ([[UIDevice currentDevice] userInterfaceIdiom] ==
    UIUserInterfaceIdiomPad) {
  self.detailViewController = (DetailViewController *)
    [[self.splitViewController.viewControllers lastObject]
    topViewController];
}
```

3. Insert the following line as the last line of the method (after `self.detailView Controller` has been set).

```
self.detailViewController.managedObjectContext =
  self.managedObjectContext;
```

4. End the `if` statement for iPad with a bracket.

5. You can now add the saving code modeled on `MasterViewController` to set `Editing: animated:` in `DetailViewController`. You can use the underscore notation for the new `_managedObjectContext` property.

```
// Save the context.
NSError *error = nil;
// Use the new managed object context
if (![_managedObjectContext save:&error]) {
  // Replace this implementation with code to
  // handle the error appropriately.

  // abort() causes the application to generate a crash log
  // and terminate. You should not use this function in
  // a shipping application, although it may be useful
  // during development.
  NSLog(@"Unresolved error %@, %@", error, [error userInfo]);
  abort();
}
```

On iPhone, the detail view controller doesn't exist yet, so here is how you set it and pass in its managed object context.

1. Find `prepareForSegue:` in `MasterViewController`. This is where the segue from the storyboard is set up.

```
- (void)prepareForSegue:(UIStoryboardSegue *)segue sender:(id)
  sender
{
  if ([[segue identifier] isEqualToString:@"showDetail"]) {
    NSIndexPath *indexPath =
      [self.tableView indexPathForSelectedRow];
    NSManagedObject *object =
      [[self fetchedResultsController]
        objectAtIndexPath:indexPath];
    [[segue destinationViewController] setDetailItem:object];
    }
}
```

2. After setting the detail item, check to see if you are on an iPhone. If so, set the detail view controller and its managed object context. Here is what the end of the method looks like now.

```
[[segue destinationViewController] setDetailItem:object];

if ([[UIDevice currentDevice] userInterfaceIdiom] !=
  UIUserInterfaceIdiomPad) {
  self.detailViewController =
    (DetailViewController*)[segue destinationViewController];
  self.detailViewController.managedObjectContext =
    self.managedObjectContext;
}
}
```

Here is what setEditing: animated: looks like in DetailViewController.m now that it's completed:

```
- (void)setEditing: (BOOL)flag animated: (BOOL)animated
{
  [super setEditing: flag animated:animated];

  if (flag == YES) {
    _partyNameField.borderStyle = UITextBorderStyleRoundedRect;
    _locationField.borderStyle = UITextBorderStyleRoundedRect;
    _dateField.borderStyle = UITextBorderStyleRoundedRect;

    _partyNameField.enabled = YES;
    _locationField.enabled = YES;
    _dateField.enabled = YES;
  } else {
    _partyNameField.borderStyle = UITextBorderStyleNone;
    _locationField.borderStyle = UITextBorderStyleNone;
    _dateField.borderStyle = UITextBorderStyleNone;

    _partyNameField.enabled = NO;
    _locationField. enabled = NO;
    _dateField.enabled = NO;

    ((Party*)_detailItem).partyName = _partyNameField.text;
    ((Party*)_detailItem).location = _locationField.text;
    //_dateField.text = [((Party*)_detailItem).date description];

    // Save the context.
    NSError *error = nil;
    if (![_managedObjectContext save:&error]) {
```

```
        // Replace this implementation with code to handle
        // the error appropriately.

        // abort() causes the application to generate a
        // crash log and terminate. You should not use this
        // function in a shipping application, although it may be
        // useful during development.
        NSLog(@"Unresolved error %@, %@", error, [error userInfo]);
        abort();
    }
  }
}
```

Retrieving Data

Now you need to do the other side of the picture: move data from the data store into the fields. The code is a complete reversal of the previous section—set the `text` attribute of a field to the appropriate attribute such as `partyName` of the managed object subclass (`Party`).

`configureView` in `DetailViewController.m` is part of the template, and even helpfully contains a comment indicating that this is the place to handle moving data into the interface. You can see that the syntax is basically the reverse used to save data. Add the code shown here, below the comment.

```
- (void)configureView
{
  // Update the user interface for the detail item.
  if (self.detailItem) {
    _partyNameField.text = ((Party*)_detailItem).partyName;
    _locationField.text = ((Party*)_detailItem).location;
    _dateField.text = [((Party*)_detailItem).date description];
  }
}
```

Although the date field isn't going to be set until the date formatting is discussed in Chapter 17, you can move its (nonexistent) value into the interface now. That will mean one less step to take later on.

Testing the App

If you haven't done so already, test the app. As you can see in Figure 10-6, when you run it as an iPad app in landscape orientation, the master view controller appears on the left and the detail view controller is on the right.

FIGURE 10-6 Run the app on the iPad simulator.

You can click Edit to edit the data as you see in Figure 10-7.

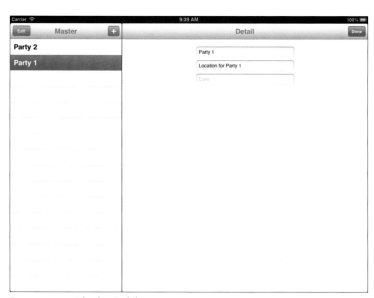

FIGURE 10-7 Edit the iPad data.

If you run the app using the iPhone simulator, the results are as you see in Figure 10-8.

FIGURE 10-8 Run the app on the iPhone simulator.

Because the data is stored in the iOS Simulator under /Library/Application Support, both simulators use the same data. In practice, the data would be stored on each device, so entering data on the iPhone would not affect data on the iPad.

If you use iCloud for both apps, the results would indeed be what you see here. Unfortunately, iCloud is beyond the basic scope of this book.

Summary

When it comes to editing, saving, and restoring data, you can see one of the best examples of how the Cocoa Touch framework makes your life easier. Most of the functional components of the process are built into the framework, ranging from the Edit-Done button to the set Editing: animated: method that works with it. As you see in this chapter, all that you need to do is use the Edit-Done button and insert the code for your data model fields and your interface elements in setEditing: animated:.

At this point, your app runs. Yes, there are additional steps to be taken such as working with the date field, but the app is starting to be presentable. At this point, it's good to step back and have a look at the debugging tools that are provided with Xcode. As bugs and glitches appear (as they always do), those debugging tools help you track them down and fix them.

With that in mind, it's on to Chapter 11, "Testing the App with the Debugger."

chapter eleven

Testing the App with the Debugger

IT IS DIFFICULT to describe the process of using the debugger because, most of the time, you need to use the debugger when something untoward has happened. The app is in an unknown and possibly unstable condition, so you need to try to analyze and recover from the problem.

In this chapter, you'll see how to deliberately introduce errors into your code so that you can "find" them with the debugger. Of course, there's not too much difficulty in finding errors that you have introduced yourself. If you are working in a class or with a group of people, you can pair off to find errors that others have introduced.

Create a new project from the Master-Detail Application template. You've used it as the basis of the Party Planner app, so you know a bit about its structure. By starting from an untouched version, you can run it with the debugger to get a sense for how the debugger works. Furthermore, if you want to create code that will generate an error, you can do so without worrying about damaging your own app.

Using Informal Debugging Techniques

A debugger or a colleague can sometimes pinpoint a problem—perhaps a missing comma—and you'll be able to be on your way again. All too often, the most vexing problems aren't that simple. Here are some of the techniques that I've used. Some are tips from other developers or teachers, and others are strategies that I've discovered work for me.

- **Take a break**—Have a cup of coffee, walk the dog, go to lunch, or rearrange the supply closet. If you're on a deadline, it's hard to do this, but in the long run, solving the problem and moving on will save you time.

- **Describe the problem**—Stop thinking about the problem; instead, describe the problem out loud. The process of verbalizing the issue may be using a different part of the brain because it seems to work in many cases. You don't need an expert to talk to (although that may help). Describing the problem to a snoring dog may even help. You just want to get out of the rut that you're in.

- **Plan for never solving the problem**—Right at the beginning consider how you will work around the problem if it can't be solved. Working on an alternative implementation may just give you enough perspective to be able to make progress.

- **Contact Apple's Developer Technical Support (DTS)**—The standard developer programs come with two technical support incidents each year. If you need more, you can buy them in groups of two ($99) or five ($249). Apple engineers will review your code and help you solve the problem. Note that questions about pre-release software can't be handled by DTS.

Exploring the Debugger from a Basic Template

Starting from an untouched project built from the Master-Detail Application template gives you a good starting point to explore. You can refer back to "Getting Started with the Template" in Chapter 4, "Designing the Party Planner App" for more information about creating the project. Figure 11-1 shows the basic settings you should have.

Use storyboards, automatic reference counting (ARC), and Core Data. Choose a universal application so that it will run on both iPad and iPhone.

Although these settings should give you a project that matches the text and figures in this chapter, remember that changes in the template projects often occur from version to version of Xcode. What you see may differ in some ways.

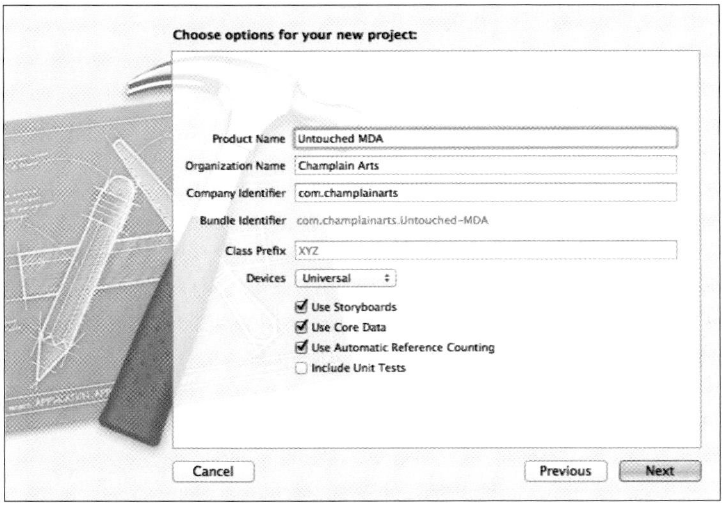

FIGURE 11-1 Create a new project with these basic settings.

Modify the `application:didFinishLaunchingWithOptions:` in `AppDelegate.m`. Add the three lines in bold to the code, as shown here.

```
// Override point for customization after application launch.
if ([[UIDevice currentDevice] userInterfaceIdiom] ==
  UIUserInterfaceIdiomPad) {
    UISplitViewController *splitViewController =
      (UISplitViewController *)self.window.rootViewController;
    UINavigationController *navigationController =
      [splitViewController.viewControllers lastObject];
    splitViewController.delegate =
      (id)navigationController.topViewController;

    // introduce an error JF
    int x = 0;
    int y = 0;
    y = 5 / x;

    UINavigationController *masterNavigationController =
      splitViewController.viewControllers[0];
    MasterViewController *controller = (MasterViewController *)
      masterNavigationController.topViewController;
    controller.managedObjectContext = self.managedObjectContext;
  } else {
```

Setting Up the Debugger

The debugger is built into Xcode. It allows you to run your app in a controlled environment so that errors that might normally cause the app to crash are caught by the debugger. This way you can inspect what is going on. There are tools available to you at that time to modify variables so that you don't have to wait to recompile your code and start over.

Finding an Error

For example, in Figure 11-2, you can see that a divide by zero has deliberately been inserted in the code. When it is encountered, the debugger takes over. At the left of the editor in Figure 11-2, the small green arrow indicates the line of code that has just been executed. Xcode posts the error at the right.

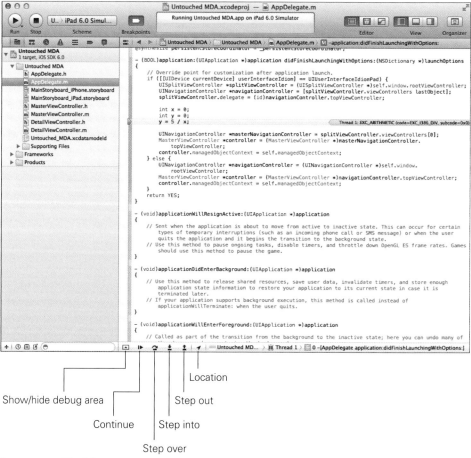

FIGURE 11-2 The debugger stops on errors.

At the very bottom of the editor, new controls and information appear. Here's what the controls do (from left).

- **Up- or down-pointing arrow**—This arrow shows or hides the Debug area. In Figure 11-2, the Debug area is hidden.

- **Right-pointing arrow**—This arrow continues execution from the line where it stopped if that is possible. In the case of a divide by zero, continuing is not possible.

- **Curved arrow**—This arrow lets you step over a line of code. Typically, you step over a line of code that calls a function or method. The function or method is executed, and then the next line in the source code is where the control stops again (unless, of course, an error has been encountered).

- **Down-pointing arrow**—This arrow lets you step into a function or method. The debugger stops on the first line of the function or method.

- **Up-pointing arrow**—This arrow lets you step out of a function or method. From wherever you are, the function or method continues operation and the debugger stops on the first line after the `return` statement.

Next to the arrows, you find a location pointer (it's pointing to what would be northeast on a compass). This opens a pop-up menu that lets you choose a location for the simulator to use.

Further to the right, you have the stack and thread structure of where the debugger has stopped.

Configuring Behaviors Preferences

The Xcode debugger has a wide variety of options that you can set. Before exploring them, here is a suggestion for the settings to get started with. Use Xcode➡Preferences to open the Preferences window shown in Figure 11-3. Select the Behaviors tab at the top.

Although there are many options to set, the format of the Behaviors preferences are all much the same. At the left side of the window, you see a variety of *triggers* that can happen as you build and run your app. When you select one of them, the *actions* shown at the right are available to you. You can turn each action on or off using its checkbox. Some actions are simple, such as bouncing the Xcode icon in the Dock when the app is inactive. Others have choices within them.

A common setting (and one that is used in the examples in this chapter) is to set actions for the *pauses* trigger when an app is running. Use the checkboxes to turn on the actions that you want, and, if there are choices, select them. In Figure 11-3, if an app pauses, the Debug navigator will be shown. You can choose from any of the navigators in Xcode or you can select whatever the current navigator is.

In addition, you can choose to show the debugger, as shown in Figure 11-4.

FIGURE 11-3 The Behaviors tab of the Preferences window.

FIGURE 11-4 If an app pauses, show the debugger.

If it is shown, the debugger appears below the editor. The controls and information shown originally at the bottom of Figure 11-2 are now at the top of the Debug area. You can drag them up or down to enlarge or reduce the size of the Debug area.

There are two sections to the debugger as you see in Figure 11-5. At the left, current variables are shown. At the right, console messages (if any) are shown. You can also view the console messages by using the Console app inside Applications/Utilities. There is also a setting to show both panes at the same time (that is the view shown in Figure 11-5) or you can set the action to use whatever the current configuration is. Controls at the top right of the Debug area let you choose among these settings when the Debug area is open.

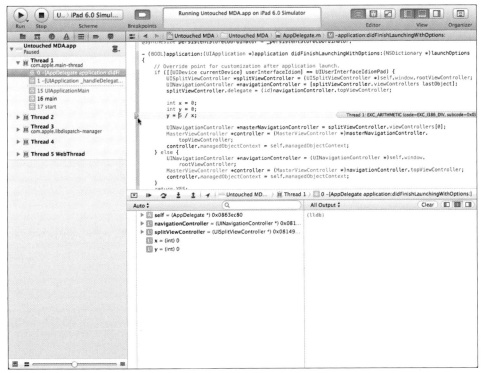

FIGURE 11-5 Use the debugger.

Setting a Breakpoint

You don't have to wait for an error to use the debugger. One of the most common ways of debugging is to set a *breakpoint*. For example, Figure 11-6 shows the divide by zero code that dropped the app into the debugger. If this were a more complex case, you might see the divide by zero, but you might want to backtrack to find out how a variable was set to zero. In that case, you might set a breakpoint just before the place where the error occurs. In Figure 11-6, a breakpoint has been set just before the code that fails. You set a breakpoint by click-ing in the *breakpoint gutter* at the left of the editor. A blue arrow indicates the breakpoint.

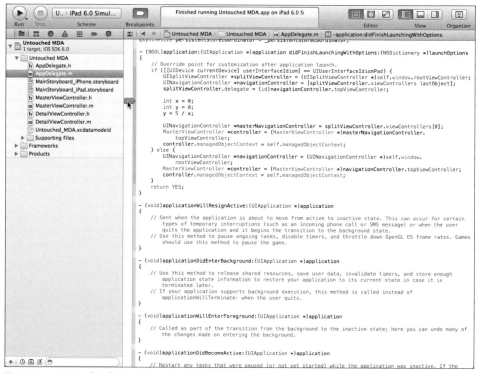

FIGURE 11-6 Set a breakpoint.

The code that causes the divide by zero is easy to locate because it is set off by spaces from the basic template code. Remember that this code is used to demonstrate what happens when an error occurs. In real life, instead of setting a variable to zero and then using it as a divisor, you're much more likely to wind up with a divisor of zero that has been set far away from where the error occurs—perhaps as a return value of a function that actually works properly but in some cases winds up being called with an invalid argument.

Inspecting Variables

If you run the app with the breakpoint in place, it will pause as shown in Figure 11-7. As before, the green arrow points to the location where the app has stopped. In this case, it is at the breakpoint.

When the debugger stops at a breakpoint, there is no error message at the right—rather, it explains that it has stopped because of a breakpoint as you see in Figure 11-7. What happens next is probably the most likely scenario you'll use as you debug your software. The breakpoint is set just before an error (divide by zero) occurs. Most commonly, you back up a line or two so you can see the state of affairs before the error occurs.

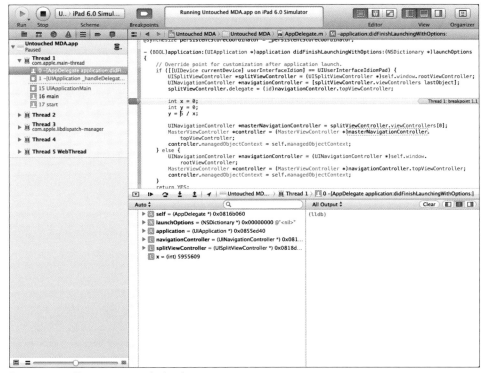

FIGURE 11-7 The app stops at the breakpoint.

In the variables pane at the left of the debugger, you see local variables and their values. In parentheses, you can also see the memory location assigned to the variable. In most cases, all you care about is whether it is allocated or not. (You can use the pop-up menu currently set to Auto at the left of the debugger to choose from local variables or all variables—local is the most common setting to start with.) When a breakpoint is set, the debugger stops just *before* the indicated line is executed. (When the debugger stops because of an error, it is *after* the line has been executed and the error has occurred.)

Look at the variables, and you'll see that the locally declared variable x is set to 5955609. That's what the debugger says, and that's probably what its current value is. However, remember that this line of code has not yet been executed, so that value is whatever happened to be in that memory location.

Use the Step Over button to move to the next line of code, as shown in Figure 11-8. The Step Over button is the curved arrow shown in Figure 11-8. Note that the value of x is now 0 because the line of code has been executed. The number 0 is shown in blue and italic to indicate that it has changed from its last display.

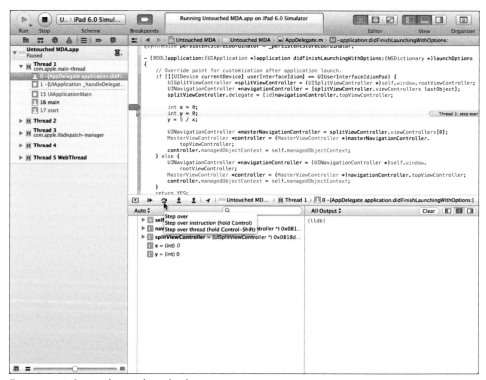

FIGURE 11-8 Step to the next line of code.

Click Step Over one more time, and you'll see that x is no longer blue and italicized. Click Step Over one more time, and you'll see what is shown in Figure 11-9. The divide by zero error reoccurs, and you cannot continue the app.

This is the standard process of tracking down an error. If something goes wrong at a certain point, look to see where the app fails. Then, set a breakpoint a line or two before the error. When the app stops at the breakpoint, check the variables to see if any of them seem to be out of line. Zeroes are always danger flags.

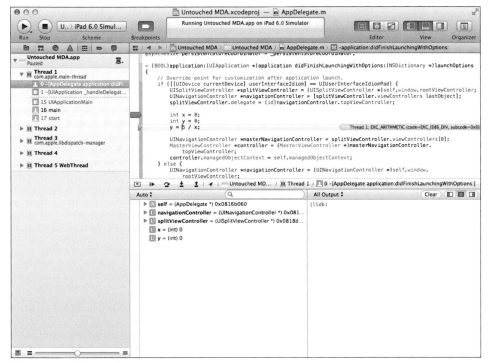

FIGURE 11-9 The error happens again.

Inspecting Objects

You can use *disclosure triangles* to look inside objects, as you see in Figure 11-10. Note that `containerView` has never been assigned or created, so it has a zero memory location. In this case, that's normal behavior, but often if you are encountering errors, it will be because an object has not been created, and those zeroes will point you on your way to solving the problem.

You can often use disclosure triangles to move through several levels of objects. For example, in Figure 11-10, `self` is an object of the `AppDelegate` class, and it is stored at memory location 0x816b060. Its disclosure triangle is closed so you don't see any of its properties.

On the other hand, the `navigationController` variable of type `UINavigation Controller` has been opened, and you can see its variables. Note that you can see the backing variables for properties (they start with the underscore).

The variables are organized by class. `navigationController` is an instance of `UINavigationController`. Directly beneath its entry, you see a closed disclosure triangle for `UIViewController`. That will display the variables of the superclass for `navigation Controller`, which is a `UIViewController`.

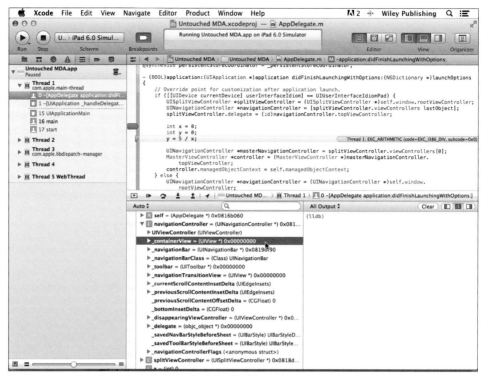

FIGURE 11-10 Use disclosure triangles to look inside objects.

Writing a Console Message

Sometimes, you want to write messages to the console rather than setting a breakpoint. There are many reasons for this, but perhaps the most common is to not have to stop at each breakpoint. As the app is executing, you can have the debugger write out values to the console and review them at your leisure—or perhaps when you have stopped at a breakpoint and want to review several steps that have just occurred.

You write out messages using the NSLog function. NSLog is a function built into the Foundation framework. It functions like an ordinary C print statement, but it has different features added to it.

The basic function is as follows:

```
NSLog (@"a format string", variable1, variable2 ...);
```

In practice, you use something such as this:

```
NSLog (@" %@", navigationController);
```

The %@ format specifier writes out an object's description or descriptionWith Locale: depending on which is available. (For that reason, although you can add text to the format specifiers, you don't need to identify an object you're printing out—it's already identified in the description text.) Other specifiers such as %@ for an unsigned int are listed at https://developer.apple.com/library/mac/#documentation/Cocoa/ Conceptual/Strings/Articles/formatSpecifiers.html. When you get into the debugging phase of your project, you may want to print out that table and leave it next to your Mac.

You can experiment with a console message by adding a line to the divide by zero code you inserted into application:didFinishLaunchingWithOptions:, as shown in Figure 11-2.

```
NSLog (@"Test NSLog: %@ ", splitViewController.delegate);
int x = 0;
int y = 0;
y = 5 / x;
```

If you set a breakpoint after the NSLog message, Figure 11-11 shows you what you will see in the debugger.

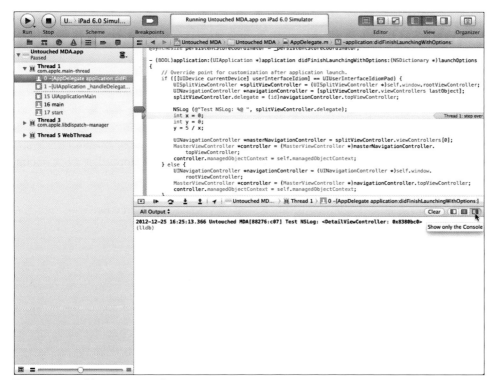

FIGURE 11-11 Write out a console message.

Notice that each console message is time-stamped. You can also add your own string messages to the output.

Editing Breakpoints

You can edit breakpoints to customize their appearance and behavior. This can save you from writing special code to assist in debugging. Much of it can be done just by editing a breakpoint.

Begin by setting a breakpoint as you would normally do. Then, Control-click on the breakpoint as shown in Figure 11-12.

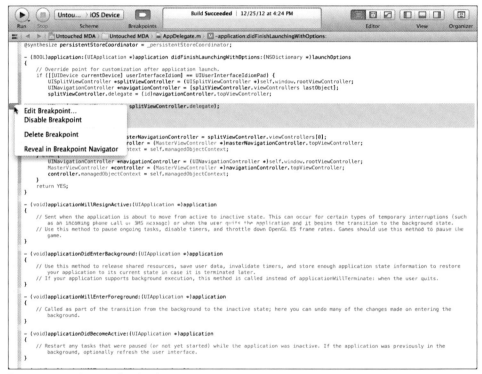

FIGURE 11-12 Start to edit a breakpoint.

You can now edit the breakpoint and its actions, as shown in Figure 11-13.

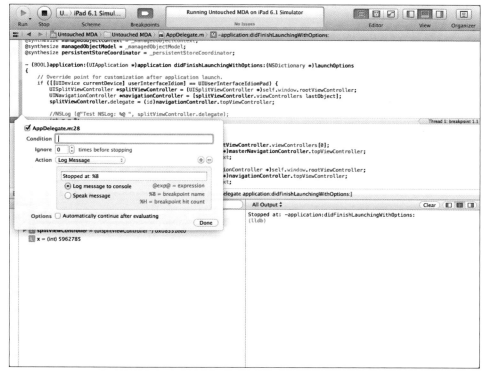

FIGURE 11-13 Edit the breakpoint and its actions.

To begin with, you can turn the breakpoint on or off with the checkbox in the upper left. If the breakpoint is disabled, the indicator is dimmed. You can configure the breakpoint to fire on a specific condition, or after a certain number of iterations. You can add customized actions, and you can have the app continue after evaluating the breakpoint. This is useful when used in conjunction with a log message. The app will just keep running and the message will be written out. In the example shown in Figure 11-13, you'll see that the name of the method is displayed in the log. No more do you have to write those diagnostics yourself.

Summary

This chapter introduces you to the debugger that's built into Xcode. You can set breakpoints and write out console messages to help diagnose problems. Most commonly, you use the debugger to spot the point in your code where an error occurs. Unless the debugger immediately shows you what's wrong, most often you use a combination of setting breakpoints to find out *where* the problem is set up, and utilizing a set of console messages to show you *what* is happening as the app runs off the rails.

part 4

Using Table and Collection Views

chapter twelve

Exploring the Table View in the Template

YOU HAVE SEEN many of the basics of app development on iOS. For most apps, the heart of the app is its interface, and you have seen how to use storyboards to create the interface. When it comes to the data that is displayed and manipulated in the interface, you have seen how to use a Core Data model to organize the data. Xcode provides tools to convert a graphically created data model into code in subclasses of NSManagedObject. The basics of view controllers and views were demonstrated in the master and detail view controllers described in the previous part. And, of course, the key aspect of saving and restoring data has also been addressed.

There's much, much more to iOS, and this part of the book shows you one of the most important sets of frameworks, classes, and tools—table views. At first, the whole idea of using table views may seem very specific and not really a major part of iOS development. Tables, after all, are just ways of formatting data—aren't they? You can manage tables with a word processor (Pages or Microsoft Word, for example). If you want to do sophisticated things with tables, Numbers, Excel, Bento, or FileMaker let you do what you need to do.

In this chapter, you see table views in action and learn about their basic components. Following that, there is a high-level description of how the concepts work together with table views. Unlike most of the other chapters in this book, this chapter is primarily conceptual: it provides the background information that you'll use in the other chapters in this part of the book.

Introducing Table Views, Protocols, and Delegates

If you want to understand why tables deserve their own part of this book—with three chapters, no less—stop thinking about tables in the context of word processing and spreadsheets. In iOS, tables are used to present tabular data—data is organized into cells that are arranged in rows and a single column. (On OS X, multiple columns are allowed.)

 Because there is only one column in an iOS table view, each row consists of a single cell. It is the cells in the table that you format and use to display data items. The table and its column are the container for the cells.

Tables are most often implemented using a UITableViewController that is paired with a UITableView that it controls. These are subclasses of UIViewController and UIView. They provide a good example of how the building blocks of Objective-C and the Cocoa Touch frameworks work together. If you approach UITableViewController head-on, it may be disconcerting at first. However, there is a reason for the structure, and, before long, you'll see how it fits together.

The components of this structure—protocols, delegates, and the basic classes of UITable View and UITableViewController—are basic Objective-C concepts that are used throughout the frameworks. Because you'll need to use two separate table views in the Party Planner app, this is a good context to use to explore these fundamental and critical concepts.

Looking at Table Views

First, it's a good idea to look at how table views are used, and the Master-Detail Application template, which is the basis of your Party Planner app, is a good place to start.

Using Views on an iPhone

In Figure 12-1, you can see the Party Planner (as it is at this stage) running on an iPhone. At the top of the window is the status bar. Just below it, is a navigation bar with an Edit button at the left and a + button at the right; its title is Master (that's the default name in the template).

FIGURE 12-1 The master view controller on iPhone.

Beneath the navigation bar, you see a `UITableView`, which is managed by a `UITable
ViewController` (as with all view controllers, you don't see the controller itself). The dim
lines across the table view separate the rows from one another whether or not there is data
to be displayed in them. (Those dim lines are the hallmark of a table view.)

In the first row, you see Party 2, with Party 1 in the second row. At the right of each row, an
accessory view, which in this case is a *disclosure indicator,* is shown. (The disclosure indicator is
discussed in the following section.)

If you tap Edit, the table view enters Edit mode, as shown in Figure 12-2.

FIGURE 12-2 You can edit a table view.

To delete a row, you tap the delete button at the left of the row and then confirm the action by tapping Delete at the right, as shown in Figure 12-3.

It's interesting to note that on iOS devices, many of the interruptions that happen on desktop computers have been banished. You don't see Cancel buttons. Rather, if you do anything but tap the button that performs an action, the action is cancelled. Similarly, whereas on a desktop computer you might be asked to confirm the deletion of an object, on iOS, it is still a two-step process, but those two steps are less verbal.

FIGURE 12-3 Deleting a row requires two steps.

After you have deleted the row (or not), tap Done and you're back to the list you saw in Figure 12-1.

From there, tap a disclosure indicator to move to the details for a given row, as shown in Figure 12-4.

Now, the navigation bar has a Back button at the left to return you to the master view controller. In the center, the title of this view is Title (that's a default value in the template), and, at the right, is an Edit button.

Tap the Edit button now, and you'll enter Edit mode for the data on the screen, as shown in Figure 12-5.

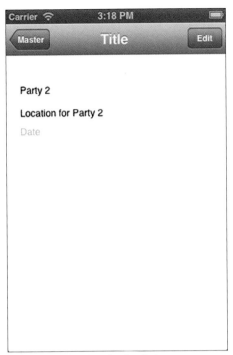

FIGURE 12-4 Look at the details for a row.

FIGURE 12-5 You can edit data.

Using Views on iPad

In Figures 12-1, 12-2, and 12-3, you see a table view. In Figures 12-4 and 12-5, you see an ordinary view. In the context of a table view that shows a number of rows of data (Figures 12-1, 12-2, and 12-3), editing means editing the table itself—adding or removing a row. When a view shows data from within a row (as is the case in Figures 12-4 and 12-5), editing means editing the data itself rather than the structure of the table.

Although the interface looks different, it is similar on iPad. The biggest difference is that instead of using a navigation controller, a split view controller is used. Thus, compare Figure 12-6 to Figures 12-1 and 12-4. Because of the larger screen, there's no need for a disclosure triangle because both the master view controller and the detail view controller can be seen at the same time.

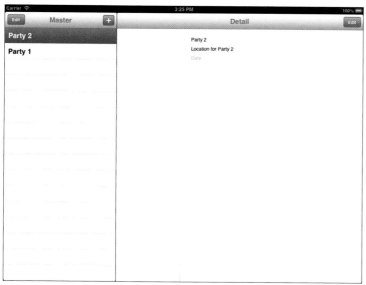

FIGURE 12-6 Edit both parts of a split view controller on iPad.

Even in portrait mode, parts of both views can be seen at the same time, as you see in Figure 12-7.

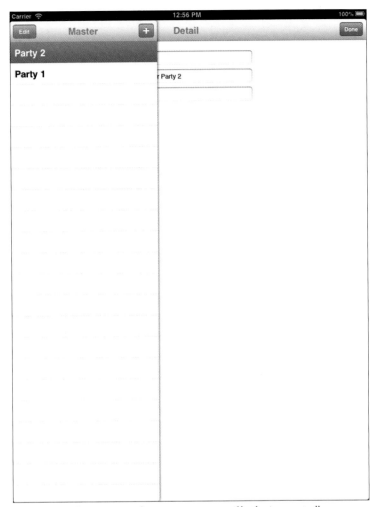

FIGURE 12-7 In portrait mode, you can see parts of both view controllers.

As you can see in Figure 12-8, each view can be edited separately.

(Note that the relevant Edit-Done button when it is in use is blue even though the color may not be reproduced on a printed page. Cocoa Touch manages the proper *focus* of the interface to indicate which view is being edited with the blue Edit-Done button.)

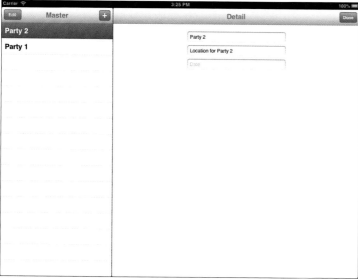

FIGURE 12-8 Edit the data view.

Figure 12-9 shows the master view controller being edited (compare this to Figure 12-3).

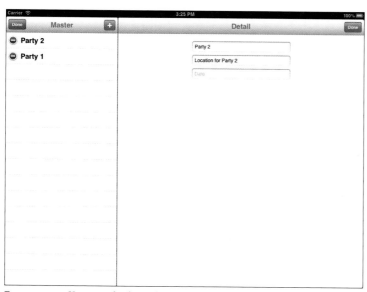

FIGURE 12-9 You can edit the table view's structure.

Using Table Views for Data Display and Editing

When a `UITableView` displays data, it is highly formatted. When you use your own interface, such as the text fields shown in Figures 12-5 and 12-9, you can place them wherever you want. Using a table view instead of individual text fields or other interface elements can make your app's interface more attractive and easy to use. You can even combine accessory views such as disclosure triangles with table view cells that display data fields.

Perhaps the best demonstration of the advantages of a table view is found in Settings. Figure 12-10 shows you the settings for Maps. One of the first things to notice is that the table view rows are *grouped* into three groups (Distances, Map Labels, and Label Size). This immediately makes the data easier to conceptualize. Also, note the absence of an Edit-Done button. If you want to change the setting for Distances from In Miles, you just tap In Kilometers, and the checkbox will move. To change the switch controlling map labels in English, just tap the switch to change it to No. (A different type of interface could let you select which language you want to use, but that's not implemented in this version of the Maps software.)

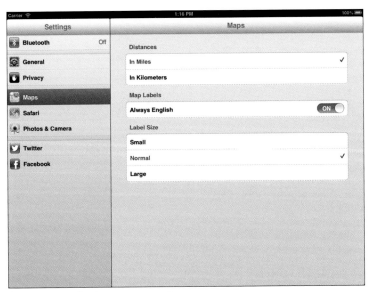

FIGURE 12-10 Settings uses grouped rows.

Settings for Safari, shown in Figure 12-11, are more complex. They use a variety of single-tap interface elements (such as the checkboxes) along with disclosure triangles for other rows.

In Figure 12-12, you can enter text directly using the keyboard. Note the Sign In button that lets you use the data immediately. (That is a simpler interface than Edit-Done; it's made possible by the context of the data. After entering a user ID and password, logging in is a natural next step.)

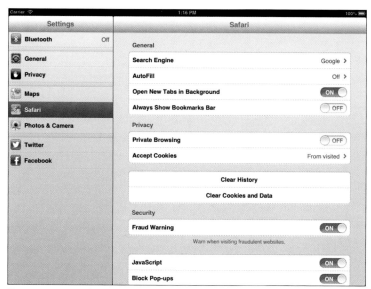

FIGURE 12-11 Safari settings are more complex, but still easy to use.

FIGURE 12-12 You can log into Twitter from Settings.

UITableView High-Level Architecture

As you have seen, `UITableView` is more than a two-dimensional set of data cells. It manages rows of data for display and entry, but it also provides accessory views to let users drill down into the data. In addition, in various circumstances it responds to Edit and Done actions. In addition to optional accessory views, table views allow you to group rows together (as in Figures 12-10, 12-11, and 12-12). Furthermore, there are many other formatting and functional features that have not yet been explored.

The UITableView manages the display and entry of data, but it doesn't do it alone—it uses helper objects in the form of a delegate and a data source to do its work. These helper objects are common in Objective-C; you'll find out more about them shortly in "Introducing Protocols and Delegates."

For full documentation, refer to "Table View Programming Guide for iOS," which is downloadable from developer.apple.com.

The UITableView comprises three inter-related objects:

- UITableView is the basic class that manages the display of the table.
- A helper object—technically a *delegate*—helps with interface management such as selections, headers, and footers, as well as deleting and reordering cells. It is responsible for many aspects of what the table view looks like. One of the delegate methods that you use most frequently is:

  – tableView:didSelectRowAtIndexPath:

  This lets you know when the user has tapped in a cell.

- Another helper object—this one a *data source*—helps with the data. It is responsible for providing the data to be displayed in the cells. One of its most frequently used methods is:

  – tableView:cellForRowAtIndexPath:

  This returns a specific cell for the table. You commonly use this method in your implementation of the data source, and, as part of that implementation, you typically insert and format the data for the cell before returning it. (Other methods let you reuse the cell with different data, but this is where the cell comes from initially.)

Thus the table view, with its overall structure, works with the delegate to manage the interface and user interactions and with the data source to manage the data. (There's more on the details of this in the following section.)

Two points are worth noting before moving on:

- As you can see from both code snippets, cells are identified by their index path. This is an NSIndexPath instance, which, on iOS, lets you locate a cell by its row and its section (see the grouped cells in Figure 12-10). You'll see NSIndexPath objects in action throughout this part of the book. Although index paths can handle very complex tables, for your work with iOS tables (remember they have a single column) the index path is what you use to determine the row and section of a specific cell.

- Remember that the table view with its delegate and data source are all managed by a view controller—UITableViewController. So that gives you a total of four objects working together to produce your table view on the iOS device screen. Just remember that each object has its own role to play. The reason for separating the implementation into these four objects is so that you avoid having an enormous object with complex relationships within it. Here, you have one object with two helper objects as well as the controller for a fourth object. The relationships are simple.

MasterViewController.m in the template implements the two helper objects. These are the methods that are implemented in the template—the pragma marks have been added to the template. (The template places them all in a Table View pragma; in the downloadable sample code for the back, the delegate and data source methods are separated.) From the method names, you can get a sense for what they do. In a nutshell, the data source works with data and the delegate works with user interaction. Read on for more details.

```
#pragma mark - Table View Data Source
- (NSInteger)numberOfSectionsInTableView:(UITableView *)tableView
- (NSInteger)tableView:(UITableView *)tableView
    numberOfRowsInSection:(NSInteger)section
- (UITableViewCell *)tableView:(UITableView *)tableView
    cellForRowAtIndexPath:(NSIndexPath *)indexPath
- (BOOL)tableView:(UITableView *)tableView
    canEditRowAtIndexPath:(NSIndexPath *)indexPath
- (void)tableView:(UITableView *)tableView
    commitEditingStyle:(UITableViewCellEditingStyle)editingStyle
        forRowAtIndexPath:(NSIndexPath *)indexPath
- (BOOL)tableView:(UITableView *)tableView
    canMoveRowAtIndexPath:(NSIndexPath *)indexPath

#Pragma mark - Table View Delegate
- (void)tableView:(UITableView *)tableView
    didSelectRowAtIndexPath:(NSIndexPath *)indexPath
```

Introducing Protocols and Delegates

Objective-C has a number of approaches to the classic object-oriented design problem of multiple inheritance. This is the problem in which you find yourself wishing that a class could be a subclass of two separate classes at the same time.

Exploring the Issue of Multiple Inheritance

For example, take a very concrete example of structuring classes to handle buildings. You could have an abstract superclass (that is, one that is never instantiated) called Building. Subclasses of it might be Residential Building, Commercial Building, and Public Building. You could also subclass the Building class based on construction materials: Brick Building, Stone Building, and Wooden Building.

Each subclass of Building would have its own characteristics and behaviors. Now, imagine that you want to build a wood-frame house. Which subclass of Building do you use? You actually want to subclass both Wooden Building and Residential Building, but in most object-oriented programming languages you have to pick a unique superclass. This is the problem of multiple inheritance.

In Objective-C, you cannot have multiple inheritance, but there are several techniques whereby you can package certain aspects of a class into a reusable set of methods. One such technique consists of *protocols* and *delegates*. Thus, to continue the analogy to buildings, you could have Brick Building, Stone Building, and Wooden Building, but the features of Residential, Commercial, and Public Buildings could be packaged up into protocols—sets of methods. You could then subclass Brick Building from Building, and add a Commercial protocol—a set of methods that could be applied to Brick, Wooden, or Stone buildings.

Protocols consist of methods—You cannot specify properties inside a protocol. However, you can specify a protocol with a method that accesses something that is normally thought of as a property. When you adopt a protocol, you implement its methods using whatever properties and instance variables you have in the class that is adopting the protocol.

 This is a fairly detailed discussion of the protocol and delegate structure. In the following section, you will see how that structure is used for `UITableView`. If you want to skip over the structure described in this section and come back to it later, that's fine. You can just take it on faith that the code described in the following section will work rather than working through the structural details.

Exploring the Protocol and Delegate Structure

Having worked with and written about iOS and its predecessors since 1997, I've had the opportunity to work with the operating systems, write about them, and help developers learn how to use them. (It's been a great experience full of surprises—I can assure you that in the late 1990s, we weren't thinking about iPhone.)

I do hate to break in, but I feel that I should let you know that what I'm about to describe is, for some people, one of the most difficult concepts to grasp. It's actually not all that complicated, but it sometimes takes a little bit of thinking about it to realize the impact. Don't worry if you have to read this section a few times. It really is not difficult once you get your mind around it.

Declaring a Delegate that Adopts a Protocol

A class often declares a delegate, which must adopt a certain protocol. When the delegate adopts a protocol, the class that declares the delegate can be assured that the delegate implements the required methods of the protocol, and the class can safely call those methods, as you will see.

UIApplication declares a delegate that adopts the UIApplicationDelegate protocol as a property of UIApplication. Here is the declaration of delegate in UIApplication.h:

```
id <UIApplicationDelegate>  _delegate;
```

You typically use it through the property in UIApplication:

```
@property(nonatomic, assign) id<UIApplicationDelegate> delegate
```

_delegate is of type id—that is, it can be any object—but the object that is assigned to _delegate must itself adopt the UIApplicationDelegate protocol. (That's the significance of the pointed brackets.)

In most of the templates, a class that conforms to the UIApplicationDelegate protocol is created for you—it's called AppDelegate.

Adopting a Protocol

Perhaps the most frequently used protocol in iOS is UIApplicationDelegate. In most of the Xcode templates for iOS, you'll find an application delegate class. In the Master-Detail Application template, it's called AppDelegate.

In the interface for AppDelegate, you can see that it's a subclass of UIResponder and also that it adopts the UIApplicationDelegate protocol, as you see at the top of AppDelegate.h:

```
@interface AppDelegate : UIResponder <UIApplicationDelegate>
```

The pointed brackets indicate the protocol(s) that are adopted by the class being declared (AppDelegate in this case).

Assigning an Object to a Delegate

If you put the code from the two previous sections together, you'll see that you can assign an object of any type to _delegate in UIApplication provided that the object you assign to _delegate adopts the UIApplicationDelegate protocol.

In most apps, this particular operation is done in `main.m`. That's part of most templates, and it's code that you don't modify. Here is the code as generated in the Master-Detail Application template:

```
//
//  main.m
//  Party Planner
//
//  Created by Wiley Publishing on 11/25/12.
//  Copyright (c) 2012 Champlain Arts. All rights reserved.
//

#import <UIKit/UIKit.h>

#import "AppDelegate.h"

int main(int argc, char *argv[])
{
  @autoreleasepool {
    return UIApplicationMain(argc, argv, nil,
      NSStringFromClass([AppDelegate class]));
    }
}
```

The last argument to `UIApplicationMain` is the `AppDelegate` class and, as you can see in the documentation, that class is assigned to the delegate. Thus, the `AppDelegate` object in your app that adopts the `UIApplicationDelegate` protocol is assigned to `delegate` in `UIApplication` at runtime, and all of the required methods of the protocol are available for `_delegate` because they are implemented in `AppDelegate`.

In a protocol declaration, its methods can be marked as *required* or *optional*. If they are not marked, they are treated as required. All of the methods in `UIApplicationDelegate` are optional.

Declaring a Protocol

The `UIApplicationDelegate` protocol is declared inside `UIApplication.h`. This is a common situation—if a class will declare a delegate that must adopt a protocol, the class usually defines that protocol.

The beginning of the declaration of the `UIApplicationDelegate` is shown here:

```
@protocol UIApplicationDelegate<NSObject>

@optional
  - (void)applicationDidFinishLaunching:
    (UIApplication *)application;
  - (BOOL)application:(UIApplication *)application
    willFinishLaunchingWithOptions:(NSDictionary *)launchOptions
    NS_AVAILABLE_IOS(6_0);
  - (BOOL)application:(UIApplication *)application
    didFinishLaunchingWithOptions:(NSDictionary *)launchOptions
    NS_AVAILABLE_IOS(3_0);
```

Note that NS_AVAILABLE_IOS(6_0) means that this method is available in iOS 6 or later. Similarly, NS_AVAILABLE_IOS(3_0) means the method is available in iOS 3 or later. For now, these are not important to worry about. If it's necessary, they are called out in the documentation.

Tracking Down the Protocol, Delegate, and Data Source Structure in UITableView

In short, a protocol consists of functionality that is implemented in whatever way a class that adopts the protocol wishes to do it. What follows is a concrete example of the process in the Master-Detail Application template (the basis for your Party Planner app). The declaration of a delegate or other helper object specifies a protocol that must be adopted by an object that is assigned to the delegate. The class that declares the delegate can then safely use any method declared in the protocol. (If the protocol includes optional methods, you should check to make certain that the method you want has actually been implemented.)

The delegate is specified by the UITableViewDelegate protocol. The data source is specified by the UITableViewDataSource protocol. (You can find full documentation in the Xcode Organizer or on developer.apple.com.) Here is the beginning of the UITableViewController declaration:

```
@interface UITableViewController : UIViewController
  <UITableViewDelegate, UITableViewDataSource>
```

You can see that it is a subclass of UIViewController and that it adopts the UITableViewDelegate and UITableViewDataSource protocols.

As noted in the previous section, UITableView is the fundamental table class in iOS. Each table view has two helper objects—a UITableViewDelegate and a UITableView DataSource. Together they form the table view itself, and, to top things off, a UITableView Controller manages the whole set of objects. In your implementation, any of these objects can be overridden. `UITableView` isn't overridden too often, but `UITableViewController` is frequently overridden. The two protocols (`UITableViewDelegate` and `UITableView DataSource`) aren't overridden—They're implemented in one or more objects that you assign to the *delegate* property in your `UITableView` (or descendant) or to the `dataSource` property in your `UITableView` (or descendant). Most frequently, these assignments are made using Interface Builder, and, in the Xcode templates such as Master-Detail Application they are already set up.

Here's the place where you need to keep track. You can specify that a class *adopts* a protocol. If a class adopts a protocol, this means that it must implement the required methods of the given protocol. A class can adopt more than one protocol. As an example, consider the declaration of `UITableViewController`:

```
@interface UITableViewController :
  UIViewController <UITableViewDelegate, UITableViewDataSource>
```

This means that an instance of `UITableViewController` or of a subclass of it must respond to all of the required messages of both of these protocols. If you subclass `UITableViewController` (which you frequently do), you have promised to implement the required methods of the two protocols.

And this is where the piece that's a little tricky comes into play.

The documentation of `UITableView` makes it very clear that you must have a data source and delegate. Here is the relevant section from the `UITableView` Class Reference.

> "A `UITableView` object must have an object that acts as a data source and an object that acts as a delegate; typically these objects are either the application delegate or, more frequently, a custom `UITableViewController` object. The data source must adopt the `UITableViewDataSource` protocol and the delegate must adopt the `UITableView Delegate` protocol. The data source provides information that `UITableView` needs to construct tables and manages the data model when rows of a table are inserted, deleted, or reordered. The delegate provides the cells used by tables and performs other tasks, such as managing accessory views and selections."

If you use the Xcode Organizer to look up the header for `UITableView` in `UITableView.h`, you'll find the two properties for these objects declared:

```
@property(nonatomic,assign)  id <UITableViewDataSource> dataSource;
@property(nonatomic,assign)  id <UITableViewDelegate>   delegate;
```

`id` is used to declare a *weakly-typed* variable or property. A weakly-typed variable is a variable of some type that is not specified in the declaration. You can use introspective functions at runtime to find out exactly what type or class it actually is. In this case, both the `dataSource` and `delegate` properties are weakly typed.

Each one *conforms* to a protocol—either `UITableViewDataSource` or `UITableViewDelegate`—but it doesn't matter what the actual class is as long as the object conforms to the relevant protocol and therefore can implement all the protocol's required methods.

It doesn't really matter where they are implemented; you must be able to set two properties (delegate and data source) to the object that implements them. With these declarations, it is possible for a `UITableViewController` (or descendant thereof) to be assigned to the delegate and/or data source property of a `UITableView`. (In most cases the controller is assigned to both properties.) What is important to note is that, although in most cases (and in the Xcode templates), the table view controller is both the data source and the delegate of the table view, that doesn't have to be the case.

Thus, in the structure of a table view you typically have:

- `UITableView` (the view)
- `UITableViewDataSource` (a protocol)
- `UITableViewDelegate` (a protocol)
- `UITableViewController` (the view controller that manages the view)

In many of the implementations, they are implemented with a `UITableView` that is designed and customized with a storyboard and with a subclass of `UITableViewController` that also conforms to the two protocols. Thus, when it comes to writing code, you often write the code only for the subclass of `UITableViewController` that also includes the two protocols.

Many protocol methods begin with a parameter for the primary object, which is `tableView` in many of the methods used here. Because `UITableViewController` is both the delegate and the data source, it already knows which table view is the subject of the method. However, this architecture will work even if some other object is processing the protocol message. In that case, the implementation of the method would need to find some way to interrogate the specific table view that is passed in. In this case, however, that isn't necessary, and, in fact, if you look at the code you'll see that the protocol methods can look at the fetched results controller to find the number of items returned from the fetch and, therefore, the number of rows in the table. At this point, you don't need to worry at all about this, but it's a useful tidbit to store away in your mind in case you want to pursue delegates and protocols in more depth later.

Looking at the Master View Controller

The listings in this section show you the structure of the master view controller in the Master-Detail Application template. This is the complete structure of the file—the code in all of the methods has been removed. You'll see how the basic `UITableViewController` class code is combined with the code for the `UITableViewDataSource` and the `UITableViewDelegate`. (The annotations can also serve as a review of the syntax discussed previously.) Remember that those protocols are adopted by `UITableView Controller` and are required for the data source and delegate in `UITableView`. Thus, an instance of `UITableViewController` can be the data source or delegate (or both) for a `UITableView`.

Looking at the .h File

This is the declaration of `MasterViewController` in the `MasterViewController.h` file:

```
@interface MasterViewController : UITableViewController
  <NSFetchedResultsControllerDelegate>
```

As you can see, `MasterViewController` adopts the `NSFetchedResultsController Delegate` protocol, which means that it has promised to implement all required methods of that protocol (as you will see in Listing 12-5). It is also a subclass of `UITableView Controller`, which, as discussed previously in this chapter, has promised to implement the required methods of the `UITableViewDataSource` protocol and the `UITableView Delegate` protocol. This means that you have three protocols to implement in the `.m` file (at least for the required methods).

Looking at the .m File

The beginning of the file, shown in Listing 12-1, includes the standard Xcode-generated comments as well as the necessary `#import` directives along with a class extension that declares the `configureCell:` method. This method is private and won't be available except to code in this file. Class extensions are now frequently used in the .m files of classes to keep methods private.

Class extensions are found in the `.m` file (before the `@implementation` section) and always have this structure:

```
@interface MasterViewController ()
...
@end
```

After the class extension, you find the implementation of `MasterViewController`. Following that, the implementation of the class begins with common methods such as

```
awakeFromNib
viewDidLoad
didReceiveMemoryWarning
```

`insertNewObject` is a common type of method to add new objects to a table view.

Listing 12-1   The beginning of MasterViewController.m

```objc
//
//   MasterViewController.m
//   Party Planner
//
//   Created by Wiley Publishing on 11/25/12.
//   Copyright (c) 2012 Champlain Arts. All rights reserved.
//

#import "MasterViewController.h"
#import "DetailViewController.h"
#import "Party.h"

@interface MasterViewController ()
- (void)configureCell:(UITableViewCell *)cell
  atIndexPath:(NSIndexPath *)indexPath;
@end

@implementation MasterViewController

- (void)awakeFromNib
{
...
}

- (void)viewDidLoad
{
...
}
```

continued

Listing 12-1   continued

```
- (void)didReceiveMemoryWarning
{
...
}

- (void)insertNewObject:(id)sender
{
...
}


- (void)configureCell:(UITableViewCell *)cell
    atIndexPath:(NSIndexPath *)indexPath
{
...
}
```

Listing 12-2 shows the code that follows immediately after Listing 12-1. The section of code is labeled "Table View" in the template, but, in fact, these are methods declared in the UITableViewDataSource protocol. Note that all of the methods in this protocol are optional except for the second and third in this listing.

You can see that they must be required. You have to know how many rows there are in at least the first section. The number of sections is not a required method: the default value is 1. cellForRowAtIndexPath: must be required: without it, nothing could be passed back to the table view because you wouldn't know what cell you were looking for. Everything else is optional.

Listing 12-2   Implementing the UITableViewDataSource methods
```
#pragma mark - Table View

- (NSInteger)numberOfSectionsInTableView:(UITableView *)tableView
{
...
}

// the following method is one of two required methods in
// this protocol JF
- (NSInteger)tableView:(UITableView *)tableView
    numberOfRowsInSection:(NSInteger)section
{
```

```
...
}

// the following method is the other of two required methods
// in this protocol
- (UITableViewCell *)tableView:(UITableView *)tableView
    cellForRowAtIndexPath:(NSIndexPath *)indexPath
{
...
}
- (BOOL)tableView:(UITableView *)tableView
    canEditRowAtIndexPath:(NSIndexPath *)indexPath
{
...
}

- (void)tableView:(UITableView *)tableView
    commitEditingStyle:(UITableViewCellEditingStyle)editingStyle
    forRowAtIndexPath:(NSIndexPath *)indexPath
{
...
}

- (BOOL)tableView:(UITableView *)tableView
    canMoveRowAtIndexPath:(NSIndexPath *)indexPath
{
...
}
```

Listing 12-3 shows the implementation of a `UITableViewDelegate` protocol method. All methods in this protocol are optional, and this is the only one that's implemented.

Listing 12-3   UITableViewDelegate protocol methods

```
- (void)tableView:(UITableView *)tableView
    didSelectRowAtIndexPath:(NSIndexPath *)indexPath
{
...
}
```

Listing 12-4 continues with code that is specific to the Master-Detail Application template. It is discussed further in Chapter 14, "Editing Table Views."

Listing 12-4   Preparing for a segue

```
- (void)prepareForSegue:(UIStoryboardSegue *)segue sender:(id)
  sender
{
...
}
```

Listing 12-5 shows the code that implements the `NSFetchedResultsController Delegate` protocol. This is the protocol that is adopted by `MasterViewController.h`. You normally only have to worry about the settings for your fetched results controller. You made the necessary updates in Chapter 4, "Designing the Party Planner App" in the "Setting Up the Data Model Section," but the method is shown here for reference (comments have been added).

Listing 12-5   Implementing the NSFetchedResultsControllerDelegate protocol

```
#pragma mark - Fetched results controller

- (NSFetchedResultsController *)fetchedResultsController
{
  if (_fetchedResultsController != nil) {
    return _fetchedResultsController;
  }

  NSFetchRequest *fetchRequest = [[NSFetchRequest alloc] init];
  // Edit the entity name as appropriate.
  NSEntityDescription *entity = [NSEntityDescription
    // set your entity to Party - JF
    entityForName:@"Party"
    inManagedObjectContext:self.managedObjectContext];
  [fetchRequest setEntity:entity];

  // Set the batch size to a suitable number.
  [fetchRequest setFetchBatchSize:20];

  // Edit the sort key as appropriate.
  NSSortDescriptor *sortDescriptor = [[NSSortDescriptor alloc]
    // set your key to partyName - JF
    initWithKey:@"partyName" ascending:NO];
  NSArray *sortDescriptors = @[sortDescriptor];

  [fetchRequest setSortDescriptors:sortDescriptors];

  // Edit the section name key path and cache name if appropriate.
  // nil for section name key path means "no sections".
  NSFetchedResultsController *aFetchedResultsController =
```

```
  [[NSFetchedResultsController alloc]
   initWithFetchRequest:fetchRequest
   managedObjectContext:self.managedObjectContext
   sectionNameKeyPath:nil cacheName:@"Master"];
aFetchedResultsController.delegate = self;
self.fetchedResultsController = aFetchedResultsController;

NSError *error = nil;
if (![self.fetchedResultsController performFetch:&error]) {
  // Replace this implementation with code to handle the error
  // appropriately.
  // abort() causes the application to generate a crash log and
  // terminate. You should not use this function in a shipping
  // application, although it may be useful during development.
  NSLog(@"Unresolved error %@, %@", error, [error userInfo]);
  abort();
}

return _fetchedResultsController;
}

- (void)controllerWillChangeContent:(NSFetchedResultsController *)
    controller
{
...
}

- (void)controller:(NSFetchedResultsController *)controller
    didChangeSection:(id <NSFetchedResultsSectionInfo>)sectionInfo
    atIndex:(NSUInteger)sectionIndex
    forChangeType:(NSFetchedResultsChangeType)type
{
...
}

- (void)controller:(NSFetchedResultsController *)controller
    didChangeObject:(id)anObject
    atIndexPath:(NSIndexPath *)indexPath
    forChangeType:(NSFetchedResultsChangeType)type
    newIndexPath:(NSIndexPath *)newIndexPath
{
...
}

- (void)controllerDidChangeContent:(NSFetchedResultsController *)
    controller
```

continued

Listing 12-5   continued

```
{
...
}

/*
comment deleted
*/

- (void)configureCell:(UITableViewCell *)cell
    atIndexPath:(NSIndexPath *)indexPath
{
...
}
@end
```

Summary

This chapter shows you how table views work. They're not just rows and columns—they let you manage behaviors such as editing and restructuring the table itself. Table views are frequently used in iOS. They're at the heart of the Master-Detail Application template, which is the basis for the Party Planner app you're building. In fact, in the next chapter you'll see how to add another table view to the detail view controller.

Settings provides a good overview of table view features. It organizes various settings and lets you drill down through them to control your iOS device and its behavior. It's this organizational aspect of tables that will be used in the following chapter.

In looking at the way that table views are implemented, you've seen how protocols are used. *Protocols* are sets of methods that are declared on their own rather than within a class. Any class can adopt a protocol, which means that the protocol's methods must be implemented by that class. Part of the usefulness of protocols is that, once declared, they can be adopted by any number of classes. This provides a way around the classic multiple inheritance issue that is common in object-oriented programming. (As a side note, it's important to note that a number of important Cocoa Touch functionalities are implemented as protocols that are widely adopted both by framework classes as well as by classes you are likely to write, such as the UITableView delegate and dataSource protocols.)

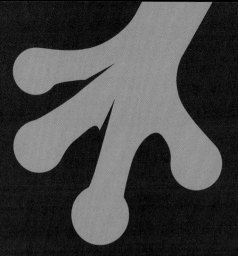

chapter thirteen

Formatting Table Cells

THE STRUCTURE OF the master view controller combines UITableView Controller as well as the two protocols that it adopts (UITableViewDelegate and UITableViewDataSource) so that MasterViewController can become the delegate and the data source of your UITableView. You've seen that structure in Chapter 12, "Exploring the Table View in the Template," and now it's time to delve into a number of the methods that make up this combined object.

A large number of the methods—particularly in the adopted protocols—are self-explanatory both in their names and their implementations. For example, here's the method that controls re-ordering table rows:

```
- (BOOL)tableView:(UITableView *)tableView
    canMoveRowAtIndexPath:(NSIndexPath *)indexPath
{
    // The table view should not be re-orderable.
    return NO;
}
```

The comment is part of the Master-Detail Application template, as are comments in many of the other basic protocol implementations in the template. The only thing that might be a little perplexing to you is the mechanics of breaking down the NSIndexPath into a row and section, but even that isn't an issue in many cases (and it's explained at the end of this chapter in the "Configuring the Detail Item" section.) This method is called as needed for each row in the table. Most of the time you want all rows to be re-orderable or for none of them to be re-orderable. Don't worry about the value of indexPath—just set the return value to NO or YES and, most of the time, you're done.

Other methods let you customize the appearance and content of the cells in the table, and those methods do require your attention. They are the subjects of this chapter.

Converting the Detail View to a Table View for iPhone

As you saw in Chapter 12, table views are a good way to organize data entry and display. Settings, for example, as shown in Figure 13-1, uses table views in a variety of ways to provide a powerful yet consistent user interface for a variety of types of data.

FIGURE 13-1 Settings uses table views to organize its interface.

In the Party Planner app as it has been built so far, you use the built-in table view for the master view controller (shown at the left in the iPad version shown in Figure 13-2). You have changed the detail view controller (shown at the right in Figure 13-2) to use editable text fields.

On iPhone, a navigation controller combines the functionality of both master and detail view controllers, as shown in Figure 13-3.

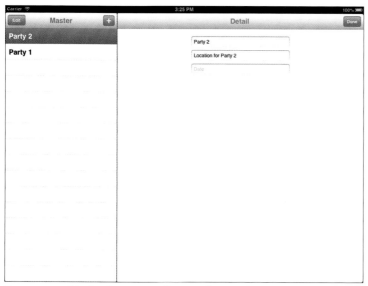

FIGURE 13-2 The detail view controller is implemented using editable text fields.

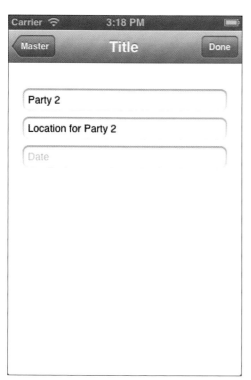

FIGURE 13-3 The master view controller on iPhone uses a navigation controller.

As you explore the workings of table views and their cells in this chapter, you'll convert the text field-based interfaces shown in Figures 13-2 and 13-3 to ones based on table views such as the Settings interface shown in Figure 13-1.

At this point, the interface for a party has three entries:

- Party name
- Location
- Date

Clearing Out the Text Fields on iPhone

Here are the steps to convert the detail view controller to a table view. As you'll see, it's a matter of removing the existing view controller with its text fields and replacing it with a table view controller with a table view. The methods that now work to configure and save the text fields need to be emptied of those references in preparation for converting them to use table views. You can leave the shells of those methods for now—it'll save some typing later on.

1. Make certain you save a copy of the project as it is now. You'll be destroying the current detail view controller and you may need to revert to it if something goes wrong.

2. In Xcode, select the iPhone storyboard. (As in previous chapters, it's easiest to work first with the iPhone storyboard and then continue with the iPad storyboard. It's not that iPhone storyboards are simpler; it's just that the screen size is smaller so it's easier to see what's going on in the storyboard as you work.)

3. In the detail scene of the detail view controller, select the three text fields (party Name, location, and date). As shown in Figure 13-4, it may be easiest to select them in the document outline.

4. Press Delete to delete them. Note that the constraints object is not selectable. When the text fields have been deleted, it is irrelevant and will automatically disappear.

5. In DetailViewController.h, select the three properties for those text fields and delete them, as shown in Figure 13-5.

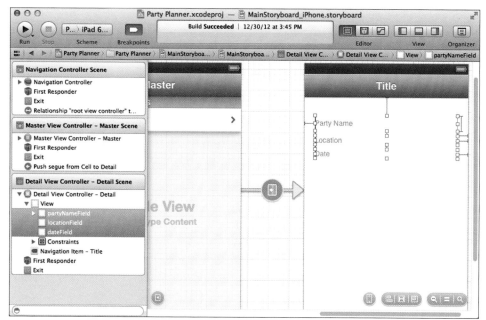

FIGURE 13-4   Select the three text fields and delete them.

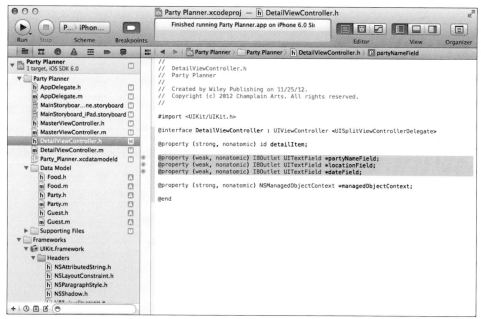

FIGURE 13-5   Delete the field properties.

6. If you build the app after you delete the properties, you will have a slew of error messages in DetailViewController.m, as shown in Figure 13-6. These are the lines of code that reference the now-deleted properties.

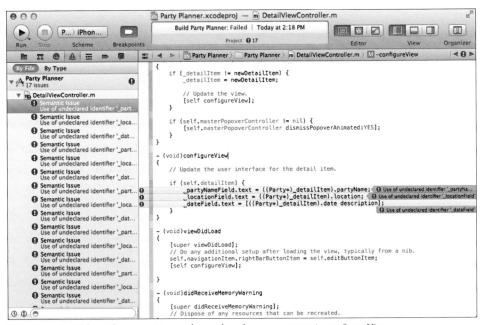

FIGURE 13-6 Without the properties you have a lot of error messages in configureView.

7. Three of them will be in configureView. configureView is no longer needed, so you can just delete it. Remember to delete the declaration from the class extension at the top of the file.

```
@interface DetailViewController ()
@property (strong, nonatomic) UIPopoverController
  *masterPopoverController;
- (void)configureView;
@end
```

For now, this class extension will become:

```
@interface DetailViewController ()
@property (strong, nonatomic) UIPopoverController
  *masterPopoverController;
@end
```

8. There's another big batch of errors using those properties in setEditing: animated:, as you see in Figure 13-7.

9. Delete those lines so that setEditing: animated: looks like Listing 13-1.

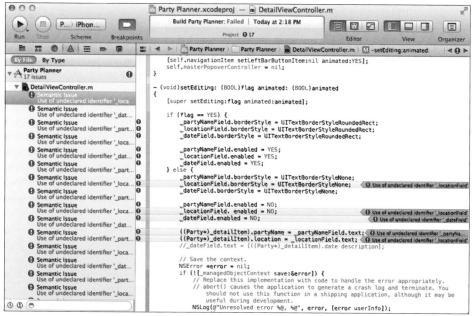

FIGURE 13-7 You also have a lot of errors in setEditing: animated:.

Listing 13-1 The altered setEditing: animated:

```
- (void)setEditing: (BOOL)flag animated: (BOOL)animated
{
  [super setEditing: flag animated:animated];

  if (flag == YES) {
    } else {
    // Save the context.
    NSError *error = nil;
    if (![_managedObjectContext save:&error]) {
      // Replace this implementation with code to handle the
      // error appropriately.
      // abort() causes the application to generate a crash log
      // and terminate. You should not use this function in a
      // shipping application, although it may be useful during
      // development.
      NSLog(@"Unresolved error %@, %@", error, [error userInfo]);
      abort();
    }

  }
}
```

There may still be two references to `configureView` that are flagged as errors. They will be removed later.

Adding the Table View on iPhone

Now you add the table view controller that contains the table view. You connect the objects to new properties as you have done previously. This sequence of steps is repeated over and over as you add new views to the storyboard, so you'll soon be quite familiar with it. As you become more familiar with these steps, you may do them in a slightly different order. As long as you do all of them, you'll be okay.

Here are the steps.

1. Delete the detail view controller from the storyboard. Before doing so, note the segue shown in Figure 13-8. You can select the segue and show it in the Attributes inspector.

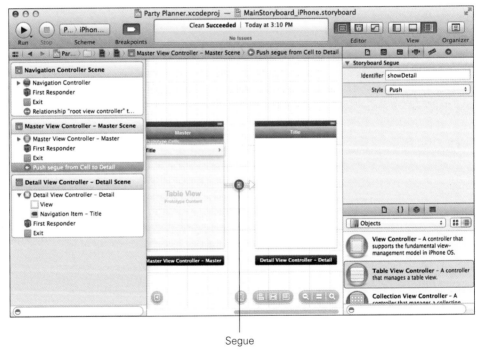

Segue

FIGURE 13-8 Delete the detail view controller.

2. Add a table view controller to the storyboard. Show the library, and drag a table view controller into it, as shown in Figure 13-9.

3. Recreate the segue from the master view controller to the new table view controller. Control-drag from the prototype cell in the master view controller to the new table view controller, as shown in Figure 13-10.

FIGURE 13-9 Add a table view controller.

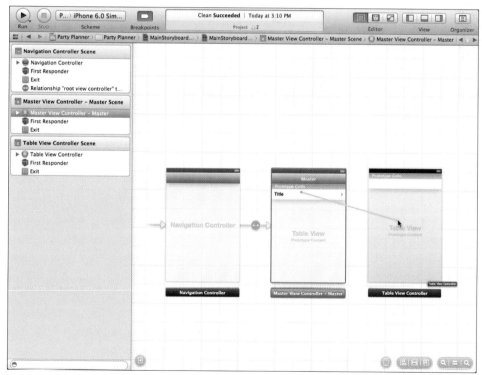

FIGURE 13-10 Recreate the segue.

4. As soon as you release the mouse button you'll be able to select the type of segue you want. It should be Push just as it was in Figure 13-8 and Step 1. See Figure 13-11. (Choose whether you want the segue to occur when the row is selected or only when the accessory is tapped.)

5. With the segue still selected, show the Attributes inspector and set its name to show Detail just as it was in Step 1 and Figure 13-8. (This is so that the existing code will still work.) Figure 13-12 shows the completed segue.

6. In DetailViewController.h, change the declaration so that DetailView Controller is a subclass of UITableViewController instead of UIView Controller. That is, from this:

```
@interface DetailViewController : UIViewController
  <UISplitViewControllerDelegate>
```

to this:

```
@interface DetailViewController : UITableViewController
  <UISplitViewControllerDelegate>
```

7. With the new table view controller selected in the storyboard, change its class in the Identity inspector to DetailViewController, as you see in Figure 13-13. (Note that this is a place where sequence matters—Step 6 must have been done before this step.)

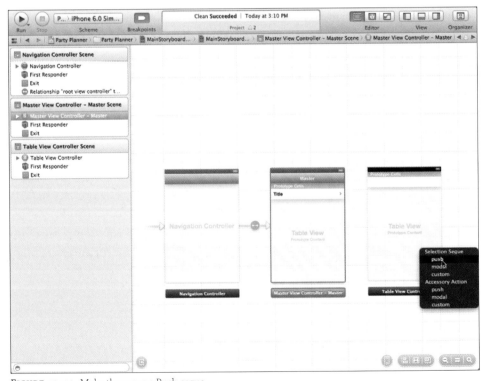

FIGURE 13-11 Make the segue a Push segue.

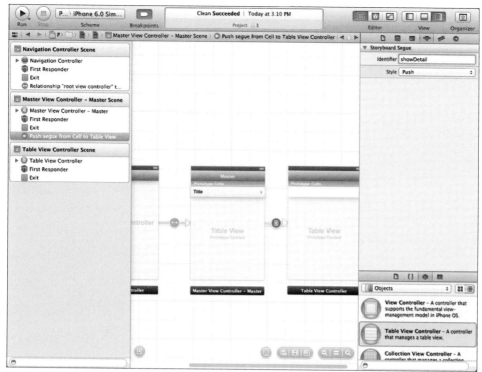

FIGURE 13-12 Add an identifier to the segue.

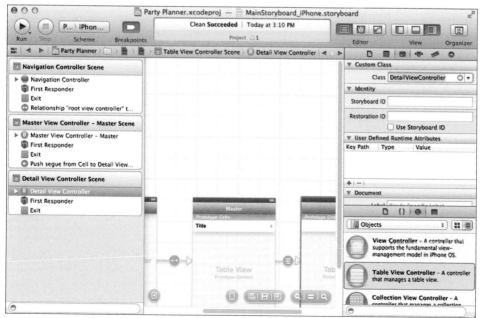

FIGURE 13-13 Change the class in the storyboard.

8. In the Attributes inspector, change the title of the new table view controller to Detail, as shown in Figure 13-14. (Note that in the document outline, what you type will not be reflected until after you press Return or otherwise leave the field. Thus, Figure 13-14 shows both halves of the operation—setting the title and the automatic updating of the document outline.)

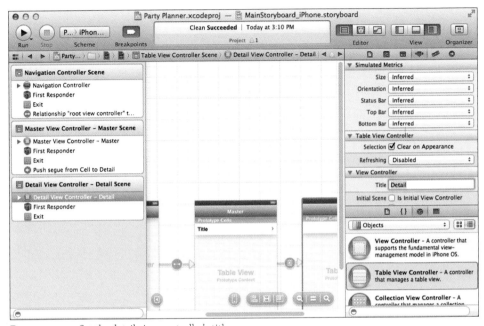

FIGURE 13-14 Set the detail view controller's title.

9. In the document outline, Control-click on the table view in the detail view controller to check that its outlets (dataSource and delegate) are both connected to the new table view controller. This new table view controller is called Detail View Controller - Detail if you have followed these steps. Figure 13-15 shows what the table view outlets should be. (UITableView declares the delegate and dataSource properties, so you must connect those properties to an object that adopts the UITableViewDelegate and UITableViewDataSource protocols. UITableViewController does so, so your subclass of UITableViewController—DetailViewController—also adopts them and implements them in the template and, later, in the code that you will write.)

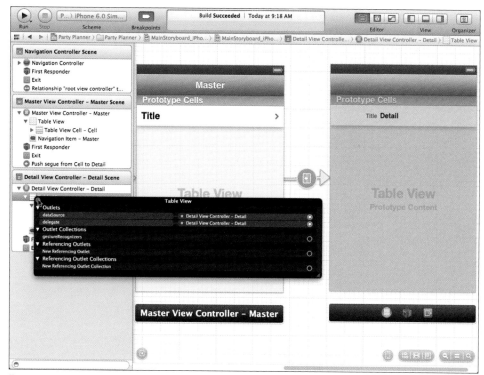

FIGURE 13-15 Check the table view outlets.

Converting the Detail View to a Table View on iPad

Converting to a table view on iPad is somewhat different than it is on iPhone. The chief reason for this difference is that on iPad, the template uses a split view controller so that both master and detail views can be seen at the same time. If you have not done so already, follow the steps in "Clearing Out the Text Fields on iPhone" because the steps involving code apply also to iPad. (If you have worked through the previous section, you're ready to continue here.)

Adding the Table View on iPad

This process is similar to the process of adding a table view on iPhone, but, as noted, there are differences because you're relying on a split view controller rather than on a navigation interface. Even if your focus is primarily on iPhone or iPad, it is worthwhile to work through both sets of steps because they will help you to understand the differences between the two environments. Furthermore, although the iPhone interface is totally reliant on the navigation structure (there is no split view controller on iPhone), the navigation interface is used heavily on both iPhone and iPad.

Here are the steps to add the table view to the iPad storyboard.

1. Save the project before you make these changes.

2. Open the iPad storyboard. As usual, you may need to adjust the workspace window. In Figure 13-16, both the navigation and status areas at left and right of the window are hidden so you can see the structure of the split view storyboard.

    From the split view's master view controller (A in Figure 13-16), you have a relationship to a navigation controller (B) and then from there, to the master view controller (C). (This master view controller is separate from the master view controller that is part of the split view controller.) From the split view's detail view controller (D), you have a relationship to a navigation controller (E) and then from there, to the detail view controller itself (F).

    In the detail view controller, you may have text fields that you have added as you did in the iPhone storyboard. You can see these in Figure 13-16.

3. Select the detail view controller, as shown in Figure 13-17. Remember to select the detail view controller and not its navigation controller (to its left); also make sure it's the detail view controller you have selected and not the view within it.

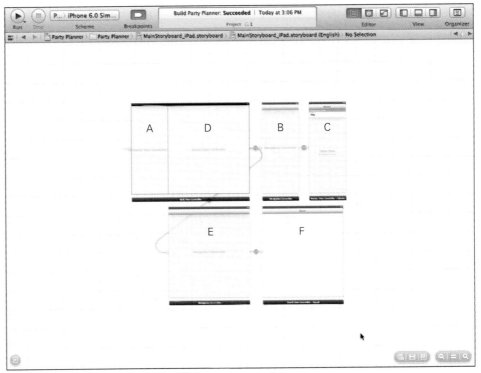

FIGURE 13-16 Open the iPad storyboard.

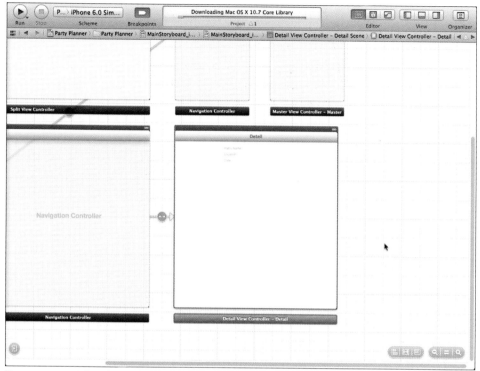

FIGURE 13-17 Select the detail view controller.

4. Delete the detail view controller. (Once it's selected, just use the Delete key on the keyboard. You can also use Edit➜Delete. Alternatively, you can show the document outline in the storyboard editor, select it there, and then delete it in either of those ways.)

5. Add a table view controller to the storyboard. Show the library, and drag a table view controller into it, as shown in Figure 13-18.

6. Recreate the relationship segue from the navigation controller to the new table view controller. Control-drag from the navigator for the detail view controller (bottom left) to the new table view controller, as shown in Figure 13-19. (Note that you have a prototype cell in the detail view controller, as shown in Figure 13-19. You will adjust its contents in the next steps, so don't worry if it doesn't show Detail yet.)

If you are comparing this process with the iPhone sequence, you'll see that the relationship segue (Root View Controller) you create in this step is comparable to the segue you created in Step 4 of "Adding the Table View on iPhone." It's comparable but not identical because instead of a Push for a selection, the segue is a Relationship—the views don't move in a split view controller.

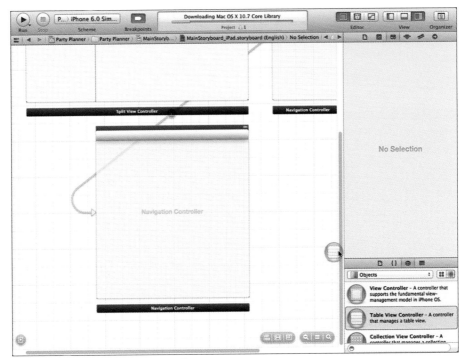

FIGURE 13-18 Add a table view controller.

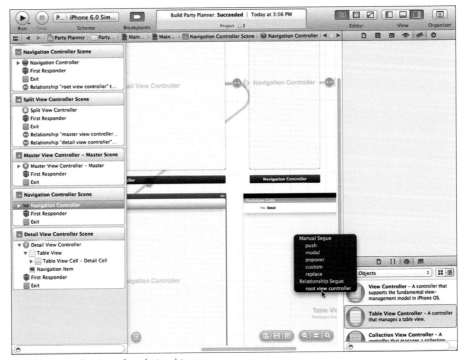

FIGURE 13-19 Recreate the relationship segue.

7. With the new table view controller selected in the storyboard, change its class in the Identity inspector to `DetailViewController`, as you see in Figure 13-20.

Note that Step 6 of "Adding the Table View on iPhone" isn't needed here. You have to adjust each of the storyboards (iPhone and iPad), but the code change from Step 6 applies to both of them.

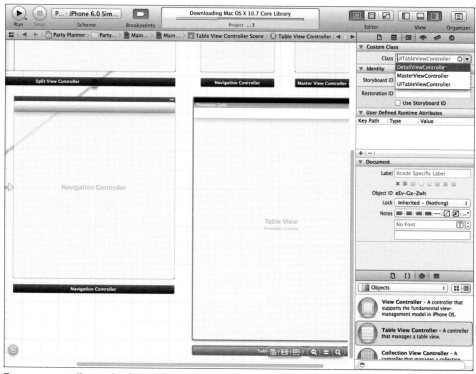

FIGURE 13-20 Change the class in the storyboard.

8. In the Attributes inspector, change the title of the new table view controller to `Detail`, as shown in Figure 13-21.

You now have a table view controller containing a table view as the detail view controller for both iPad and iPhone.

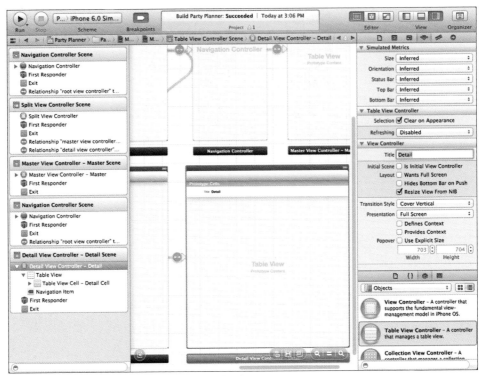

FIGURE 13-21 Set the new detail view controller's title.

Preparing the Prototype Cell
in the Storyboard

As a reminder, Figure 13-22 shows the master view controller in action on iPhone (the master view controller is on the left; the detail view controller is on the right).

Prototype cells provide basic formatting. You can modify the formatting as you go along, but most of the time, you use and reuse the prototype cell over and over in the table. This provides some performance efficiencies, and it also can make the look and behavior of the table more consistent. In this example, a single prototype cell will be used for the detail view table. In fact, that is the same structure that you already have in the master view controller. Open the iPhone storyboard and locate the master view controller. Select the prototype cell and show the Attributes inspector, as you see in Figure 13-23.

FIGURE 13-22 Master and detail view controllers in the template.

This is the Basic style; there is a disclosure indicator as an accessory view. Perhaps most important, the prototype has an identifier—in this case `Cell`. You use that identifier to access this cell from your code in `MasterViewController.m`.

If you select the prototype cell in the new detail view controller, you'll see that it is a Custom style, with no accessory view. (You can see this in Figure 13-24.)

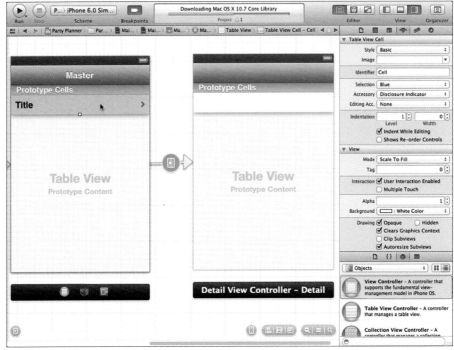

FIGURE 13-23 Examine the master view controller prototype cell.

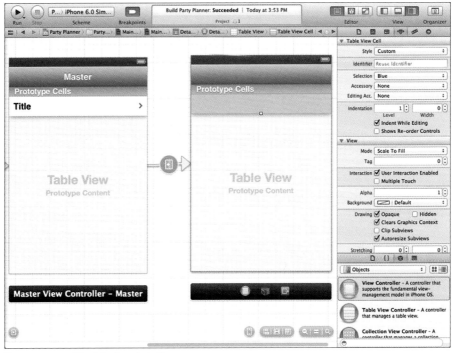

FIGURE 13-24 The default style is Custom.

You can experiment with different styles. For now, choose Left Detail and no accessory view, as shown in Figure 13-25. Also, provide an identifier such as Detail Cell.

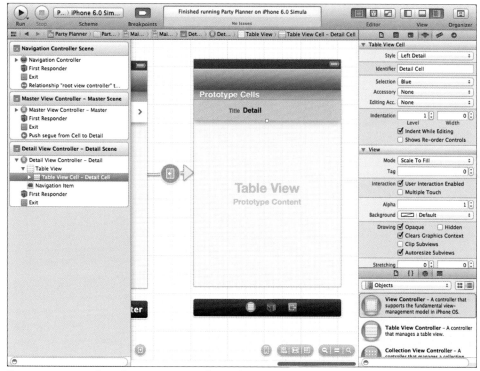

FIGURE 13-25 Set the style to Left Detail and provide an identifier.

Apply the same settings to the prototype cell in the detail view controller for iPad.

Configuring and Returning a Single Table Cell

Every cell in a table view is set individually using the `tableView: cellForRowAtIndex Path:` method of the `UITableViewDataSource` protocol. That method returns a `UITableViewCell` for the specified index path. It locates the cell using the cell identifier that you set in the storyboard. It frequently also fills in data to the cell it returns, but all that's required is that it return a cell.

In your storyboard, you create one or more prototype cells for your table view. Those prototypes provide the basic formatting and styling of the cell. (You can have several prototype cells.)

This section shows you how to combine a prototype cell with data and return them all as a cell to be shown in the table. The sequence of events is just that:

1. Create a prototype cell in the storyboard,

2. On demand, combine a prototype cell with the necessary data.

3. Return the cell and its data for display in the table view.

In fact, when you look at the code that you wrote to work with the text fields in the previous version of Party Planner, you'll see that the second and third steps in this sequence are already there. Yes, you have to rewrite them to use the table view cells instead of the text fields, but you have a good basis on which to build. In the previous section, you deleted the text field code, so now it's a matter of replacing it.

Setting the Detail Item

In the Master-Detail Application template, there is a property in `DetailViewController.m` that contains the selected object:

```
@property (strong, nonatomic) id detailItem;
```

Because it is of type `id`, it can be an instance of any class, so this code can be used as-is in any apps that you build based on this template.

It is useful to examine exactly how this property in the detail view controller is set. That examination shows you a number of basic features of Objective-C and the Cocoa Touch frameworks. Don't worry, this is not long and complex topic. Rather, this is a set of code snippets and design patterns that will help you in many cases throughout your development of iOS apps.

The issues that you follow in tracking down how the detail item is set are:

- **Property accessors**—Whether you write the accessors or allow Xcode to create them for you, they manage getting and setting property values.

- **Segues**—You'll learn the difference between relationship segues and storyboard segues.

Using Accessors for Declared Properties

A declared property such as `detailItem` actually encompasses a number of components. Starting with Xcode 4.4, declared properties are *synthesized* automatically. Previously, this was done with a `@synthesize` compiler directive in the `.m` file. Synthesizing a property manages two aspects of the property:

- **Backing variable**—Every property is backed by an instance variable (or *ivar*). With automatic synthesis of declared properties, the backing variable is declared automatically, and it is named by prefixing the property name with an underscore. Thus, the backing variable for the `detailItem` property by default is `_detailItem`. If the property is declared in the `.h` file, objects that import the .h file can access it.

The backing variable is visible within the .m file when you use the default naming. That means that from the .m file—and not from instances of the class that just use the information in the .h file—you can get to the property by using _myProperty. In all cases you can also get to the property by using dot syntax (see the following section).

• **Accessors**—When you use the dot notation (myInstance.myProperty), Xcode generates two *accessors* that, by default, retrieve or set the value of the backing variable. (Depending on their function, they are called *getters* or *setters*.)

The accessors are invoked with dot notation. You can write your own accessors that can do more than simply access the value of the backing variable.

You can also provide customized names for the accessors. For example, for a property called myProperty with type id, the default getter is:

- (id)myProperty;

The default setter is:

- (void)setMyProperty:(id)newProperty

Note that in the default getter and setter, the lowercase property name is adjusted to uppercase within the setter method name.

If you write your own accessors that do more than simply access the value of the backing store, the consequences of using dot notation compared to using the backing variable (_myProperty) may be different. This is explained in the following section.

In the Master-Detail Application template, the detailItem property in DetailView Controller.h is set with this code in DetailViewController.m:

```
- (void)setDetailItem:(id)newDetailItem
{
    if (_detailItem != newDetailItem) {
        _detailItem = newDetailItem;

        // Update the view.
        [self configureView];
    }

    if (self.masterPopoverController != nil) {
        [self.masterPopoverController dismissPopoverAnimated:YES];
    }
}
```

You'll see that this method adheres to the default syntax for a declared property setter, and therefore it is the default setter for the detailItem property. If you set a breakpoint at the beginning of this method, you'll see that this method is called when you assign a value to the property using dot notation; you don't have to call this method directly. Furthermore, this method is a good example of a setter that does more than just access the backing variable—it configures a view and also manages a popover. The view will be discussed more in the following section.

After the detail item is set, `configureView` is called to update the interface. This code is specific to the template. Now that you're using a table view for the detail view, you should use a more general method to update the view. Instead of the template's `configureView`, change that line to

```
[self.tableView reloadData];
```

Make the same change to `viewDidLoad`.

This is a framework method for `UITableViewController`. This code asks the table view to reload its data (hence the name). With this one change to `setDetailItem:`, you are ready to proceed.

Segues: Exploring the Difference Between Relationship and Action/Manual Segues

In iOS storyboards, you create a segue by Control-dragging from one view controller to another. As storyboards and segues have evolved over the last few versions of Xcode, two varieties of segues have come into focus. Both types were shown previously in Figure 13-19.

- **Action/manual**—An action or manual segue (Apple documentation uses both terms) is a segue typically initiated by a user action. Sometimes, it is initiated indirectly by a user action, but, at the bottom, you'll usually find a user action. Action/manual segues describe something that *happens*.

- **Relationship/containment**—Other segues are drawn in the same way, but they represent a state—something that *is* rather than something that *happens*.

This matters because the navigation interface of the Master-Detail Application template is based on navigation—user actions. The split view controller version of the app for iPad is based on relationships. Both the master view controller and detail view controller are present at the same time. They may not be visible together, but there is no moment of transition from master view controller to detail view controller as there is on the iPhone/navigation interface version.

This matters if you are building an app on this template or if you are building your own app that must use both types of interfaces (and, as noted, this means almost any universal app that runs on both iPhone and iPad). Because of this difference in functionality, there is different code for setting the detail item in the detail view controller. The code is in the `MasterViewController.m`, because that is where the detail view controller is set up.

For a navigation interface (typically the iPhone interface), you set the detail item in `prepareForSegue:sender:`. Here is the default code:

```
- (void)prepareForSegue:(UIStoryboardSegue *)segue sender:(id)
  sender
{
  if ([[segue identifier] isEqualToString:@"showDetail"]) {
    NSIndexPath *indexPath =
      [self.tableView indexPathForSelectedRow];
  NSManagedObject *object = [
    [self fetchedResultsController] objectAtIndexPath:indexPath];
  [[segue destinationViewController] setDetailItem: object];
  }
}
```

The detail view controller's detail item is set in the last line:

```
[[segue destinationViewController] setDetailItem:object];
```

In the case of the split view controller on iPad, `prepareForSegue:sender:` is not called because, as you saw in Figure 13-19, the relationship segue makes the detail view controller the root view controller instead of launching an action segue. Thus, you override `tableView:didSelectRowAtIndexPath:` in `MasterViewController.m` (but remember that this is a `dataSource` protocol method that is implemented by the master view controller).

```
- (void)tableView:(UITableView *)tableView
  didSelectRowAtIndexPath:(NSIndexPath *)indexPath
{
  if ([[UIDevice currentDevice] userInterfaceIdiom] ==
    UIUserInterfaceIdiomPad) {
      NSManagedObject *object =
        [[self fetchedResultsController]
          objectAtIndexPath:indexPath];
      self.detailViewController.detailItem = object;
    }
}
```

The detail view controller's detail item is set in the last line of this method. In both cases, this code is in the template.

Using a Custom Subclass of NSManagedObject for the Detail Item

You can make your life easier by changing `detailItem` from an `id` to an instance of `Party`. This will mean that you will not have to coerce the item each time you access it.

Coercing Objects

In object-oriented programming, you can subclass objects. For example, most objects in Cocoa Touch are subclasses of NSObject. NSManagedObject is one such subclass. As you saw in Chapter 8, "Building on the Data Model," you can create a subclass of NSManagedObject for the entities in your data model. Party, for example, is a subclass of NSManagedObject; it is also a subclass of NSObject. When you know the class hierarchy of an object, you can *coerce* it to any of the classes or subclasses that it is. For example, given an object called myObject that happens to be declared as an NSManagedObject, you can coerce it to be a Party object (provided that you know it is). Here is the code:

```
(Party*)myObject
```

Coercing objects can make code more readable. Other benefits may occur at runtime.

Here are the steps to change detailItem from an id to an instance of Party:

1. Add a forward declaration for Party at the top of DetailViewController.h:

   ```
   @class Party;
   ```

2. Import the .h file at the top of DetailViewController.m:

   ```
   #import "Party.h"
   ```

3. Change the property declaration in DetailViewController.h from id to Party*.

4. In the two assignment lines in MasterViewController.m called out in the previous snippets, coerce object to (Party *) object, as in

   ```
   self.detailViewController.detailItem = (Party *)object;
   ```

With these two methods in place, you are ready to proceed.

Even if you are implementing only one of the universal versions, it can be easier to make both of these changes now. That way, if you come back to add iPhone to iPad or vice versa, you won't have to remember to make this change. And, in the meantime, it does no harm.

Configuring the Detail Item

Now that the detail item is set, you can combine the data with the interface. This is easier than using the code to set individual fields. In Chapter 12, you saw how to set each text field in `configureView`:

```
- (void)configureView
{
  // Update the user interface for the detail item.

  if (self.detailItem) {
    _partyNameField.text = ((Party*)_detailItem).partyName;
    _locationField.text = ((Party*)_detailItem).location;
    _dateField.text = [((Party*)_detailItem).date description];
  }
}
```

Removing configureView

Instead of addressing the view and each of its fields, a utility method can let you set each row. `configureView` is no longer needed, so remove its declaration from the class extension at the top of `DetailViewController.m` and remove its definition from the body of that file. (You may already have done this as described in the section "Clearing Out the Text Fields on iPhone.")

Implementing the Data Source Protocol for the Detail View Controller

There are two required methods in `UITableViewDataSource` and they are `tableView:InSection:` and `tableView:cellForRowAtIndexPath:`

You may want to add these methods to a new section prefaced with

```
#pragma mark - Table View Data Source Protocol
```

How you organize your source code files is up to you. In the sample code that you can download, the #pragma directives move around from chapter to chapter. This reflects what seems to be a real-life pattern. Instead of constructing a massively structured file from the start, the file grows as code is added. The #pragma directives are added and the code is reorganized as it makes sense to do so.

- `tableView: numberOfRowsInSection:` —In the master view controller, the number of rows in the main section of the table view depends on the number of items in the fetched results controller, as is the case in the master view controller on the left in Figure 13-2. In cases when you are using the table view for formatting rather than for accommodating a variable number of rows, you can hard-code the number of rows (see Figure 13-3).

  Add `tableView: numberOfRowsInSection:` to `DetailViewController.m`. Compare to Figure 13-3 to see why the return value is 3:

  ```
  - (NSInteger)tableView:(UITableView *)tableView
      numberOfRowsInSection:(NSInteger)section
  {
      return 3;
  }
  ```

- `tableView:cellForRowAtIndexPath:` —You have to implement the `UITableView DataSource` protocol method `tableView:cellForRowAtIndexPath:` in order to return each cell on demand. A utility method can work with it. Thus, as shown in the following section, if you implement a method called `configureCell:at IndexPath:`, you can call it from `tableView:cellForRowAtIndexPath:`. Add `tableView:cellForRowAtIndexPath:` with the prototype cell identifier added, along with the call to `configureCell: atIndexPath:` to `DetailView Controller.m`.

  ```
  - (UITableViewCell *)tableView:(UITableView *)tableView
    cellForRowAtIndexPath:(NSIndexPath *)indexPath
  {
    UITableViewCell *cell = [tableView
      dequeueReusableCellWithIdentifier:@"Detail Cell"
      forIndexPath:indexPath];
    [self configureCell:cell atIndexPath:indexPath];
    return cell;
  }
  ```

Implementing the Table View Delegate Protocol for the Detail View Controller

All of the options in this protocol are optional, so you don't need to worry about any of them for now. (You will implement some of them in the next two chapters.)

Consider how you implement `configureCell: atIndexPath:`. This is not a data source protocol method, so you may want to put it in a `pragma` with your other methods. It should be declared in the class extension at the top of `DetailViewController.m` so that the class extension now looks like this:

```
@interface DetailViewController ()
@property (strong, nonatomic) UIPopoverController *
  masterPopoverController;
- (void)configureCell:(UITableViewCell *)cell
  atIndexPath:(NSIndexPath *)indexPath;
@end
```

Add the definition of `configureCell: atIndexPath:` to `DetailViewController.m`.
It may look a bit daunting at first, but it's really just a sequence of nearly identical case
statements, as you will see.

```
- (void)configureCell:(UITableViewCell *)cell
  atIndexPath:(NSIndexPath *)indexPath
{
  switch ([indexPath row]) {
    case 0:
      cell.detailTextLabel.text =
        [self.detailItem.partyName description];
      cell.textLabel.text = @"Party Name";
      break;

    case 1:
      cell.textLabel.text = @"Location";
      cell.detailTextLabel.text =
        [self.detailItem.location description];
      break;

    case 2:
      cell.textLabel.text = @"Date";
      cell.detailTextLabel.text = @"value";
      break;

    default:
      break;
    }
}
```

The heart of the `switch` statement is found in the `NSObject` UIKit Additions Reference.
There you will find three methods to pull out the `NSInteger` components of the
`NSIndexPath` objects:

```
@property(nonatomic, readonly) NSInteger row
@property(nonatomic, readonly) NSInteger section
@property (nonatomic, readonly) NSInteger item;
```

Depending on the style of your prototype table cell, you set the text label or detail text label to the label and the other one to the value. Note that for the date—which is not yet set—the string constant *value* is displayed. For the other data elements, you use the properties of the `Party` class you created rather than the key-value method for retrieving data. Furthermore, the `description` method is used to return a text string.

Summary

This chapter shows you how to format table view cells rather than have to create and set text fields individually. The result is neater and easier for users to manage; in addition, it can be easier for you to write.

You may think that formatting table cells is a very specialized topic, but, in fact, it's one of the most frequent tasks that you'll perform. Whether you are displaying data or letting users manage settings and preferences, being able to quickly convert data from a persistent data store to a clear interface is a very common task.

As the Party Planner app stands at this point, you can enter data and display it. Thanks to Core Data, your data is stored when you create a new party. However, there is no way to save any changes that you make. That will be resolved in the next chapter.

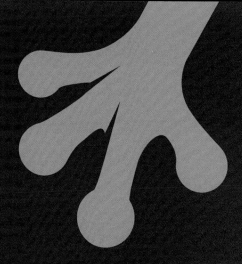

chapter fourteen

Editing Table Views

ONE OF THE most attractive features of table views is that there is a great deal of built-in functionality for editing them. Editing a table view means editing the view's structure, which can consist of adding or removing rows as well as rearranging them. Editing the *content* of a table view is not very much different from editing the text fields (and other interface elements) in a UIView. (You find out more about editing table view content in Chapter 17, "Back to the Storyboard: Enhancing the Interface.")

The default behavior of the master view controller in the Master-Detail Application template (and your Party Planner app) enables you to add and delete rows in the table view. However, you can't rearrange the rows in that table view. By now, you have probably noticed that in the illustrations of Party Planner at this point, there are two parties: Party 2 and Party 1. They are displayed in that order, and for many people, that doesn't make sense. Some automated sorting (alphabetical, by date, or the like) would be preferable to a sequence that appears out of order.

Depending on the data that you are displaying in a table view, you may want to sort the rows in some understandable way, or you may want to allow users to rearrange them. Your choice is dependent on what the data is and how much of it there is. If you are planning to display a list of 100 items, some form of automated sorting makes sense. For a smaller list, manual sorting and arrangement may make more sense. In the case of parties, for example, you may want the ones that you're working on to be at the top of the list. That might include a party for today as well as a big party that you're planning for next summer. That type of order is something that only a user can do well.

Regardless of how you feel about sorting the list of parties, you should know how to sort the rows in a table view. It's something that frequently comes up, and it's a fundamental skill for the iOS app developer. Once you know the technique, you can help the user rearrange the parties in the master view controller. And, just to emphasize the point of how common this is, when you add table views to display lists of guests and menu items (coming up in Chapter 17), those tables, too, can be rearranged by users.

There are two aspects to rearranging table rows:

- You need to store the row order so that it persists over time.
- You need to implement the reordering interface features. (Mostly, this means turning on options in the data source protocol.)

When you've rearranged the rows as you like them, you then need to save the new sequence.

Modifying the Data Model to Store Row Sequence

There are three parts to this process:

- Understanding the existing row ordering
- Adding a `displayOrder` attribute to the data
- Refreshing the data store

Looking at the Fetched Results Controller Ordering

In the master view controller table view—as in many similar table views—the order of the rows is determined by the sort descriptor in the fetched results controller. This can be one of the key functions of the fetched results controller. For example, in Listing 14-1 you can see the code for the fetched results controller in the master view controller as it should look now. (It returns a fetched results controller if it exists, and, if it doesn't, it creates it.) Note that it creates and sets a sort descriptor.

There are three primary components of the Core Data stack. The data model describes your data; the persistent store coordinator manages its storage in one or more persistent stores (such as an SQLite store); and a managed object context provides temporary storage for managed objects retrieved with the persistent store coordinator using the data model. A fetch request interacts with the Core Data stack to retrieve data, which is often then managed by a fetched results controller. Fetched results controllers typically are used to manage a master view's list of objects.

The comments in the template guide you to the main parts of the code.

- Set the entity name. In this case, it's `Party`. In the Master-Detail Application template, it started out as `Event`.

- Setting the batch size can help you optimize performance. For most beginning iOS apps, just leave it as it is.

- Edit the sort key. At this point, it is now `partyName`, and the sort order is `ASCENDING:NO`. Look at your data model to find the attribute on which you want to sort.

- The section name, key path, and cache name referenced in the fourth comment are not needed for most basic apps so you can ignore them.

Listing 14-1 shows the `fetchedResultsController` code.

Listing 14-1   fetchedResultsController

```
- (NSFetchedResultsController *)fetchedResultsController
{
  if (_fetchedResultsController != nil) {
    return _fetchedResultsController;
  }

  NSFetchRequest *fetchRequest = [[NSFetchRequest alloc] init];
  // Edit the entity name as appropriate.
  NSEntityDescription *entity =
    [NSEntityDescription entityForName:@"Party"
    inManagedObjectContext:self.managedObjectContext];
  [fetchRequest setEntity:entity];

  // Set the batch size to a suitable number.
  [fetchRequest setFetchBatchSize:20];

  // Edit the sort key as appropriate.
```

continued

Listing 14-1   continued

```
NSSortDescriptor *sortDescriptor =
  [[NSSortDescriptor alloc]
  initWithKey:@"partyName"
  ascending:NO];
NSArray *sortDescriptors = @[sortDescriptor];

[fetchRequest setSortDescriptors:sortDescriptors];

// Edit the section name key path and cache name if appropriate.
// nil for section name key path means "no sections".
NSFetchedResultsController *aFetchedResultsController =
  [[NSFetchedResultsController alloc]
  initWithFetchRequest:fetchRequest
  managedObjectContext:self.managedObjectContext
  sectionNameKeyPath:nil cacheName:@"Master"];
aFetchedResultsController.delegate = self;
self.fetchedResultsController = aFetchedResultsController;

NSError *error = nil;
if (![self.fetchedResultsController performFetch:&error]) {
  // Replace this implementation with code to handle the
  // error appropriately.
  // abort() causes the application to generate a crash log
  // and terminate. You should not use this function in a
  // shipping application, although it may be useful during
  // development.
  NSLog(@"Unresolved error %@, %@", error, [error userInfo]);
  abort();
}

return _fetchedResultsController;
}
```

Adding a displayOrder Attribute

If you want to make it possible for the users to rearrange the rows, you'll need to add a display Order attribute to the data store. Users will reorder the row in the master view controller's table view by dragging them; the displayOrder attribute will be calculated and stored.

Here are the steps to add the attribute. Before beginning, make certain that you have a backup copy of the project. Because this involves changing the data model and some other rather major (but simple) changes, you should have a copy that you can fall back to if necessary. Then proceed with these steps. (For more details, review Chapter 8, "Building on the Data Model," where this process is explained more fully.)

1. Select the data model as shown in Figure 14-1.

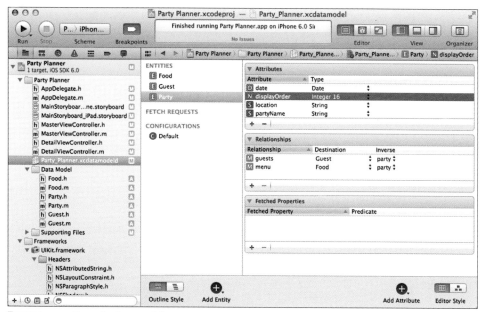

FIGURE 14-1 Open the data model.

2. Select the Party entity.

3. Click + at the bottom of the Attributes table to add a new attribute.

4. As you see in Figure 14-1, change its name to displayOrder and its type to Integer 16.

5. Create a new subclass of NSManagedObject for Party. You already have one, but this new one will overwrite it and add the displayOrder attribute. Choose Editor→ Create New NSManagedObject Subclass, as shown in Figure 14-2.

6. If you have selected an attribute for the entity, you are asked which entities to create, as shown in Figure 14-3. In this case, you can either select Party or all of them. If you have made changes to any of the subclasses created previously, don't recreate them unless it's absolutely necessary: your changes will be lost. However, in a case such as this where you have no changes to the previously generated subclasses, your choice doesn't matter. Then click Next.

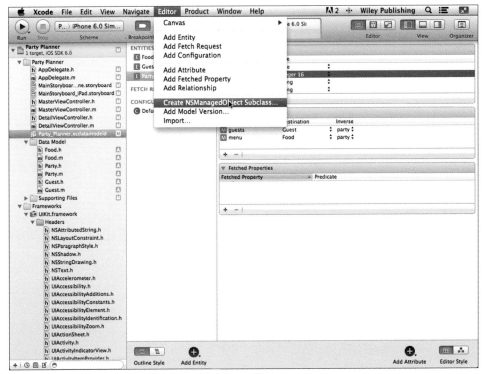

FIGURE 14-2 Recreate the Party subclass of NSManagedObject.

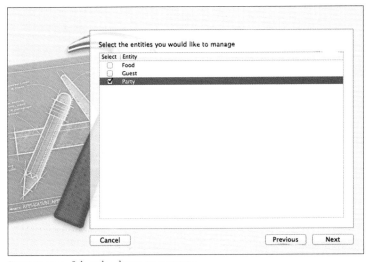

FIGURE 14-3 Select the classes to generate.

7. As shown in Figure 14-4, select the group to add the new subclass to. If you have followed the steps in this book, `Data Model` will be your choice.

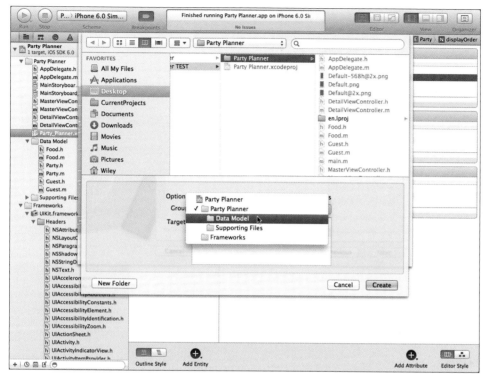

FIGURE 14-4 Select the group for your new subclass.

8. You'll be warned that files will be overwritten, as shown in Figure 14-5. Just check to make certain that they are the files you expect.

FIGURE 14-5 Confirm the files to be overwritten.

9. As shown in Figure 14-6, you can see that the `Party` class now contains the `displayOrder` property. (Remember, data model *attributes* are class *properties*.)

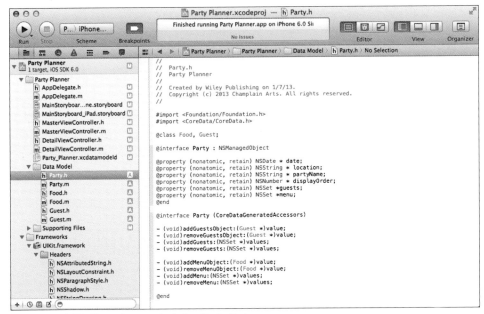

FIGURE 14-6 The Party class now includes displayOrder.

Refreshing the Data Store

Follow the steps in the sidebar entitled "Creating and Removing the Database" in Chapter 8 to remove the existing data store. (All of your test data will be removed at this stage.) You should be able to run the app without noticing any difference in its behavior from the way it was before you added the `displayOrder` property.

Enabling the Table View Reordering Features

The table view in the master view controller has access to the reordering features that are built into `UITableView` (or, more specifically, built into its `UITableViewDataSource` protocol). To enable reordering, you need to take two steps. These changes are in `MasterViewController.m`. You may want to put them in a separate #pragma section such as

```
#pragma mark - Table View Data Source
```

Here are the changes:

1. In `tableView:canMoveRowAtIndexPath:`, change the result from NO to YES so that it looks like this:

```
- (BOOL)tableView:(UITableView *)tableView
    canMoveRowAtIndexPath:(NSIndexPath *)indexPath
{
    // The table view should not be re-orderable.
    return YES;
}
```

2. Implement an empty `tableView:moveRowAtIndexPath:toIndexPath:` method (it is part of the `UITableViewDataSource` protocol). The template doesn't include this method at all, and for the interface to be enabled, you need the method. It doesn't have to do anything, as is the case with this code.

```
- (void)tableView:(UITableView *)tableView
    moveRowAtIndexPath:(NSIndexPath *)sourceIndexPath
    toIndexPath:(NSIndexPath *)destinationIndexPath {
}
```

At this point, you can build and run the app. You should see the re-ordering buttons in each row, as shown in Figure 14-7. You should be able to reorder the rows and see them move appropriately in the master view controller. But there's more to do.

All that's left is to implement `tableView:moveRowAtIndexPath:toIndexPath:` and to save the newly calculated `displayOrder` data.

If you have followed the steps in this chapter and recreated the database to include the `displayOrder` property, you will notice that the names of the previous `Party` entities have been removed and replaced with the default timestamps. Chapter 17 shows you how to change this code.

Moving the Rows and Saving the New Order

There are two tasks to be accomplished here:

- You need to rearrange the elements in the table view so that they are in the new order.

- You need to calculate and store the new `displayOrder` attribute.

Rearranging the Elements in the Table View

A table view's data source (that is, an object adopting the `UITableViewDataSource` protocol that is set to the table view's `dataSource` property) provides the data for the table view.

How that is done, is up to the data source. (This is typical behavior for an object that adopts a protocol: the protocol specifies *what* happens but not *how* it happens.) Frequently, the elements of the table view are stored in an array, but, particularly in large table views, the data is retrieved only on an as-needed basis.

Because the elements of a table view are stored in an array, they normally can't be rearranged. That is because NSArray is an *immutable* class: once you have created an instance, you cannot modify it. As is the case with many of the Cocoa Touch collection classes, there is a companion class that is mutable—NSMutableArray. NSMutableArray is a subclass of NSArray: it adds methods to mutate an NSArray.

You may think that if you are going to need to modify an array that it must be an instance of NSMutableArray. Strictly speaking that is true, but there is a commonly used design pattern that handles this situation very elegantly and efficiently. If your modifications to an array are going to be constant and will happen throughout your app, then a mutable array is quite likely the best choice. However, if your changes are confined to a specific area, such as reordering the master view controller's data, the following strategy is often a good choice.

An immutable collection class (such as NSArray) has many opportunities for optimization in the compiler and at runtime. If the section of your app where you need mutability can be identified, you can create a mutable copy of the array for use there. Modify the mutable array as needed, and then, when you have finished, transfer the mutable array to an immutable NSArray.

At first blush, this may seem like extra work, and it is. However, experience and benchmark tests have convinced many developers that the efficiencies and optimizations achieved by using NSArray objects where possible outweigh the added cost of creating a temporary NSMutableArray.

This is all made possible by the following class method of NSArray:

```
+ (id)arrayWithArray:(NSArray *)anArray
```

Using Fetched Results Controllers as Data Sources

When you are using Core Data with a table view, a fetched results controller is frequently the data source. A fetched results controller has a number of features that make it well-suited to support a master view controller and its list of detail items. Methods of the NSFetchedResultsController let you easily access the results of the fetch. You can access the results using the fetchedObjects property, which can help you build a master view controller's list very easily. A fetched results controller contains not only the results of the fetch that is part of the controller, but it also contains a property for the managed object context. Thus, a fetched results controller can give you the elements of the Core Data stack that you need to display and save the results of the fetch.

There are other methods that let you create an array from a list of objects or from a file, but `arrayWithArray:` is the simplest way to switch from a mutable array to an immutable array and vice versa. And here is where a fetched results controller comes into the picture. `NSFetchedResultsController` lets you access the results of the fetch with the following property:

```
@property (nonatomic, readonly) NSArray *fetchedObjects
```

Because this is an immutable array, it isn't updated as you add, delete, or modify data. Thus, if you're going to be modifying your set of fetched objects, you'll need to copy `fetched Objects` to a mutable array.

An immutable array can (and often does) contain objects. Those objects can be modified while they are in the immutable array. It is the array itself that cannot be modified. Changing a property value in one of the array elements is not a change to the array itself as the insertion or deletion of an element would be.

The main steps in rearranging the elements of the table view now can fall into place.

1. Declare an `NSArray` to contain the parties in `MasterViewController.m`. This can live easily in the class extension at the top of `MasterViewController.m`. Add the `orderedParties` property to that section as shown here.

   ```
   @interface MasterViewController ()

   @property (strong, nonatomic) NSArray *orderedParties;

   - (void)configureCell:(UITableViewCell *)cell
       atIndexPath:(NSIndexPath *)indexPath;
   @end
   ```

2. Populate `orderedParties`. You add this method to `MasterViewController.m`.

   ```
   - (void)loadOrderedPartiesArrayFromFetchedResultsController {

     NSSortDescriptor *sortDescriptor =
       [[NSSortDescriptor alloc]
         initWithKey:@"displayOrder"
         ascending:YES];
     NSArray *sortDescriptors = [[NSArray alloc]
       initWithObjects:&sortDescriptor
       count:1];
   ```

```
NSMutableArray *myOrderedPartiesArray = [[NSMutableArray
  alloc]
  initWithArray:[self.fetchedResultsController
fetchedObjects]];
[myOrderedPartiesArray sortUsingDescriptors:sortDescriptors];
_orderedParties = myOrderedPartiesArray;
}
```

You can reuse this code in many places. It creates a mutable array from your fetched results controller and then sorts the array. The only line you need to customize is

```
initWithKey:@"displayOrder"
```

3. Use `loadOrderedPartiesArrayFromFetchedResultsController`. A good place to do that is in `viewDidLoad`, as shown here.

```
- (void)viewDidLoad
{
  [super viewDidLoad];
  // Do any additional setup after loading the view,
  // typically from a nib.

  [self loadOrderedPartiesArrayFromFetchedResultsController];

  self.navigationItem.leftBarButtonItem = self.editButtonItem;

  ...more code follows in the template
```

4. Now that you have filled your array, use it to display the data rather than using the fetched results controller. In `MasterViewController.m`, `configureCell:atIndexPath:` currently looks like this:

```
- (void)configureCell:(UITableViewCell *)cell
    atIndexPath:(NSIndexPath *)indexPath
{
  NSManagedObject *object =
    [self.fetchedResultsController objectAtIndexPath:
        indexPath.row];

  cell.textLabel.text = [[object valueForKey:@"partyName"]
    description];
}
```

The first line gets an object from the fetched results controller. Change it to use the array and row from indexPath:

```
NSManagedObject *object = [_orderedParties
  objectAtIndex: indexPath.row];
```

5. Run the app. When you tap Edit on the master view controller, you should be able to rearrange the rows. There's still more to do, as you'll see in the next section.

Calculating and Saving the displayOrder Property for a Move

The last step in this process is calculating the new value for `displayOrder` and saving it as necessary. Each of those steps is implemented in its own method. The code in those methods is used over and over in Cocoa Touch apps that use table views. As you will see, there are minor customizations you may need to make to reuse the code, but the logical structures are reusable.

Here are the steps to calculate and save the `displayOrder` attribute:

1. You already have an empty shell of `tableView:moveRowAtIndexPath:toIndex Path:` in `MasterViewController.m`. Now add the implementation code as shown here.

```
- (void)tableView:(UITableView *)tableView
  moveRowAtIndexPath:(NSIndexPath *)sourceIndexPath
  toIndexPath:(NSIndexPath *)destinationIndexPath {

  NSMutableArray *myParties =
    [NSMutableArray arrayWithArray:_orderedParties];

  Party* party = [myParties objectAtIndex: sourceIndexPath.
                    row];
  [myParties  removeObjectAtIndex: sourceIndexPath.row];
  [myParties  insertObject:party atIndex:destinationIndexPath.
                    row];

  NSInteger start = sourceIndexPath.row;
  if (destinationIndexPath.row  < start) {
    start = destinationIndexPath.row;
  }

  NSInteger end = destinationIndexPath.row;
  if (sourceIndexPath.row > end) {
    end = sourceIndexPath.row;
  }

  // this is the code that acts displayOrder
  for (NSInteger i = 0; i <= end; i++) {
    party = [myParties objectAtIndex:i];
  party.displayOrder = @(i);
  }
```

```
// Because NSMutableArray is a subclass of NSArray,
// you can assign an instance of NSMutableArray to
// an NSArray variable.
_orderedParties = myParties;
}
```

If you have taken a basic programming course, this code may look familiar. This is routine boilerplate code that is used for rearranging elements in an array. Half a century ago this code (or code very much like it) was written in FORTRAN and COBOL on mainframe computers.

To reuse this code, simply replace references to parties with whatever objects you are dealing with. You'll notice at the beginning of the method that a new local NSMutableArray is created from the NSArray that you loaded from the fetched results controller. The mutable array can be reordered and, in the next step, saved.

2. Implement setEditing: animated: in MasterViewController.m with this code. This method is called when you tap the Edit-Done button. (You can set a breakpoint on it to confirm that.) When the button displays Edit, this method is called with editing set to YES. When the button displays Done (that is, while you are editing), the method is called with editing set to NO. The _orderedParties array is correctly ordered now, but the displayOrder property needs updating, and that is done here.

To reuse this code, note the comment about providing a more meaningful error message. You'll see how to do that in Chapter 15, "Telling Users the News: Alerts and NSError."

```
- (void)setEditing: (BOOL)editing animated:(BOOL)animated
{
  [super setEditing: editing animated:animated];

  // If editing is finished, save the managed object context
  if (!editing)
  {

    NSManagedObjectContext *context = self.
managedObjectContext;
    NSError *error = nil;
    if (![context save:&error]){
      // Replace this implementation with code to handle the
      // error appropriately.
      // abort() causes the application to generate a crash
      // log and terminate. You should not use this function
```

```
    // in a shipping application, although it may be useful
    // during development.
      NSLog(@"Unresolved error %@, %@", error, [error
  userInfo]);
      abort();
    }
  }
}
```

3. Change `tableView:didSelectRowAtIndexPath:` to run off of the ordered array. Here is how it should look now:

```
- (void)tableView:(UITableView *)tableView
  didSelectRowAtIndexPath:(NSIndexPath *)indexPath
  {
    if ([[UIDevice currentDevice] userInterfaceIdiom] ==
      UIUserInterfaceIdiomPad) {
        Party *party = (Party*)
          [_orderedParties objectAtIndex: indexPath.row];
          self.detailViewController.detailItem = party;
    }
}
```

4. Change `configureCell:atIndexPath:` to also run off the ordered array. Here is how it should look now:

```
- (void)configureCell:(UITableViewCell *)cell
  atIndexPath:(NSIndexPath *)indexPath
  {
    Party *party = (Party*)
      [_orderedParties objectAtIndex: indexPath.row];

    cell.textLabel.text = party.partyName;
}
```

5. Finally, in `fetchedResultsController` in `MasterViewController.m`, make certain that you sort the fetched results on `displayOrder` and change `ascending` to `YES`. Here is the relevant section of code with the change made:

```
// Edit the sort key as appropriate.
NSSortDescriptor *sortDescriptor = [[NSSortDescriptor alloc]
  initWithKey:@"displayOrder" ascending:YES];
NSArray *sortDescriptors = @[sortDescriptor];
```

Adding a New Object

If you run the app on an iPad now, you should be able to rearrange the rows, but you'll notice that when you add a party, it's not shown in the list until the next time you run the app—that is, until the next time `loadOrderedPartiesArrayFromFetchedResultsController` runs. The solution to this is to update the `orderedParties` array.

 This is a good example of what you should watch out for in testing. Because the split view controller is used on the iPad template and a navigation controller is used in the iPhone template, views are presented differently. The problem appears only on iPad. The code change provided in this section works on both iPad and iPhone.

You can correct this problem by reloading the sorted array in `insertNewObject:`. When you do so you'll also need to set the `displayOrder` property of the new object. Here are the steps:

1. After you create the new object and set its `partyName` property, set its `displayOrder` property to the count of elements in the sorted array. As you see in this code, you'll have to coerce the count, which is an unsigned integer to an NSNumber, which is the type of `displayOrder`. Note, too, that `displayOrder` is zero-relative, so setting it to the count—which is always one value higher than the last zero-relative displayOrder—will work properly.

    ```
    newManagedObject.partyName = [[NSDate date] description];
    newManagedObject.displayOrder =
        [NSNumber numberWithUnsignedInteger:[_orderedParties count]];
    ```

2. Reload the sorted parties array as shown here:

    ```
    // Reload orderedParties
    [self reLoadOrderedPartiesArrayWithNewObject:
        newManagedObject];
    ```

    Note that this line of code will generate an error message. It uses a new method that is not yet implemented. (You'll find the code right after this set of steps.)

3. Because you'll be changing the number of objects in the sorted parties array, change the `tableView: numberOfRowsInSection:` method to run off that array. Here is how it should look now:

    ```
    - (NSInteger)tableView:(UITableView *)tableView
        numberOfRowsInSection:(NSInteger)section
    {
        return [_orderedParties count];
    }
    ```

This is how the `insertNewObject:` method looks now:

```
- (void)insertNewObject:(id)sender
{
  NSManagedObjectContext *context =
    [self.fetchedResultsController managedObjectContext];
  NSEntityDescription *entity =
    [[self.fetchedResultsController fetchRequest] entity];
  Party *newManagedObject =
    [NSEntityDescription insertNewObjectForEntityForName:
      [entity name] inManagedObjectContext:context];

  // If appropriate, configure the new managed object.
  newManagedObject.partyName = [[NSDate date] description];
  newManagedObject.displayOrder =
    [NSNumber numberWithUnsignedInteger:[_orderedParties count]];

  // Reload orderedParties
  [self reLoadOrderedPartiesArrayWithNewObject: newManagedObject];

  // Save the context.
  NSError *error = nil;
  if (![context save:&error]) {
    // Replace this implementation with code to handle the error
    // appropriately.
    // abort() causes the application to generate a crash log and
    // terminate. You should not use this function in a shipping
    // application, although it may be useful during development.
    NSLog(@"Unresolved error %@, %@", error, [error userInfo]);
    abort();
  }
}
```

You need to implement the `reLoadOrderedPartiesArrayWithNewObject:` method referred to in Step 2. This is very similar to `loadOrderedPartiesArrayFromFetched ResultsController` except that it's loaded from the `orderedParties` array. In addition the new object is added.

```
- (void)reLoadOrderedPartiesArrayWithNewObject: (Party *)newParty {

  NSSortDescriptor *sortDescriptor = [[NSSortDescriptor alloc]
    initWithKey:@"displayOrder" ascending:YES];
  NSArray *sortDescriptors = [[NSArray alloc]
    initWithObjects:&sortDescriptor count:1];
```

```
NSMutableArray *myOrderedPartiesArray =
  [[NSMutableArray alloc] initWithArray:_orderedParties];

// add the new object
[myOrderedPartiesArray addObject: newParty];

[myOrderedPartiesArray sortUsingDescriptors:sortDescriptors];
_orderedParties = myOrderedPartiesArray;
}
```

Deleting an Existing Object

Deleting an object is simpler than adding a new one. You do have to manage the two parallel
arrays (the fetched results controller array and the sorted objects array), but you don't have
to worry about re-ordering the sorted objects array. If the array is ordered correctly at the
beginning, simply removing an object from it will leave the remaining objects correctly
sorted. However, you will need to update the `displayOrder` property values. Here are
the steps:

1. Add the method to `MasterViewController.m`.

   ```
   - (void)removeObjectFromOrderedPartiesArray: (Party *)
     removeParty {

     Party * party = nil;

     NSMutableArray *myOrderedPartiesArray =
        [[NSMutableArray alloc] initWithArray:_orderedParties];
     [myOrderedPartiesArray removeObject: removeParty];

     // recalculate displayOrder
     NSInteger end = [myOrderedPartiesArray count] - 1;
     for (NSInteger i = 0; i <= end; i++) {
        party = [myOrderedPartiesArray objectAtIndex:i];
        party.displayOrder = @(i);
     }
     _orderedParties = myOrderedPartiesArray;
   }
   ```

2. This data source protocol method is called when committing changes. You need to call
   your new method there, as indicated in the comment.. Here is how the code should
   look now:

   ```
   - (void)tableView:(UITableView *)tableView
     commitEditingStyle:(UITableViewCellEditingStyle)editingStyle
   ```

```
forRowAtIndexPath:(NSIndexPath *)indexPath
{
  if (editingStyle == UITableViewCellEditingStyleDelete) {
    NSManagedObjectContext *context =
      [self.fetchedResultsController managedObjectContext];
    [context deleteObject:[_orderedParties
      objectAtIndex: indexPath.row]];

    // remove from Ordered Parties ADD THIS CODE jf
    [self removeObjectFromOrderedPartiesArray:[_
        orderedParties
      objectAtIndex: indexPath.row]];

    NSError *error = nil;
    if (![context save:&error]) {
      // Replace this implementation with code to handle the
      // error appropriately.
      // abort() causes the application to generate a crash
      // log and terminate. You should not use this
      // function in a shipping application, although it
      // may be useful during development.
      NSLog(@"Unresolved error %@, %@",
        error, [error userInfo]);
      abort();
    }
  }
}
```

3. You need to update `tableView:numberOfRowsInSection:` as you did in Step 3 of "Adding an Object" previously in this chapter. If you have followed along, that code is already in your project.

Summary

This chapter shows you how to manage editing of a table view—in particular, the techniques for re-ordering rows in the table. There are several ways you can do this. In all of them, you have the challenge of using the built-in `UITableView` methods (and those of the associated protocols) to manage the visual appearance of the table while at the same time (or, perhaps, just before saving) you manage a `displayOrder` attribute in each row that lets you store and retrieve the ordered rows.

This is a good example of how you frequently work with Cocoa Touch. The framework provides a rich environment to manage the app's interface. Sometimes, you subclass the framework classes, but more often, you implement or subclass specific methods that customize some of a class's behavior. The challenge is knowing what to subclass. The documentation (particularly the class reference documents that you can view in the Xcode Organizer) is a great place to start. However, it's a tall order to memorize every detail of every class. There are several ways to feel more comfortable.

One of the techniques that's helped me along is to periodically step back and look at the big picture. Yes, the details of managing a `displayOrder` attribute are specific to a table view, but from a broader perspective, managing a derived data element that needs to be set just before data is stored in `setEditing: animated:` is a fairly frequent occurrence. If you look at every technique in isolation you have thousands of things to learn. By abstracting and generalizing, you can make yourself more comfortable.

This is difficult to do at times, because you'll naturally be focused on the task at hand and might resist this periodic stepping back, but it does help you learn the basic principles, architecture, and design patterns of Cocoa Touch as well as of Objective-C.

part 5

Interacting with Users

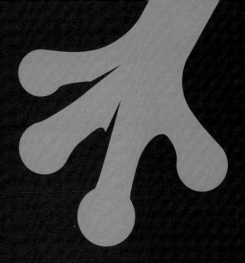

chapter fifteen

Telling Users the News: Alerts and NSError

THIS PART OF the book focuses on user interaction. You've already seen how to interact with users through view controllers and interface elements, but the user interaction discussed in this part of the book is a different type. These interactions are initiated by the app itself. Some of them not only are initiated by the app but they also take precedence over what the user may be trying to do at the time. The user indirectly initiates other types of app-initiated interactions. For example, as you will see in Chapter 17, "Back to the Storyboard: Enhancing the Interface," when a user creates a new object such as a party, it is common to immediately ask the user to provide a name for that object. The user action of creating a new object is followed by the app-initiated request for a name.

There are a variety of tools you can use to communicate with users. This chapter provides an overview of presenting information *to* the users. In Chapter 16, "Getting Input from Users: Alerts and Action Sheets," you find a discussion of the primary tools for getting information *from* users: modal views and popovers (popovers are available only on iPad).

Of course, alerts, action sheets, modal views, notifications, and badges are each different elements of the Cocoa Touch framework. Nevertheless, they are all used to implement communication with the user, and that interaction is two-way. Although a modal view may be the easiest way to get several needed items of information from a user (name, address, and phone number, for example), an alert with a brief message and a single OK button also sends data from the user to the app. The OK button sends the information that the user has seen the alert (and, presumably, has read it).

Reviewing User Interaction on iOS

iOS and its human interface guidelines dramatically changed the way people thought about and used computers. (To be fair, iOS is only one piece of a major transition to mobile computing, but, with the codification of the iOS Human Interface Guidelines, the engineers at Apple have played an outsized role in shaping expectations for the interfaces of today.)

When computers and application programs were primarily oriented to desktop and laptop computers, they were much more talkative than today's mobile apps. It was common for an app to stop and ask you if you really wanted to do something. Apps periodically informed you of what they were doing whether or not you wanted to know.

There are many reasons why this style of user interaction has fallen out of fashion (or at least is much less widely used than it was a decade or two ago). Perhaps the biggest reason for cutting down on messages from apps is the fact that today's user is likely to be multi-tasking. If you are running an enormous spreadsheet app and are sorting a spreadsheet with thousands of rows and columns, periodic updates as to progress are welcome. Without them, you sit there staring at your computer screen wondering if anything is going on. (And time is a tremendously subjective concept. When you're sitting there staring at a motionless screen, a fraction of a second can easily seem like an hour.)

On the other hand, if you start to sort your enormous spreadsheet and immediately send an email to a friend or check a restaurant review (or both), you generally rely on the fact that things will just keep working. In this type of multi-tasking environment, the user's assumption often is that things will work out and if they don't, the app will alert the user. Users don't usually expect routine updates. They expect the software to do its job.

Throughout modern interfaces including iOS, the messages from the OS are shortened. Perhaps the most significant change is in the use of alerts and other interface elements to replace dialogs on desktops and laptops. On many dialogs, users expect to see two buttons: OK and Cancel. On iOS, Cancel buttons often are not found. Tap anywhere outside the alert, and it goes away. This means that with some exceptions, a message from the OS doesn't freeze the system and demand that you answer it. Yes, you can implement this freezing functionality, but it is generally frowned upon.

If you want a general approach to designing good user interactions, don't think of them as providing information to the users. Instead, think of them as asking the users to *choose*.

Getting information is a passive activity, whereas making a choice is an active one. And, as is the case with Cancel buttons and their absence, not making a choice is a form of action. On iOS, not making a choice generally means that the user has tapped somewhere else—moved on to another action. Obviously, this has ramifications for your code. It is easier to program when you control the computer, but when you let the user control the computer, you have to work around whatever constraints the user sets up for you.

Analyzing an Alert

In the code you have seen so far based on the Master-Detail Application template, there is standard code (actually a comment) that appears in various places where the managed object context is stored.

Thinking About a Save Alert

Here is how the Save alert comment appears in `MasterViewController.m` in the set Editing: animated: method:

```
- (void)setEditing:(BOOL)editing animated:(BOOL)animated
{
    [super setEditing:editing animated:animated];

    // If editing is finished, save the managed object context
    if (!editing)
    {
        NSManagedObjectContext *context =
          self.managedObjectContext;
        NSError *error = nil;
        if (![context save:&error]){
            // Replace this implementation with code to handle the
            // error appropriately.

            // abort() causes the application to generate a crash
            // log and terminate. You should not use this function
            // in a shipping application, although it may be useful
            // during development.
            NSLog(@"Unresolved error %@, %@",
              error, [error userInfo]);
            abort();
        }
    }
}
```

How would you go about implementing the suggestions in that comment? The following sections give you some ideas.

Planning to Handle the Error

This is a good example of a message that your app will generate that is only indirectly due to a user's action. The `setEditing: animated:` message is sent to a view controller in order to change its editing state. An Edit-Done button invokes it automatically. When you are editing a view, the button title changes to Done, and the message is sent with a value of NO for `editing` (`editing` is the value to which you want to set the view controller).

Getting the User's Perspective

If an error occurs, you need to alert the user and provide a graceful way out. However, if you trace through the code, you can see that the proximate user action that indirectly causes the error if there is one, is tapping the Done button. Before you can start to work with an error, you have to perform this kind of analysis so that you (and the user) understand that although the error may be a failure to save the managed object context, the user action is tapping Done.

In fact, because it is a standard practice in iOS apps that use Core Data to save the managed object context when it is necessary (rather than asking a user to decide when to save it), it is easy to get this discontinuity. Most users probably don't even consider the fact that tapping Done invokes a Save operation on the persistent data store.

Adding the Error's Perspective

At this point, you know more than the user does—perhaps much more. The beginning of the code that handles the error contains two lines that set error handling in motion throughout Cocoa Touch apps:

```
NSError *error = nil;
if (![context save:&error]){
```

A local `NSError` variable is declared and set to `nil`. Then, a method is called that may return an error. Here is the `managedObjectContext save` method:

```
- (BOOL)save:(NSError **)error
```

Note that the `error` parameter is a pointer to a pointer to the object (that is, it has two asterisks rather than the single asterisk used for pointers to objects themselves). This means that the object that is returned in `error` can be other than the object that is passed in. In many cases where this syntax is used, the object that is passed in is nil, and the returned object is created by the method that returns it (`save` in this case).

save returns a BOOL of YES if the save is successful. If it is not successful, a value of NO is returned, and a new NSError object is created and returned in error. At this point, you can look inside the NSError object returned in error to find out more about the error. There are three properties of NSError that are important for you to use in finding out what has happened, but in practice, as you'll see in the following section, you don't have to get involved with these details.

- domain is an NSString—Domains identify the area where the error occurred. The basic domains identify the Mach core of OS X (the kernel), POSIX file routines, Carbon, and Cocoa Touch. Most of the time, you will be dealing with the Cocoa Touch domain. Additional domains can be declared by frameworks or even by developers. From your point of view, the domain rarely matters. All that matters is that there is a domain returned as a property in every NSError object.

- code is an NSInteger—Within a domain, there are numeric error codes. Thus, when you have a domain identified by the NSError object, the NSInteger for the error code has meaning. (In other words, for the error code value of 17, different domains ascribe different errors to that value.)

- userInfo is an NSDictionary—As is the case with all dictionaries, userInfo is a set of key/value pairs. In the case of an NSError object, they are used to identify the error and provide possible solutions and next steps.

Here are the parts of NSError that you deal with directly.

- localizedDescription is an NSString.

- localizedFailureReason is an NSString.

- localizedRecoveryOptions is an NSArray consisting of NSString objects. The strings are designed to be the names of buttons in an alert window that presents the error information. The first (zeroth) element should be the title of the right-most and default button; the subsequent strings are the buttons moving leftward from the default button.

- localizedRecoverySuggestion is an NSString that is suitable for the second sentence in an alert (that is, the more detailed version of the error messages).

The information is there, but, as you will see in the following section, you may not need to use it to communicate with the user. You have more specific information to pass on in many cases.

Adding Your Perspective

With the information from the NSError object, you have a great deal of information. You can use it for debugging and for communicating with the users. However, you may have more information than is needed in many cases. That's where you come in.

As you track down errors during your development process, you often need to look into the NSError objects—sometimes on a case-by-case basis. Gradually, during development, you identify and squash bugs that will not recur during production. During this process, you become more and more familiar with your software and what can go wrong. For example, in the Party Planner app as it stands now, there is a non-fatal bug that you may have discovered for yourself.

When you select an item in the master view controller, the data for that item is displayed in the detail view controller, and it is highlighted in the master view controller. When you first launch the app, no elements of the master view controller are selected. The detail view controller properly shows a placeholder message, but there are cases in which the absence of a selected object in the master view controller can cause problems. You can remedy this by either restoring the selection from the last use of the app or by arbitrarily automatically selecting the first item in the master view controller. Once you know that the absence of a selected object in the master view controller can cause problems, you can go over your code to make certain that there is always such a selected object.

It is this type of condition that is unlikely to be caught by an NSError object. You, however, understand that you built in an assumption that is not always supported in practice. What can be very important about your perspective is that you can combine the actual error information with your knowledge of the app. This means that you can set up two separate communication channels—the detailed one can go into the app's console messages, and the user-oriented channel can go to the user.

If you think of these two complementary data flows, you should recognize that the first data flow is for you, and the second is for the user. The first one may provide you with information about what to do, or it may provide you with the raw data to find that information. The flow to the user, however, should provide the critical information that the user needs to know and act on—what to do now.

What You Must Do to Handle Errors

You have seen the basic overview of handling errors that may occur. There is a great deal of information that you can use for yourself and convey—often with edits—to the users. There is one task to do now and to continue to do as you develop your app.

Any time you call a method that can return an NSError object (as shown in the code snippet at the beginning of the chapter), make certain that you handle the error. In the code sample shown here as well as in many of the Xcode templates, handling the returned error is indicated by a comment. Those comments must be heeded, and you must do something with that error information. Sometimes you can't handle the error yet because handling an error may require code you have not yet written. One habit you can get into is to insert a standard comment into your code as you encounter possible error conditions. A comment such as this will work:

```
// handle error
```

Even better is something like this

```
// handle error: no master view controller item selected
```

If you use the same comment consistently, you can search your code to find all the error messages. You can even update them as in the following:

```
// handle error: no master view controller item selected. JF done
```

Depending on how you manage the development process, you may want to delete these notes to yourself when they're done, or you may want to mark them as done—possibly with a date. You can also keep that information as comments in your Git repository. In some cases, revisions are listed in comments at the beginning of a file.

All that really matters is that these to-do items get done.

Implementing a Data Store Error Alert

With the default code you have in the template, you can experiment with alerts. Of course, you'll need an error to trigger the alert, and that requires you to actually generate an error. It's often easy enough to inadvertently trigger an error when you don't want to, but generating an error on demand can be perversely difficult. This section shows you a process that many developers use for testing. If you follow these steps, do so in a copy of your Party Planner app after you have saved the actual version in a safe place.

If you are using a source code version control system such as Git, this would be a good place to create a branch from your main code. You can then delete the branch when you're done with your experiment. Another technique is to simply compress your entire project folder into a ZIP archive. That way, you can recreate it at will. Furthermore, because it's a ZIP archive, there's little chance that you'll accidentally modify the wrong files: the project files aren't visible when they're in a ZIP archive.

Handling a Non-Error Error

One way to find and handle an error is to take the code that checks for an error, and reverse the check. Thus, the line in the template that checks to see if the BOOL result of the Save method is not YES can be reversed. Here is the template code:

```
NSManagedObjectContext *context = self.managedObjectContext;
NSError *error = nil;
if (![context save:&error]){
```

Reverse the test by removing the exclamation point that removes the NOT from the test. (You may want to comment out the old line of code so that you can revert to it later.)

```
NSManagedObjectContext *context = self.managedObjectContext;
NSError *error = nil;
if ([context save:&error]){
```

If you follow through the template code, you'll see that in the case of an error, there's a log message created; after that the app aborts.

```
NSLog(@"Unresolved error %@, %@",
        error, [error userInfo]);
abort();
```

Remove (or comment out) the abort statement. Set a breakpoint on the log message and run the app to make certain that it enters the error code, as shown in Figure 15-1.

FIGURE 15-1 Reverse the test for an error.

Step over the next line and you'll see the log message as shown in Figure 15-2.

This is fine as far as it goes, but the log message only displays the text. The NSError object and its userInfo property are both null—not unexpected because you reversed the test and the save actually succeeded. However, for testing the basic functionality of error handling, this is perhaps the fastest way to accomplish your goal.

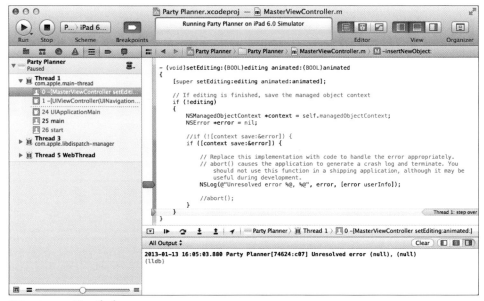

FIGURE 15-2 View the log message.

Posting the Alert

The comment in the template suggests that you deal specifically with the error, and this section shows you one way of doing so. It is the simplest to implement, but that simplicity comes at the cost of a user interface that is not as good as it can be. (Don't worry; the next chapter shows you how to refine it.)

The simplest way of communicating to the users is with an *alert,* as shown in Figure 15-3.

Until the user dismisses the alert, the app is frozen (that's the sub-optimal part of it). Furthermore, in the example shown here, this alert merely talks *to* the user: there is no option for the user to continue.

When you want to use an alert, you use an instance of `UIAlertView`. You create the instance, allocate it, initialize it, and then show it. You can do those four steps in two lines of code, but here are the steps shown individually. (The shorter version follows.)

1. Declare an `UIAlertView` instance:

    ```
    UIAlertView *alertView;
    ```

2. Allocate it:

    ```
    alertView = [UIAlertView alloc];
    ```

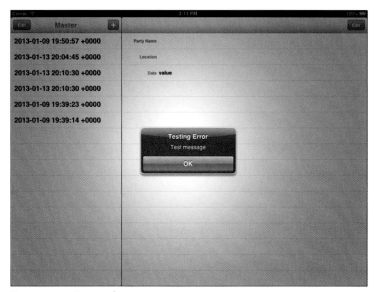

FIGURE 15-3 Post an alert.

3. Initialize it. As you can see in Figure 15-4, as you type, Xcode prompts you with the method header.

```
alertView = [alertView initWithTitle:@"Testing Error"
  message:@"Testing Message"
  delegate:nil
  cancelButtonTitle:@"OK"
  otherButtonTitles: nil];
```

4. Show the alert.

```
[alertView show];
```

Here is the two-line version:

```
UIAlertView *alertView =
  [[UIAlertView alloc]initWithTitle:@"Testing Error"
    message:@"Testing Message"
    delegate:nil
    cancelButtonTitle:@"OK"
    otherButtonTitles: nil];
[alertView show];
```

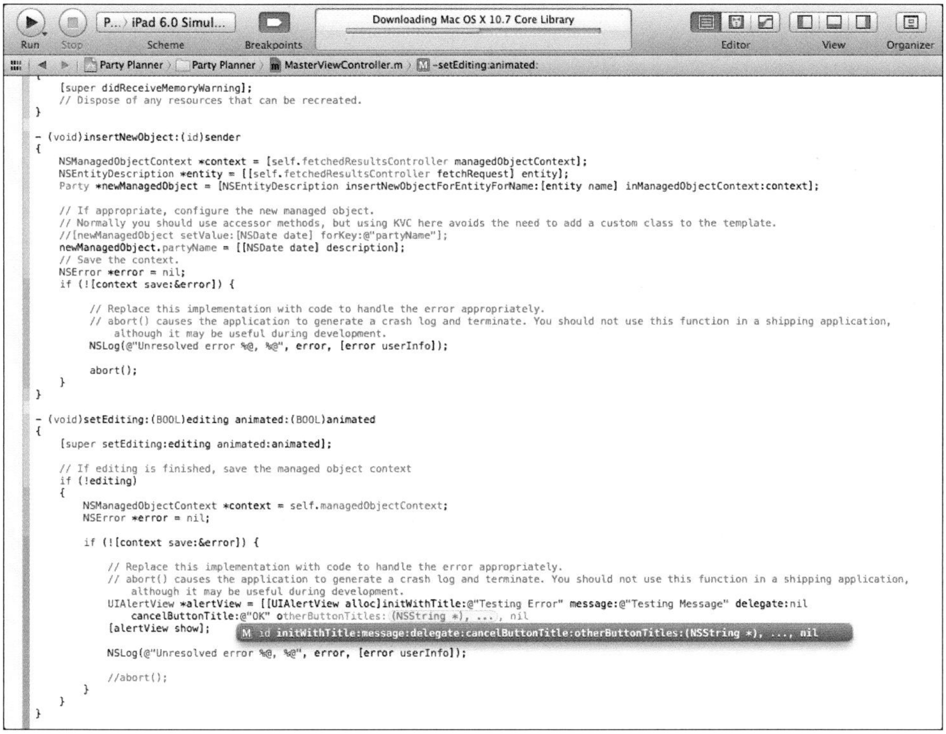

```
        [super didReceiveMemoryWarning];
        // Dispose of any resources that can be recreated.
    }

    - (void)insertNewObject:(id)sender
    {
        NSManagedObjectContext *context = [self.fetchedResultsController managedObjectContext];
        NSEntityDescription *entity = [[self.fetchedResultsController fetchRequest] entity];
        Party *newManagedObject = [NSEntityDescription insertNewObjectForEntityForName:[entity name] inManagedObjectContext:context];

        // If appropriate, configure the new managed object.
        // Normally you should use accessor methods, but using KVC here avoids the need to add a custom class to the template.
        //[newManagedObject setValue:[NSDate date] forKey:@"partyName"];
        newManagedObject.partyName = [[NSDate date] description];
        // Save the context.
        NSError *error = nil;
        if (![context save:&error]) {

            // Replace this implementation with code to handle the error appropriately.
            // abort() causes the application to generate a crash log and terminate. You should not use this function in a shipping application,
            //     although it may be useful during development.
            NSLog(@"Unresolved error %@, %@", error, [error userInfo]);

            abort();
        }
    }

    - (void)setEditing:(BOOL)editing animated:(BOOL)animated
    {
        [super setEditing:editing animated:animated];

        // If editing is finished, save the managed object context
        if (!editing)
        {
            NSManagedObjectContext *context = self.managedObjectContext;
            NSError *error = nil;

            if (![context save:&error]) {

                // Replace this implementation with code to handle the error appropriately.
                // abort() causes the application to generate a crash log and terminate. You should not use this function in a shipping application,
                //     although it may be useful during development.
                UIAlertView *alertView = [[UIAlertView alloc]initWithTitle:@"Testing Error" message:@"Testing Message" delegate:nil
                    cancelButtonTitle:@"OK" otherButtonTitles:(NSString *), ..., nil
                [alertView show];      M id initWithTitle:message:delegate:cancelButtonTitle:otherButtonTitles:(NSString *), ..., nil

                NSLog(@"Unresolved error %@, %@", error, [error userInfo]);

                //abort();
            }
        }
    }
```

FIGURE 15-4 Xcode prompts you with the method header.

Adding a Log Message

No matter what type of user message you use, you typically write a companion message to
the log. This is critical during your development process when you are running on the simulator. When you move to production, you often remove these messages for apps. When you
are building an app for a non-public purpose (such as an in-house app), you may leave log
messages in. Also you may have the ability to send messages to a corporate web service where
they can be logged.

Now that you have seen the structure of the NSError object, you can examine the message
that writes it out to the log. NSLog takes a format string followed by a comma-delimited list
of items to be written out according to the format string. Here is the code in the template:

```
NSLog(@"Unresolved error %@, %@", error, [error userInfo]);
```

The format string consists of these items:

- `Unresolved error` is text that is displayed as entered.
- `%@` displays the description of an `NSObject`—there are two of these.

Following the string are two objects that correspond to the `%@` formats:

- `error` is the `NSInteger` error code in the `NSError` object.
- `userInfo` is the dictionary returned in the `NSError` object. All of its key/value pairs will be displayed.

Summary

This chapter shows you how to handle the simplest error condition: one in which you alert the user to something that has happened. It is the simplest form of communication, and, partly because of that, it is the most blunt instrument you can use to communicate with the user. You have seen how to use the `NSError` object, which provides information about the error that has occurred, and you have seen how to extract the numeric error code and user dictionary of all items returned from the error.

In the next chapter, you'll learn about more complex ways of communicating with users. They're a bit more trouble for you, but they're much easier for the users. The alerts shown in this chapter freeze the app in place, thus preventing anything else from happening until the alert is dismissed. In the next chapter, you'll see how to use multiple buttons to dismiss and alert and how to use action sheets. In all of these cases, this will mean that rather than telling the users what has gone wrong, you'll be able to offer the user actions to take to ameliorate or work around the problems.

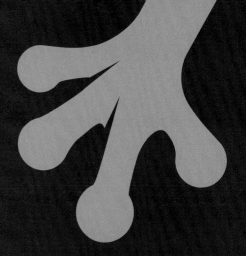

chapter sixteen

Getting Input from Users: Alerts and Action Sheets

PROVIDING INFORMATION TO users about what's happening with your app is an important part of the user experience. As pointed out in Chapter 15, "Telling Users the News: Alerts and NSError," software in general is much less talkative and verbose than it used to be. In part this is because software, computers, and users are all more sophisticated about what's going on. No longer do you need to ask a user to confirm every little step in a process because you and the user can more frequently assume—correctly—that things have gone as planned.

When you do need to notify the user of some issue, an alert is a blunt-force tool. It brings the app to a halt until the user dismisses it. In this chapter, you'll begin to learn about the more flexible tools for communicating with the users. Rather than use the simple alert discussed in the previous chapter and shown in Figure 16-1, you'll see how you can allow the user to communicate to you.

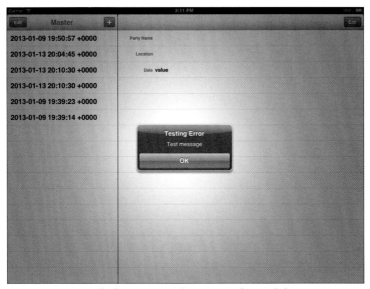

FIGURE 16-1 A simple alert presents information with a single button.

The basic tools are:

- **Alerts with multiple buttons**—As soon as the user can choose between more than one button, you have provided a communication channel from the user to the app as shown in Figure 16-2. With one button, the only communication is that the user has seen the alert, but now the user is empowered to make a choice and take an action.

FIGURE 16-2 Alerts can have multiple buttons.

- **Action sheets**—These dispense with the alert text: they consist only of a title and a set of buttons, as shown in Figure 16-3. The buttons have to be self-explanatory.

FIGURE 16-3 Action sheets consist only of actions.

- **Modal views**—These are standard views that are presented modally. The layout of text, images, and user interface controls is up to you.

In all of these cases, you get information back from the user. In the case of alerts, the communication is often initiated by the app after something untoward has happened. With action sheets and modal views, it is commonly the case that the user has tapped a control to initiate the conversation (creating a new email message, exporting data to a destination to be determined by an action sheet, and so forth).

Using Modes on iOS

One of the guidelines developers for the original Mac were advised to adopt was to minimize the use of *modes*—separate parts of a program with their own rules and even functionality. In the mid-1980s, one of the complaints most often voiced about personal computers was that it was too easy to fall into a mode from which you could not escape. Worse, you might not even realize that you were in a mode that, not unlike a science fiction device, altered the environmental rules (for example, making it impossible to close a window).

Nevertheless, modes—and particularly modal dialogs—are an important tool. Yes, they put the user into a place from which only escape is possible (perhaps by clicking OK or Cancel), but sometimes you want the user to do nothing except handle that issue.

continued

continued

This need to stop the user from doing anything except handle a specific issue is a valid need at times, and it is in this context that modes are frequently overused. You should consider whether there is some other way to handle the issue.

In fact, the human interface guidelines recommend the use of modal views in a very specific case. One guideline is that there should be a single path to each view. If you have a view that is presented in a number of different contexts, it often is preferable to present it either modally or in one of the alert or action sheet styles. That separates it from the uniquely locatable main content of your app.

As you'll see in this chapter, alerts and modal views behave similarly on iPhone and iPad. Action sheets, however, behave differently on iPhone and iPad. On iPhone, they are typically placed at the bottom of the screen, while on iPad, they are displayed in a popover.

Using Alerts with Multiple Buttons

In Chapter 15, you learned the basics of a one-button alert. The first step to making your alerts more useful to users (and, thus, to you) is to allow multiple buttons to be used. This means that rather than presenting information to the user and asking the user to click a button which can only signify that the alert has been presented, you can ask the user to make a decision—continue with an action or stop it, for example.

Adding the Buttons

Most developers and users probably would suggest that whenever you leave a choice to a user, the app is more useful. Of course, when you leave a choice to a user, you have the responsibility to explain what that choice is. A choice such as "denormalize the database" or "invert the data matrix" is not particularly user-friendly. What you may find is that coming up with the wording of the choice that you present takes a good deal of time, but it also helps you understand the user and the app.

Listing 16-1 shows the code you used in Chapter 15 to present an alert.

Listing 16-1   Showing an alert

```
UIAlertView *alertView =
  [[UIAlertView alloc]initWithTitle:@"Testing Error"
    message:@"Testing Message"
    delegate:nil
```

```
    cancelButtonTitle:@"OK"
    otherButtonTitles: nil];
[alertView show];
```

The otherButtonTitles parameter appears to be set to nil. However, if you look in the documentation, you'll see that otherButtonTitles is actually a list of button titles that is terminated by nil. (A function that accepts a variable number of arguments is called a *variadic function*. This is a broad computer science concept and in Objective-C, it applies both to functions and to methods.) To add two additional buttons to the alert view, provide the following list:

```
otherButtonTitles: @"Cancel", @"Info", nil
```

The result is shown in Figure 16-2.

Handling the Buttons

If you run the app and get into the alert code (remember the simplest way is to make the test trigger if there is no error), you'll see that any of the buttons dismisses the alert. (Do remember for your testing to comment out the abort() call.)

You have to figure out how to determine which button was tapped before the alert disappears.

Once again, a delegate object is used. This delegate adopts the UIAlertViewDelegate protocol. As always with a protocol, the object that adopts the protocol must implement all required methods, but how it does so is up to the object that adopts the protocol.

In the case of the UIAlertViewDelegate protocol, all of the methods are optional. The one that is most frequently used is

```
- (void)alertView:(UIAlertView *)alertView
    clickedButtonAtIndex:(NSInteger)buttonIndex
```

Here are the steps for implementing the delegate. It is common for the object that poses the alert view to name itself as the delegate.

1. In MasterViewController.h, add the UIAlertViewDelegate protocol to the class declaration as in the following code:

   ```
   @interface MasterViewController : UITableViewController
       <NSFetchedResultsControllerDelegate, UIAlertViewDelegate>
   ```

2. You can reuse the `setEditing: animated:` method to show an alert view, as you see in this annotated code.

```objc
- (void)setEditing: (BOOL)editing animated:(BOOL)animated
{
  [super setEditing: editing animated:animated];

  // If editing is finished, save the managed object context
  if (!editing)
    {
      NSManagedObjectContext *context = self.
        managedObjectContext;

      NSError *error = nil;

      // reverse this line by removing ! for testing
      if ([context save:&error]){
      // if (![context save:&error]){ -- unreversed line
      // Replace this implementation with code to handle the
      // error appropriately.
      // abort() causes the application to generate a crash
      // log and terminate. You should not use this function in
      // a shipping application, although it may be useful
      // during development.

      // Experiment with alert view
      UIAlertView *alertView = [[UIAlertView alloc]
        initWithTitle:@"Testing Error" message:@"Testing
        Message"
        delegate:self
        cancelButtonTitle:@"OK"
        otherButtonTitles: @"Cancel", @"Info", nil];
      [alertView show];

      // NSLog (@"Unresolved error %@ %@", error, [error
      // userInfo]);
      //abort(); comment out for testing
      }
    }
}
```

3. Implement any of the protocol methods. As noted previously, the most common one simply responds to a tap. Here it is:

```
- (void)alertView:(UIAlertView *)alertView
    clickedButtonAtIndex:(NSInteger)buttonIndex
{
  // set a breakpoint here for testing
  // check the value of buttonIndex to determine what to do
}
```

4. Run the app and observe the values that are shown in the debugger. (Remember that if you have followed the code example shown here, the Done button will cause the alert to be shown.) You'll see that the bottom-most button (`cancelButtonTitle` or OK in this case) is always zero. Numbering then resumes with 1 on the top-most button (Cancel in this case) and continues down the buttons (Info is 2 in this case).

You can do any processing you want in this method. The alert is dismissed automatically after you exit the delegate method. There is no `dismiss` method to call.

Using Action Sheets

Action sheets provide a set of buttons for user choices. Particularly on iPhone, they look a bit like multi-button alerts without the alert message. However, their behavior is different in some important ways. In this section, the alert view shown in the previous section is turned into an action sheet. (You'll see the code later in this section.)

Looking at Action Sheets

Recall that Figure 16-3 showed an action sheet on an iPad with a split view controller in landscape mode. Figure 16-4 shows the same action sheet on an iPad in portrait mode.

If you compare Figure 16-3 with Figure 16-4, you may well wonder if there's a mistake: they look different. Specifically, there's a Cancel button in Figure 16-4 and there is none in Figure 16-3. You specify a Cancel button title when you create an action sheet. When the action sheet is displayed on an iPad in landscape mode, it is centered on the screen. Its behavior is like that of a popover—tapping anywhere except inside the popover dismisses it. Thus, there's no need for a Cancel button.

When an action sheet is displayed on an iPhone or an iPad in portrait mode, the Cancel button is displayed and its behavior is needed because tapping anywhere outside the action sheet has no effect: it's a *modal* presentation.

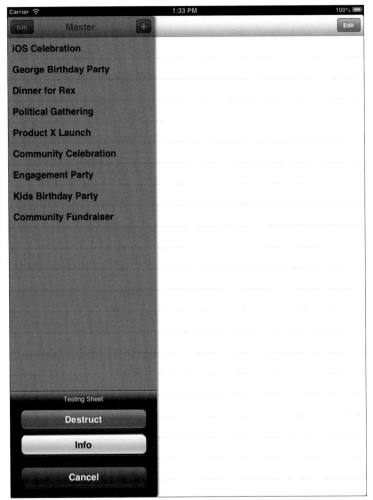

FIGURE 16-4 Action sheets display differently in portrait mode than in landscape mode on iPad.

Managing Action Sheets

Action sheets are handled in much the same way as alerts. You implement a delegate that adopts the `UIActionSheetDelegate` protocol. Here are the steps for implementing the delegate and using it. As with alerts, it is common for the object that poses the alert view to name itself as the delegate.

1. In `MasterViewController.h`, add the `UIActionSheetDelegate` protocol to the class declaration as in the following code:

```
@interface MasterViewController : UITableViewController
    <NSFetchedResultsControllerDelegate, UIActionSheetDelegate >
```

2. Implement any of the protocol methods. The most common one simply responds to a tap. It is similar to the method shown previously in Figure 16-2. Just as you did there, you may want to implement a shell of the method and place a breakpoint in it.

```
- (void)actionSheet:(UIAlertView *)actionSheet
    clickedButtonAtIndex:(NSInteger)buttonIndex
{

}
```

3. Use a variation of the alert code shown previously in Listing 16-1 to create and show the action sheet.

```
UIActionSheet *actionSheet = [[UIActionSheet alloc]
                                initWithTitle:@"Testing Sheet"
                                delegate:self
                                cancelButtonTitle:@"Cancel"
                                destructiveButtonTitle:@"Destruct"
                                otherButtonTitles:@"Info", nil];
[actionSheet showInView:self.view];
```

This produces the results shown previously in Figures 16-3 and 16-4.

Two points are worth nothing. First, there is still a nil-terminated list of button titles. In addition, two special buttons are called out: a Cancel button and a destructive button. In practical terms, Cancel is the bottom button on iPhone or on a landscape mode iPad with a split view controller.

The destructive button may or may not be destructive in the sense of destroying data. What it definitely is—on both iPhone and iPad—is red so that it warns the user that something serious will happen if it's tapped. Either of these special buttons may be set to nil.

4. As before, place a breakpoint in the delegate code and run the app. Observe the values that are shown in the debugger. You'll see that the buttons are 0 for the destructive button, 1 to whatever for the other buttons, and the final number (2 in this case) for the bottom Cancel button on iPhone.

You can do any processing you want in this method. The alert is dismissed automatically after you have finished your work.

Summary

Chapter 15 showed you how to talk to your users, and this chapter has shown you how to receive information from them. There still is plenty to talk about in terms of the user interface. There are many ways to present views to users and many ways to have interface elements present those views. There is more to say on popovers, and much to say on modal views. You are not limited to the brief messages and limited space for buttons on alert views and action sheets.

You already have used the tool that lets you link interface elements to one another and to your code: the storyboard. In the next chapter, you'll see how to return to your storyboard editing to implement more sophisticated data entry tools for users.

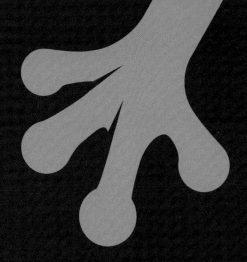

chapter seventeen

Back to the Storyboard: Enhancing the Interface

YOUR DEVELOPMENT OF the Party Planner app began in Chapter 5, "Walking Through the iPhone Storyboard" as you explored and then enhanced the storyboard in the Master-Detail Application template. Storyboards appeared for the first time in iOS 5; in iOS 6 they were dramatically refined and enhanced. Along the way, the engineers at Apple also implemented new features and concepts such as container views (they existed all along, but the explicit concept and the details of which container view class can appear in another container view class arrived in iOS 5).

After an overview of the Xcode templates, this chapter shows you how to work with the template interface elements to add buttons and other controls. These elements allow you to implement additional functionality in the Party Planner app.

Cleaning Up Some Loose Ends

In Chapters 15, "Telling Users the News: Alerts and NSError," and 16, "Getting Input from Users: Alerts and Action Sheets," you experimented with user interaction tools and techniques. To continue on with the Party Planner app, start from a copy of the version of Party Planner that you created (or downloaded) at the end of Chapter 14, "Editing Table Views." Test it to make certain that it works as it did then. You'll be adding some new features and functionality in this chapter, so make certain you're starting from a known app.

Setting Up New Objects

There are a few changes you may want to make at this time before you get started. In `MasterViewController.m`, you may still have these lines of code to set the name for a new object:

```
// If appropriate, configure the new managed object.
// Normally you should use accessor methods, but using KVC here
// avoids the need to add a custom class to the template.
// [newManagedObject setValue:[NSDate date] forKey:@"partyName"];

newManagedObject.partyName = [[NSDate date] description];
```

You can get rid of unnecessary lines and create a better default name for new party objects with this code:

```
// If appropriate, configure the new managed object.
// Normally you should use accessor methods, but using KVC here

newManagedObject.partyName = @"New Party"];
```

Using Storyboards Today

For many developers today, storyboards are the heart of the development process. They let you create a draft of an interface that can help to document your ideas both for yourself, other developers, potential funders and managers, and even for end users. (In this way storyboards for iOS function very much the same way as storyboards for movies, commercials, and video games.) The storyboard provides the structure of the interface; you can extend and customize it with a variety of options for the storyboard elements as well as by subclassing the various user interface objects that become part of your storyboard.

As you have implemented new features and functionality in the Party Planner app, you may have come to understand how you work with the Cocoa Touch frameworks. A single feature often consists of several components that may be a subclass of a framework object here, an option in a different object there, and perhaps a segue on the storyboard that sets things in motion. The days of writing line after line of computer code are far behind us.

What is also behind us is the pre-storyboard development process on iOS. The built-in Xcode templates give you powerful starting points for your apps. (Chapter 4, "Designing the Party Planner App," contains a list of the templates.) Over the last few versions of iOS and Xcode, both the IDE and the OS have been refined; at the same time, developers and users have explored new features and functionality with iOS devices. What is now available in Cocoa Touch, Xcode, and, particularly, in the Xcode templates is a more mature environment than was available several years ago. It's worthwhile to keep in mind that the iPhone first shipped in June of 2007 and the iPad first shipped in April of 2010. They are still remarkably new.

For many developers, the templates provide a ready-to-use shell of an app. There is no question that advanced developers today often build their own navigation interfaces or tab bar controllers, but many developers use the interfaces that are built into the templates. Those templates also provide built-in navigation bars (and sometimes toolbars). These are sitting there just waiting for you to add your own interface controls.

Many long-time iOS developers could tell you that you start your iOS app development from an Xcode template several weeks ahead of where they were used to starting a few years ago. You have seen the Master-Detail Application template; this section explores the Tabbed Application and Utility Application templates. The focus is on those aspects of the interface that you can use in your own apps. There also are some tips on the differences in interface design between iPhone and iPad. Later in this chapter, you'll see how to put these into practice.

Using the Utility Application Template

This template provides two view controllers. As you can see in Figure 17-1, on iPhone, they appear to be the front and back of a single object. Note that the template has been modified with some additional interface elements from the library so that you can get an idea of how you can work with the template.

In Figure 17-2, you see the iPad version.

FIGURE 17-1 The Utility Application template on iPhone.

FIGURE 17-2 The Utility Application template on iPad.

Figure 17-3 shows the iPhone storyboard.

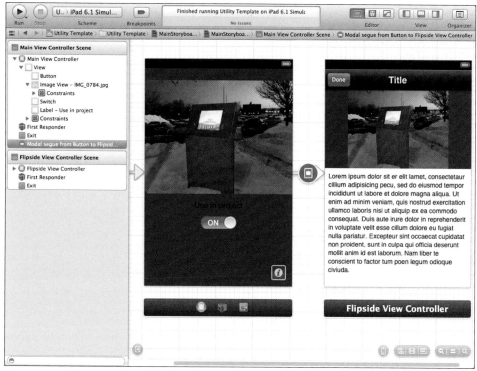

FIGURE 17-3 iPhone storyboard for the Utility Application template.

Figure 17-4 shows the iPad storyboard.

Figures 17-1 through 17-4 show one of the City of Plattsburgh's PlattInfo kiosks. PlattInfo is a network of walk-up touch-screen kiosks powered by FileMaker. Jesse Feiler is Software Architect for PlattInfo. PlattInfo artwork by Kelly Chilton (hey@kellychilton.com or www.kellychilton.com). You can find out more about PlattInfo at PlattInfo.com.

Even without seeing the names of the two views (main view and flipside view), there's little doubt as to which is the subsidiary view. On iPhone, the button in the lower right of the main view with the italicized i flips the view over. In the navigation bar on the flipside view, there's a Done button that flips the view back to the main view with the italicized i button in the lower right. It's little touches like this that help the user navigate. The Done button suggests that that view is transient. On iPad, it is shown in a popover.

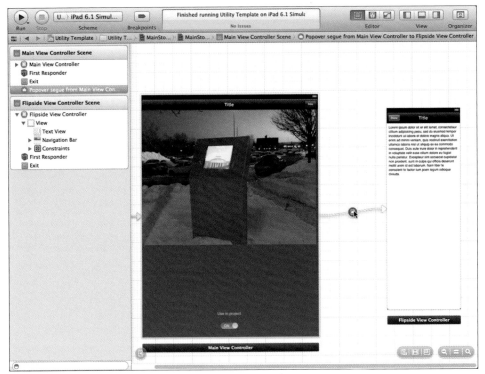

FIGURE 17-4 iPad storyboard for the Utility Application template.

Note that on iPad there are navigation bars on both views; on iPhone, there's no navigation bar on the main view. Space is so precious on the iPhone that using the i in the lower right is a better choice than a navigation bar—particularly one that exists only to put a single button on it.

Comparing iPad and iPhone Interfaces

In the Utility Application template, you can see that the interfaces differ between iPad and iPhone. The idea of a two-sided view fits well onto the small screen of an iPhone. Each "side" of the view logically is the same size as the other side. (You can refer to this as a *visual metaphor* if you want.) When you move to the larger screen of iPad, you can display much more information on the screen. Thus, in the iPad version of the template, instead of two equal-sized views, you have a larger primary view and a smaller view that is shown in a popover at the upper right. The idea of multiple views using popover or split view controllers is possible on iPad and, in fact, it is a very powerful tool for you to use.

Using the Tabbed Application Template

The Tabbed Application template illustrates another way of handling multiple views. They are controlled from a tab bar at the bottom of the view. Figure 17-5 shows the iPad version.

FIGURE 17-5 The Tabbed Application template on iPad.

Figure 17-6 shows the iPhone version.

You can see that on iPhone there is no bar at the top: the full screen is available for use. Of course, there is a trade-off: the tabs at the bottom take up space. Tabs let users switch between different perspectives on data. Unlike navigation bars or toolbars, they are used only to select which of several views is shown.

In Figure 17-7, you can see the document outline of the iPad version. Note that in the document outline, you can see that in the first view there's a toolbar and in the second view there's a navigation bar. Navigation bars implement the stack behavior of pushing and popping views. They also have a fairly structured layout for the buttons. Toolbars are much less structured. If you have a bar that requires a number of buttons, it usually works best as a toolbar.

FIGURE 17-6 The Tabbed Application template on iPhone.

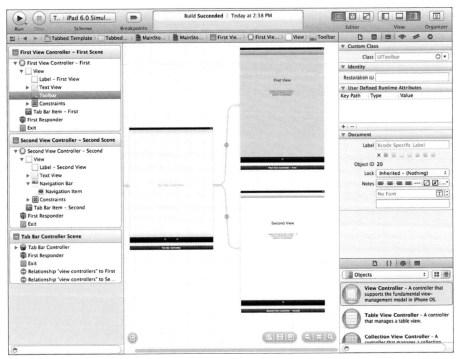

FIGURE 17-7 Look at the document outline for iPad.

Editing Basic Party Data

Now you can address the main point of this chapter: entering and saving data in your Party Planner app. As you'll see, you'll use interface elements and controls such as the ones you have seen in the figures of this chapter. As a first step consider Figure 17-8: it allows you to edit the basic party data.

FIGURE 17-8 Edit the basic party data.

What you're seeing in Figure 17-8 is a *modal view* presented in the *form* style. Modal means that the view controller stays there until it is somehow removed programmatically: there is no close box or button for the users.

This may sound strange when you can see both a Save and Cancel button in the navigation bar, but the point is that those are *bar button items* just like the Done buttons in Figures 17-1, 17-2, and 17-3. Bar button items are special types of buttons designed for use in a navigation bar or toolbar. They are linked to actions in your code, and it is those actions that dismiss the modal view. The modal view is removed programmatically, and it's your code (not framework code) that does that.

Reusing the Basic Detail Data Code

In many ways, the contents of the modal view may remind you of Figure 10-1, which is reproduced here as Figure 17-9.

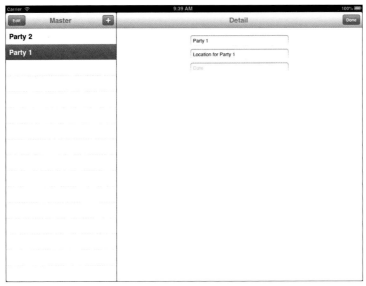

FIGURE 17-9 This example reuses the Chapter 10 view.

This is the version of the app from Chapter 10, "Saving and Restoring Data," before you added the table view interface. The table view interface is an excellent way to manage and display data, but when you want to update the data, sometimes the view in Figures 17-8 or 17-9 is best. Reusing the view from Chapter 10 can save you time and effort; it also provides a good illustration of how storyboards can make your life easier.

What you can do is to add a detail disclosure accessory to a table cell that displays data. That accessory will bring up an editable view that uses individual text fields, as is the case in Figures 17-8 and 17-9. You can use the technique described here to bring up separate views for each field or you can bring up an editable view that combines several fields—the techniques are the same. You'll also see how to use a variation of this technique to handle the related records for menus and guests.

Basically, what you can do is to take the existing storyboard and add the `DetailView Controller` from Chapter 10 to it so that it is displayed as a modal view. The only issue that you have is that you already have a `DetailViewController`. What you'll do in the following steps is copy Chapter 10's `DetailViewController` and rename it `Editable DetailViewController`. Then you'll add it to the project and the storyboard.

1. Copy the `DetailViewController.h` and `DetailViewController.m` files from your copy of the Chapter 10 project or from the downloadable code. Place them in their own folder somewhere on your computer.

2. Open them in Xcode.

3. Close any open projects and other files. The only files you want open are these two.

4. In the Search navigator, search for `DetailViewController`. There should be six occurrences.

5. In the Search navigator, switch to Replace and choose to replace all six occurrences with `EditableDetailViewController`, as shown in Figure 17-10.

   Note that normally when you rename an object you use Edit➡Refactor➡Rename. That doesn't work in this case because you want to make the change only in these two files.

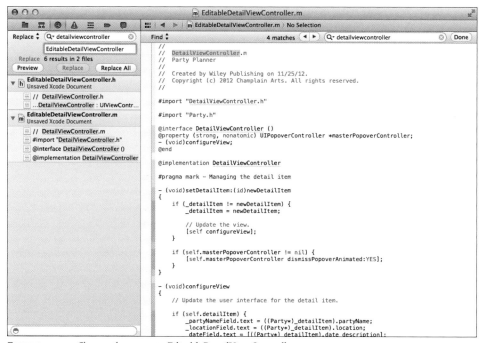

FIGURE 17-10 Change the name to EditableDetailViewController.

6. Verify the changes, and then close and save the files.

7. Rename the files `EditableDetailViewController.h` and `EditableDetail ViewController.m`.

8. Launch Xcode and open your Party Planner project.

9. Use File➡Add Files to add these renamed files back to your Party Planner project, as shown in Figure 17-11. Make sure to copy them into the destination and add them to your target (see the checkboxes at the bottom of the sheet in Figure 17-11).

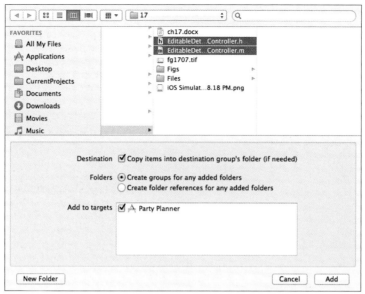

FIGURE 17-11 Add the renamed files.

10. Verify that the files are in the project. You can now delete the renamed files.

Editing the Storyboard

Now that you have the `EditableDetailViewController` class in your project you can create an instance in your storyboard. Here are the steps to do so:

1. Drag a view controller from the library onto the iPad storyboard. In previous examples you've started with the iPhone storyboard, so this gives the iPad storyboard equal time.

2. In the Identity inspector, change its class to `EditableDetailViewController`.

3. Select the existing `DetailViewController`, as shown in Figure 17-12. Position the new `EditableDetailViewController` to its right.

4. Add three text fields that will be connected to the `dateField`, `locationField`, and `partyNameField` properties in `EditableDetailViewController`. (The properties should be there already in the file that you copied. This is described in Chapter 9, "Building the Detail Data View.")

5. Control-drag in the document outline to connect the `EditableDetailView Controller` to each of the three text fields in turn, as shown in Figure 17-13.

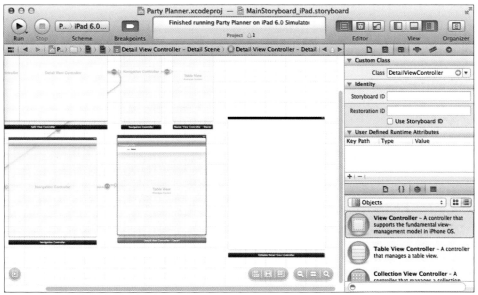

FIGURE 17-12 Add a view controller.

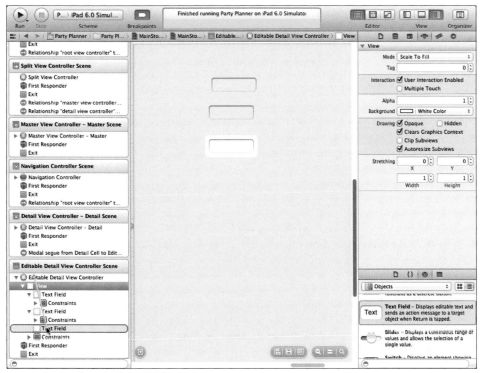

FIGURE 17-13 Connect the text fields.

6. As you connect each one, set its label. A good convention would be to change the label of the text field that's connected to `dateField` to `editableDateField`.

7. Control-click on `EditableDetailViewController` in the document outline to review its outlets. If any stray connections are left over from the previous incarnation of this file, remove them so that only the text fields in this new view are referenced. Figure 17-14 shows what the connections should look like now.

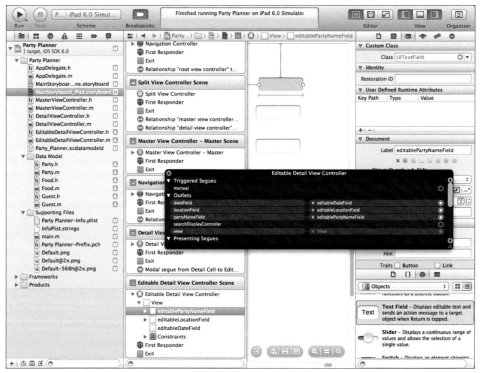

FIGURE 17-14 Update the connections.

8. Add labels next to the text fields or set their placeholder text in the Attributes inspector so that people know what data goes where.

9. In order to get to the new `EditableDetailViewController`, add a detail disclosure accessory to the prototype cell on the `DetailViewController`, as shown in

Figure 17-15. Select the prototype cell (there's only one at this point), and set its accessory to Detail Disclosure.

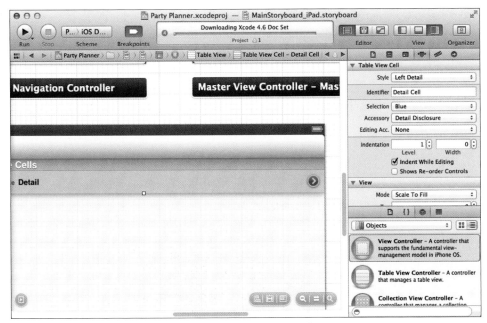

FIGURE 17-15 Add a detail disclosure accessory to the prototype cell.

10. Command-drag from the detail disclosure accessory to the new `EditableDetail ViewController`. This will create a segue. Select the segue and set its values using the Attributes inspector, as shown in Figure 17-16. The values should be:

- **Identifier**—`editableDetailsSegue`
- **Style**—`Modal`
- **Presentation**—`Form Sheet`
- **Transition**—`Default`

11. Use the Animates checkbox.

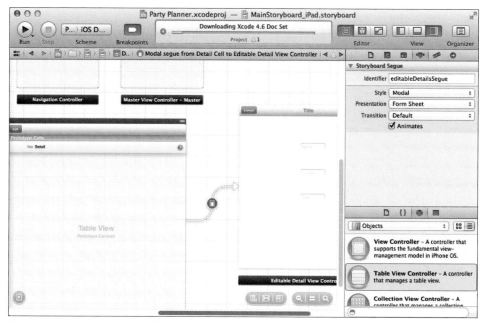

FIGURE 17-16 Connect the detail disclosure accessory to the editable view.

Adding the Segue to the Code

You use segues in storyboards to describe the transition from one view controller to another graphically. Almost all the time, you match the storyboard segue to code that handles the data side of that transition. That code normally appears in `prepareForSegue: sender:` for the view controller that initiates the segue (the `sender`).

You saw this in `MasterViewController` where `prepareForSegue: sender` was used to move the managed object context and the detail item itself to the destination view controller. Along the way, you typically coerce the segue's source and destination view controllers to your subclasses of `UIViewController`. Also, to make this work, you typically import the `.h` files for your subclasses.

Here's the code from `MasterViewController`. It's for comparison only—it's already in your project.

```
- (void)prepareForSegue:(UIStoryboardSegue *)segue sender:(id)
  sender
{
  if ([[segue identifier] isEqualToString:@"showDetail"]) {
    NSIndexPath *indexPath = [self.tableView
      indexPathForSelectedRow];
```

```
NSManagedObject *object = [[self fetchedResultsController]
   objectAtIndexPath:indexPath];
[[segue destinationViewController]
   setDetailItem:(Party*)object];
if ([[UIDevice currentDevice] userInterfaceIdiom] !=
   UIUserInterfaceIdiomPad) {
      self.detailViewController = (DetailViewController*)[segue
         destinationViewController];
   self.detailViewController.managedObjectContext =
      self.managedObjectContext;
   }
  }
}
```

For the segue from `DetailViewController` to `EditableDetailViewController`,
which you just added, add this line at the top of `DetailViewController.m`.

```
#import "EditableDetailViewController.h"
```

Now add the `prepareForSegue: sender:` method to `DetailViewController.m`.

```
- (void)prepareForSegue:(UIStoryboardSegue *)
                  segue sender:(id)sender {
  if ([[segue identifier] isEqualToString:
    @"editableDetailsSegue"]) {
      ((EditableDetailViewController*)segue.
        destinationViewController).managedObjectContext =
      ((DetailViewController*)segue.sourceViewController).
        managedObjectContext;
      ((EditableDetailViewController*)segue.
        destinationViewController).detailItem =
      ((DetailViewController*)segue.sourceViewController).
        detailItem;
   }
}
```

Adding the Navigation Bar and Buttons

You'll want a navigation bar with Save and Cancel buttons at the top of your view, as shown
previously in Figure 17-8. Here are the steps to add the navigation bar and the buttons:

1. Make certain that `EditableDetailViewController` is centered in the storyboard.

2. You have to enlarge the view so that it is full size in order to add the navigation bar.

3. From the library, drag a navigation bar to the top of `EditableDetailView` `Controller` and place it all the way to the left (it should snap into place). You may need to do this in two steps: first drag it to the top of the view, and then move it to be flush with the left edge. The size of your computer display and the mouse/trackpad parameters as well as your finger dexterity will determine whether it's one step or two.

4. Add a bar button item from the library to the left side of the navigation bar (it will snap into place).

5. With the button selected, set its identifier to Cancel in the Attributes inspector, as shown in Figure 17-17.

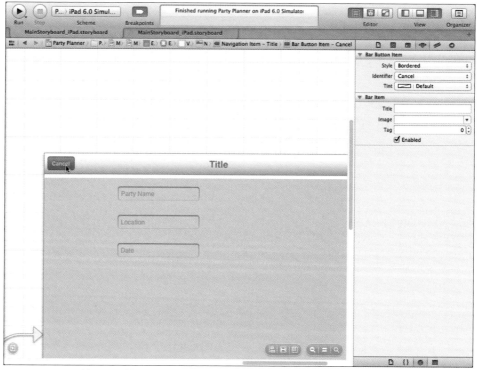

FIGURE 17-17 Add a Cancel button at the left.

6. Similarly, add another button to the right side of the navigation bar and set its identifier to Save.

7. Using the assistant editor, make certain that the storyboard and `EditableDetail` `View.h` are both visible.

8. Control-drag from the Cancel button to the interface. You'll be given a choice of creating an outlet, an outlet collection, or an action, as shown in Figure 17-18.

9. Use the pop-up menu to select Action, and then name it `cancel` (remember that method names are always lowercase). Figure 17-19 shows the interface.

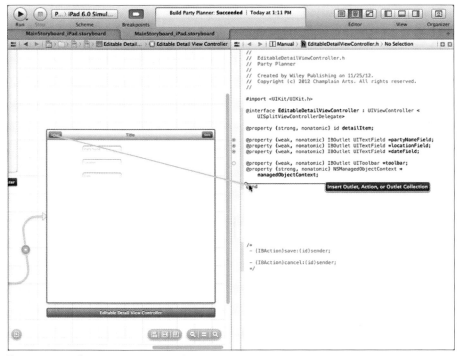

FIGURE 17-18 Start to create a new action.

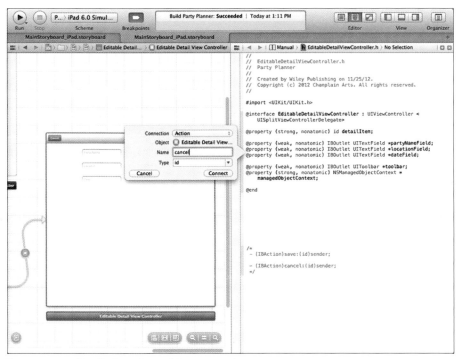

FIGURE 17-19 Specify the action and its name.

10. Similarly, create a save method.

11. In EditableDetailView.m, you'll see the shells of these two methods (they should be at the bottom of the file). Add the code shown here to those method shells. Note that they are identical except that save calls setEditing: animated:.

```
- (IBAction)cancel:(id)sender {
    [self.presentingViewController
        dismissViewControllerAnimated:YES completion:NULL];
}

- (IBAction)save:(id)sender {
    [self setEditing: NO animated:YES];
    [self.presentingViewController
        dismissViewControllerAnimated:YES completion:NULL];
}
```

Handling the Date Field

There's just one more thing to do. All along, that date field has been conspicuous by not being used. It's time to use it.

The reason that the date field requires special handling is that the field in the data model is a date field, and the field in the interface is a text field. You'll need to convert the string that's in the text field to a date and vice versa. As is so often the case with Cocoa and Cocoa Touch frameworks, decades (literally) of use has given rise to a large number of utility classes and methods. One such class is NSDateFormatter. Its job is to convert strings to dates and dates to strings while applying various formatting techniques. The full documentation is quite extensive, but you can use the code shown here without modification (except for the name of the text field and the name of the Core Data field).

Converting the Text Field String to a Date

This conversion is needed in EditableDetailViewController.m in setEditing: animated:. There is already code there from DetailViewController. Find the section of code that moves the contents of the text fields to the Party object:

```
((Party*)_detailItem).partyName = _partyNameField.text;
((Party*)_detailItem).location = _locationField.text;
```

Now, create a date formatter and use it to convert the text field to a date:

```
NSDateFormatter *dateFormat = [[NSDateFormatter alloc] init];
[dateFormat setDateFormat: @"MM dd yyyy"];
```

```
NSDate* date = [dateFormat dateFromString:_dateField.text];

((Party*)_detailItem).date = date;
```

As noted, you can use and reuse this code; just change the name of the text field and the name of the property. Also note that the formatting string is used precisely, so if you want slashes or hyphens in it, include them in the string.

Converting a Date to a Text Field String

The reverse transformation needs to take place in `DetailViewController.m` because that's where the data is displayed in the detail view. The code is in `configureCell: atIndexPath:`. Look for this code:

```
case 1:
  {
    cell.textLabel.text = @"Location";
    cell.detailTextLabel.text =[_detailItem.location description];
  }
break;
```

Now, rewrite case 2 to match the following code. Note that you'll need to make this case into a block with the brackets to avoid a compiler error. Some people simply use the brackets for all case statements. Remember that the date format delimiters (be they spaces, hyphens, or anything else) must match the data string.

```
case 2:
  {
    cell.textLabel.text = @"Date";
    NSDateFormatter *dateFormat = [[NSDateFormatter alloc] init];
    [dateFormat setDateFormat: @"MM dd yyyy"];
    cell.detailTextLabel.text = [dateFormat
      stringFromDate:self.detailItem.date];
    break;
  }
```

Handling Relationships to Guests and Food

You still need to add new properties and fields and those steps are the same as you have done here. But what about guests and menus, which require relationships? There are two ways to handle relationships in the interface.

Handling Relationships with Static Fields

When you have a relationship that has a limited number of elements, you can create fields for each one. For example, if you typically have something like half a dozen or a dozen menu items, you can create the appropriate number of text fields and handle them just like the text fields you've already used. You now have classes for guests and menus, so just create a new instance of whichever one you need from the appropriate text field.

For more details, see "Core Data Recipes" on `developer.apple.com`, which uses this technique for ingredients.

Handling Relationships with a Table View

If the number of related items is large, you may want to let the user manage a related table that can have any number of rows. "Core Data Books" on `developer.apple.com` uses this technique for books. However, you don't have to go that far: the master view controller in the Master-Detail Application template does exactly the same thing when you add a new party.

In this section, you add a new field to the detail view—that field will contain the number of guests in a related table. In this implementation, the row in the detail view with the number of guests not only tells you how many guests there are but also provides a home for a detail disclosure accessory view, which will take you to a table view where you can add the guests (this will be `GuestViewController`). Food can work the same way with the related table containing menu items.

 This section shows you the steps to follow to implement the related table. As noted, you have done these steps previously throughout the book, so they are presented here quickly.

Grouping the Detail View

It makes sense to group the detail view so that the related tables are shown in a separate section. There are four steps to grouping the detail view:

1. Set the grouping style.

2. Add a second prototype cell to the storyboard.

3. Update the code.

4. Connect the `GuestViewController` to the accessory view.

Set the Grouping Style

Open the iPad storyboard and select the table view in `DetailViewController`. Using the Attributes inspector, change the style to Grouped, as shown in Figure 17-20.

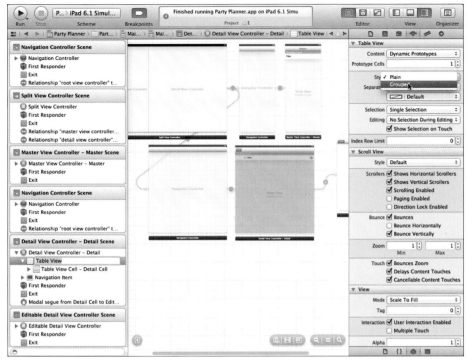

FIGURE 17-20 Group the rows.

Add a Second Prototype Cell

Change prototype cells to 2 rather than 1. You will use a second prototype cell for the group information. The reason you need this separate prototype is so that you can connect its detail view accessory to the new `GuestViewController`. Select the new prototype cell and set its identifier to Grouped Cell in the Attributes inspector (the original prototype cell is called Detail Cell).

Update the Code

In `DetailViewController.m`, you need to change `cellForRowAt: indexPath:` to use the new prototype cell for section 1.

```
- (UITableViewCell *)tableView:(UITableView *)tableView
  cellForRowAtIndexPath:(NSIndexPath *)indexPath
{
  UITableViewCell *cell;
  switch ([indexPath section]) {
    case 0:
      {
      cell = [tableView dequeueReusableCellWithIdentifier:
        @"Detail Cell" forIndexPath:indexPath];
      break;
      }
```

```
  case 1:
  {
  cell = [tableView dequeueReusableCellWithIdentifier:
    @"Guest Cell" forIndexPath:indexPath];
  break;
  }
}
[self configureCell:cell atIndexPath:indexPath];
return cell;
}
```

Likewise, change `configureCellAt:  indexPath:` to accommodate the new section. Notice the need to convert the `NSUInteger` to a string for the result of count.

```
- (void)configureCell:(UITableViewCell *)cell
    atIndexPath:(NSIndexPath *)indexPath
{
    switch ([indexPath section]) {
      case 0:
        {
        switch ([indexPath row]) {
          case 0:
            {
            cell.detailTextLabel.text =
              [self.detailItem.partyName description];
            cell.textLabel.text = @"Party Name";
            break;
            }

          case 1:
            {
            cell.textLabel.text = @"Location";
            cell.detailTextLabel.text =
                [self.detailItem.location description];
            break;
            }

          case 2:
            {
            cell.textLabel.text = @"Date";
            NSDateFormatter *dateFormat =
              [[NSDateFormatter alloc] init];
            [dateFormat setDateFormat: @"MM dd yyyy"];
            cell.detailTextLabel.text = [dateFormat
                stringFromDate:self.detailItem.date];
```

```
            break;
            }

            default:
              break;
            }
      break;
      } // section 0

    case 1:{
       cell.textLabel.text = @"Guests";
       NSUInteger theCount = [self.detailItem.guests count];
       cell.detailTextLabel.text =[NSString stringWithFormat:
         @"%d", theCount];
       } // case of section 1 -- only all rows will use this
   } //end of switch for cases
}
```

Now change the style in the code to reflect the number of rows and sections. This code needs to be added; it wasn't needed when you only had one section because that's the default.

```
-  (NSInteger)numberOfSectionsInTableView:(UITableView *)tableView {
        return 2;
}
```

Change `tableView: numberOfRowsInSection:` to return 3 for section 0 and 1 for the new section 1 (section numbers are zero-relative):

```
-  (NSInteger)tableView:(UITableView *)tableView
    numberOfRowsInSection:(NSInteger) section
{
  switch (section) {
    case 0:
      {
      return 3;
      break;
      }

    case 1:
      {
      rcturn 1,
      break;
      }
  } // end switch
  return 1; // default shouldn't get here
}
```

Implementing the Guest View Controller

GuestViewController is another UITableViewController—just like DetailView
Controller. Its structure and conventions mirror those of DetailViewController.

Begin by creating a new Objective-C class using File➔New➔File, as shown in Figure 17-21.

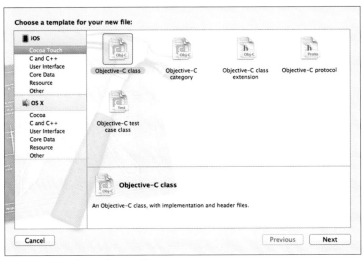

FIGURE 17-21 Create the new file.

Name it GuestViewController and make it a subclass of UITableViewController, as
shown in Figure 17-22.

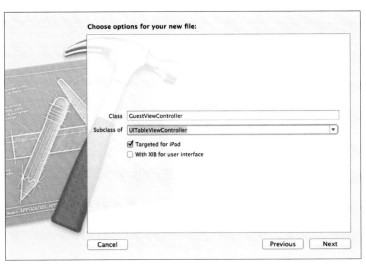

FIGURE 17-22 Specify the class name.

Save it and add it to your project, as shown in Figure 17-23.

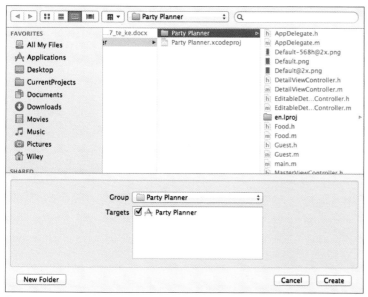

FIGURE 17-23 Save the file.

GuestViewController.h

Inside this new class, you'll need the detailItem (the current Party) and the managed view controller. Just as you have done before, when you connect the new view with the storyboard, you'll set this values from the view that presents it. Thus, DetailViewController in its prepareForSegue: sender: method will do the work to set up GuestViewController.

Here's how the header file should look (remember to add the forward declaration for Party):

```
#import <UIKit/UIKit.h>
@class Party;

@interface GuestViewController : UITableViewController

@property (strong, nonatomic) Party * detailItem; //jf
@property (strong, nonatomic) NSManagedObjectContext
  *managedObjectContext;

@end
```

GuestViewController.m

You need to implement a sorted guests array in memory just as you've done before with `sortedParties` in `MasterViewController`. When you download the code for the end of this chapter, you should take a few minutes to look it over; it should look very familiar.

 Because this code is repetitive, it's not shown again here. You can find it in the downloadable files.

Connect the Guest View Controller to the Accessory View

In the iPad storyboard, create a new table view controller from the library. Position it to the right of `DetailViewController` (perhaps below `EditableDetailViewController`). Change its class to `GuestViewController` and set up the prototype cell. You might call it **Guest Cell** because you'll need the identifier for shortly.

Connect the detail disclosure accessory view in the second prototype cell of `DetailView Controller` to `GuestViewController`. Make the connection a Push segue so that the navigation bar will be shown at the top.

Create an Add button at the right of the navigation bar by dragging a bar button item from the library and setting its class to Add. Then, Control-drag from it to `GuestView Controller.h` to create an Add method.

Update `prepareForSegue: sender:` in `DetailViewController.m` to pass the `detailItem` and managed object context down to `GuestViewController` for this segue.

At the top of `DetailViewController.m`, add:

```
#import "GuestViewController.h"
```

Then add code so that `prepareForSegue: sender:` looks like this:

```
- (void)prepareForSegue:(UIStoryboardSegue *)segue sender:(id)
  sender {
  if ([[segue identifier] isEqualToString:
  @"editableDetailsSegue"])
  {
    ((EditableDetailViewController*)segue.
      destinationViewController).managedObjectContext =
      ((DetailViewController*)segue.sourceViewController).
      managedObjectContext;

    ((EditableDetailViewController*)segue.
      destinationViewController).
```

```
    detailItem =
      ((DetailViewController*)segue.sourceViewController).
        detailItem;
  } else {
    if ([[segue identifier] isEqualToString: @"guestViewSegue"])
    {
      ((GuestViewController*)segue.destinationViewController).
        managedObjectContext =
        ((EditableDetailViewController*)segue.
          sourceViewController).
        managedObjectContext;
      ((GuestViewController*)segue.destinationViewController).
        detailItem =
        ((EditableDetailViewController*)segue.
          sourceViewController).
         detailItem;
    } // if
  } //else
}
```

The final step is to apply these changes to the iPhone storyboard. It's basically a process of repeating the steps. Because the properties and actions were created when you updated the iPad storyboard, it should just be a matter of making the connections.

Summary

This chapter returns to the starting point: the user interface in your storyboard. As you implement new features in your apps, you'll find yourself repeating the steps you've seen in this book. Control-dragging on a storyboard to create a new outlet or action will become second nature. Xcode provides you with declarations and shells for your methods: you just have to write the code.

As you explore more of the classes in Cocoa Touch, you'll find yourself repeatedly subclassing existing classes and implementing delegates. These processes happen over and over again. You'll come to realize that when you want to implement new functionality, it often is merely a few lines of code; the call to super to get the basic class functionality does most of the work.

iOS and Cocoa Touch are a new way of developing software for many people. Don't try to map these new tools and techniques to older technologies you know. Adopt them, enjoy them, and use them to provide what Apple so often describes as a "beautiful experience."

Index

programming concepts
about, 16–17
messaging in Objective-C, 19–21
objects in Objective-C, 17–18
project navigator
about, 42–43
controls, 44–47
finding missing files, 44
groups, 43–44
projects
about, 36–37
building, 31
creating, 68–72
running, 31
Xcode, 36–37
properties
connecting
about, 178–179
interface elements to, 164–170
creating, 178–179
dataSource, 283
declaring for classes, 104
defined, 17
detailItem, 193, 266–270, 345
fetchedObjects, 284
fetchedResultsController, 156, 159–160, 277–278
IBAction, 105
IBOutlet, 104, 105, 167, 168, 181
managedObjectContext, 161, 186
navigationItem, 188
rootViewController, 162
UIApplication, 233
userInfo, 301, 303–305
weakly-typed, 237
property accessors, 266
@property compiler directive, 104
protocols
about, 231–232
adopting, 233
declaring
about, 234–235
delegates that adopt, 233
structure, 232
prototype cell, preparing in storyboard, 262–265

Q
quantity of data, 65–66
Quick Help, 50, 105

R
rating your apps, 61, 64
reading reviews, 19
rearranging elements in table view, 283–287
refining relationships, 139–140
refreshing data store, 282
registering as developers, 15–16
related items pop-up menu, 27–30
relationship segues, compared with action/
manual segues, 268–269
relationships
building, 136–141
creating, 136–139
handling
with static fields, 340
with table views, 340–343
inverse, 137
refining, 139–140
Relationships table, 74
relative to build products setting, 50, 107
relative to developer directory setting, 50, 107
relative to group setting, 49, 107–108
relative to project setting, 50, 107, 108
relative to SDK setting, 50, 107
removing
configureView, 271
database, 142
existing connections, 166–167
renaming classes/files, 107
reordering features, of table view, 282–283
requirements, describing for apps, 61, 64
research, 8–9
resizing panes, 49
restoring data. *See* data, saving and restoring
retrieving data, 183, 198
return statement, 205
returning single table cells, 265–274
reusing basic detail data code, 327–330
reviewing user interaction on iOS, 298–299
reviews, reading, 9
right-pointing arrow, 205
root view controller, 93

views. *See also* Interface Builder
  accessory, 346–347
  detail
    about, 11
    converting to table view for iPhone, 246–257
    converting to table view for iPad, 257–262
    grouping, 340–343
  detail data
    about, 153–154
    connecting interface elements to properties, 164–170
    creating iPad interface, 180–181
    layout, 170–180
    `Party` class, 154–164
  detail view controller
    building, 142–151
    implementing data source protocol for, 271–272
    implementing table view delegate protocol for, 272–274
  Guest view controller
    connecting to accessory view, 346–347
    implementing, 344–347
  master, 11
  master view controller
    about, 238
    `.h` file, 238
    `.m` file, 238–240
  modal, 311
  root view controller, 93
  split, 10–11
  split view controller
    about, 89
    creating, 96
  table
    about, 88, 219–227, 275–276
    adding new objects, 290–292
    adding on iPad, 257–262
    adding on iPhone, 252–257
    converting detail view for iPhone, 246–257
    converting detail view for iPad, 257–262

  delegate protocol, implementing for detail view controller, 272–274
  delegates, 231–237
  deleting existing objects, 292–293
  enabling reordering features, 282–283
  handling relationships with, 340–343
  `MasterViewController`, 238–244
  modifying data model to store row sequence, 276–282
  moving rows and saving new order, 283–289
  protocols, 231–237
  `UITableView` high-level architecture, 219–231
  using for data display and editing, 218–229
  using on iPad, 225–227
  using on iPhones, 220–224

W

weakly-typed variable/property, 237
websites
  Apple Developer, 7
  DTS (Developer Technical Services), 15
  example code, 3
  icons, 60
  iTunes Connect Developer Guide, 58
  PlattInfo, 323
  Treehouse, 4
  Worldwide Developers Conference (WWDC), 120
workspace window
  about, 26–27
  code completion, 39, 41–42
  Editing preferences, 39
  File inspector, 49–50
  Fix-It feature, 40–41
  handling indentation, 39–40
  inspectors, 50–51
  jump bar, 27–30
  libraries, 51
  project navigators, 42–47
  Quick Help, 50
  search navigator, 47–48

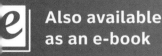